THE ARCHAEOLOGY OF
MEDIEVAL BRITAIN

Series Editor: Dr Helen Clarke

Medieval Fortifications

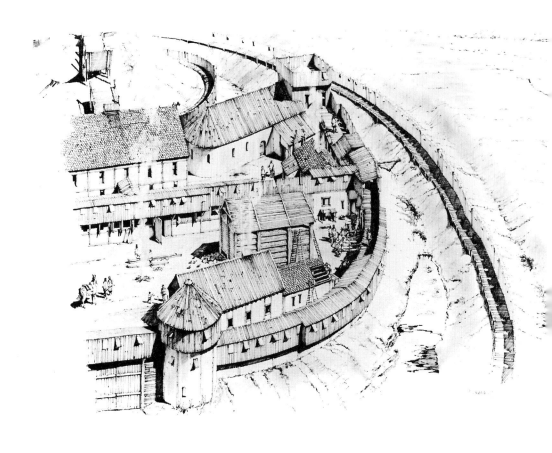

Frontispiece Peter Scholefield's reconstruction drawing of how the northern half of the bailey at Hen Domen may have appeared *c.* 1150

MEDIEVAL FORTIFICATIONS

—————— J O H N R. K E N Y O N ——————

LEICESTER UNIVERSITY PRESS
(a division of Pinter Publishers)
Leicester, and London

For Chris, Pippa and Joanna

First published in Great Britain in 1990 by Leicester University Press (A division of Pinter Publishers Ltd)

Paperback edition published in 1991.

Editorial offices
Fielding Johnson Building, University of Leicester, University Road, Leicester, LE1 7RH

Trade and other enquiries
25 Floral Street, London, WC2E 9DS

British Library Cataloguing in Publication Data
A CIP cataloguing record for this book is available from the British Library

ISBN 0-7185-1289-8
ISBN 0-7185-1392-4 (Pbk)
Photoset in North Wales by
Derek Doyle & Associates, Mold, Clwyd.
Printed and bound in Great Britain by
Biddles Ltd.

Contents

Foreword

The series *The Archaeology of Medieval Britain*, in which this is the first publication, will consist of a number of books presenting the most up-to-date surveys of the archaeological evidence for specific aspects of Britain in the middle ages. The core period to be covered in depth is from the Norman Conquest of 1066 to the Reformation, but there are no hard-and-fast chronological boundaries and example will be drawn from before and after the period where appropriate. The books will not be narrowly site– or object–orientated, emphasizing rather the social and economic aspects of the subjects in question, and they will be of interest to archaeologists and historians alike. Their style of presentation and their lavish illustrations will also make them attractive to general readers interested in their medieval heritage.

Each topic will be covered by an expert in that field, whose depth and breadth of knowledge will throw new and exciting light on the middle ages. Archaeological excavations in recent decades will be used as the basis for wideranging conclusions and synthesis.

John R. Kenyon here inaugurates the series with a survey of medieval fortifications. His wide experience and knowledge of the subject has enabled him to provide a fresh approach to a subject which has been discussed by many authorities over the years. He shows here what a great contribution archaeology has made to the understanding of the defended sites of medieval Britain and his work is a most suitable introduction to a series which aims to explain and underline the importance of archaeology in the interpretation of an historic period.

Helen Clarke
University College London, December 1989

Preface and acknowledgements

One of the advantages of being given the opportunity to write this book has been that I have been able to rediscover for myself the wealth of information on castles and town defences that lies scattered in excavation reports. Naturally, one is very familiar with the key sites which have contributed so much to castle studies, such as Abinger, Castle Acre, Hen Domen and Castlehill of Strachan, but this book has led me to look at all reports and summaries which have appeared since 1945. Not all excavations have produced outstanding results by any means, but even where the work has been on a small scale enough may have been learnt to explain the function of a particular building, or how a castle or a town wall was constructed and ditch crossed. So I have found the last few months particularly instructive, and my thanks, therefore, must first go to Helen Clarke, the editor of this series, and Leicester University Press for inviting me to present this study. The advice and criticism of Helen Clarke has been invaluable, and I am very grateful for the various suggestions she has made for the improvement of the text.

Various drafts of the chapters were also read by my good friends Richard Avent and Derek Renn, and many of their comments have been incorporated, but, naturally, any errors that remain are the responsibilty of the author. I am also grateful to the National Museum of Wales for the support that it has given me. My thanks must go as well to those people who over the years have supplied me with offprints of their publications, as this made it considerably easier to undertake the research at home. If I have misinterpreted any aspect of the results which have appeared in reports, my apologies go to the authors concerned.

The book was written in the evenings and at weekends over a two-year period from April 1987; family life, therefore, suffered to a large extent! The work could not have been done without the tolerance of my wife Chris and daughters Pippa and Joanna, and so this book is dedicated to them. Chris also read some of the text, and I have gratefully accepted the improvements that she suggested.

Various individuals and institutions provided me with photographs, or have permitted me to make use of line drawings. I wish to thank the following for these figures:

R. Avent, 11.1; P.A. Barker and the Hen Domen Archaeological Project, frontispiece, 1.18, 1.19, 4.3, 5.1–5.3; Bedfordshire County Council Photographic Unit, 9.1; G. Beresford, 4.4; Birmingham City Museum and Art Gallery, 7.3, 7.4; Bristol Museum and Art Gallery (Department of Archaeology), 10.5; British Archaeological Association, 1.16, 2.8, 3.2; L.A.S. Butler, 2.5; Cadw: Welsh Historic Monuments, 1.1, 1.2, 2.9, 3.4, 4.7, 6.3, 7.5, 8.4; Cambridge University Collection of Air Photographs, 1.3, 3.5; Cardiff Archaeological Society, 5.9; R.D. Carr, 7.1; Centre de Recherches Archéologiques Médiévales, Caen, 4.5, 5.10; Cornwall Archaeological Society, 5.11; B.W. Cunliffe, 9.2; B.K. Davison, 1.12; P.L. Drewett, 4.2, 4.8; English Heritage, 1.8, 1.9, 5.4, 5.5; G. Ewart, 1.10; G. Fairclough, 3.3; Glamorgan– Gwent Archaeological Trust, 1.14,

5.6; Gloucester City Museum and Art Gallery, 9.4, 9.5, 10.4; R.A. Higham, 2.3; Historic Buildings and Monuments, Scottish Development Department, 3.9, 4.6; T. James, Dyfed Archaeological Trust, 10.3; T.J. Miles, 4.7; National Museum of Wales, 8.5, 9.3; Oxfordshire Architectural and Historical Society, 3.1, 10.2; C. Platt, 1.6; Powysland Club, 3.6; Royal Archaeological Institute, 1.7, 2.6, 2.7; Royal Commission on Ancient and Historical Monuments in Wales, 1.13; Royal Commission on the Ancient and Historical Monuments of Scotland, 1.5, 1.11, 3.7; Royal Commission on the Historical Monuments of England, 8.1; Society for Medieval Archaeology, 6.1, 10.1; Society for Post-Medieval Archaeology, 5.8; Society of Antiquaries of London, 2.1, 8.3; Society of Antiquaries of Scotland, 5.7; Somerset Archaeological and Natural History Society, 1.15; South Staffordshire Archaeological and Historical Society, 1.17; Southampton City Council (City Museum), 6.2; C.J. Spurgeon, 3.8; M.W. Thompson, 2.2; University of Wales Press, 2.10; Victoria and Albert Museum, 1.4; Wakefield Art Galleries and Museums, 2.11, 4.1, 7.2; Winchester Excavations Committee, 2.4, 8.2.

My sincerest thanks also to Fiona Gale for preparing the majority of the line drawings.

It should be noted that the following figures are Crown copyright: 1.1, 1.2, 1.5, 1.11, 2.9, 3.7, 3.9, 4.6, 6.3, 7.5, 8.1. Figures 1.10, 1.13, 3.4, 4.7 and 8.4 are based on Crown copyright plans.

Preface to paperback edition 1991

While the hardback edition was in press, and subsequent to its publication, a number of reports were published to which reference is given below.

One of the important excavations cited in the book was that of Goltho in Lincolnshire, and the reader should be aware that Beresford's dating of the various phases has been called into question in a review article by Everson (1988), where it is also argued that the site itself may not be the true medieval 'Goltho' but the manor of Bullington. Everson suggests that the first castle dates to the 1130s, with the second castle phase, when the bailey was infilled, considerably later.

The publication of the results of the excavations of the Roman amphitheatre at Silchester, Hampshire, includes a section on the medieval occupation (Fulford 1989). The design of the amphitheatre was such that it had potential for conversion into a castle ringwork, and it seems that it may have been so adapted in the first half of the twelfth century, during the civil war years of the reign of King Stephen. There was evidence for a hall and one other building, as well as a palisade.

Stuart Rigold's interpretation of Eynsford, Kent, has been called into question in an article by Horsman (1988, published 1990). More recent work on the castle suggests that the early tower which Rigold associated with the early castle may belong to a settlement possibly dating to the beginning of the eleventh century, that is to say pre-castle, and that the building may have been a hall on stone foundations rather than a tower.

Reports on excavations at five other masonry castles have also been published, including Tamworth and Nottingham. Work on Tamworth, Staffordshire, in 1972 and 1974, concentrated on the gatehouse (McNeill 1987–8). The gate, somewhat shallow-fronted with a short passage, was built possibly some time in the second half of the thirteenth century. It is unusual in that there was no building behind the gate itself, such as a hall-block, which would have made it a true gatehouse, but this entrance was simply linked to a building to one side. The gate contained a number of arrowslits, and postholes excavated in the basement may represent the original position of scaffold timbers used when the gate was under construction. The results of the Nottingham Castle Project which ran from 1976 to 1984 have been published (Drage 1989), and the report includes a detailed history of the castle together with several reconstruction drawings of the castle at various phases of its development. The excavations concentrated on the middle bailey curtain wall, mural towers and the bridge. Among the finds was a quantity of decorated window glass and carved stonework, as well as a breach-loading cannon of wrought iron dating to the late fifteenth or early sixteenth century.

The reports on two other masonry castles are concerned with thirteenth-century native Welsh castles. The latest account of the work undertaken at Dryslwyn, Carmarthenshire, provides details of the results up to 1988 (Caple 1990). The main phases of the castle apparently date to the period up to the capture of the castle by the English in 1287, and in spite of the rich documentary evidence for the English rebuilding and occupation there remains surprisingly little archaeological evidence for the final occupation of Dryslwyn, from the late thirteenth to the early fifteenth century. The castle was to be stripped of all its fixtures and fittings, and following a widespread fire the walls of the inner ward were partly demolished. Like Dryslwyn, Llywelyn ap Gruffudd's Dolforwyn was eventually to end up in English hands. The report on the excavations is to appear in three parts, of which the first has now appeared (Butler 1989), and it is this report which should be consulted for definitive information regarding the rectangular keep. More recent work on the bailey and its circular tower has been described in two other recent articles (Butler 1990; 1991).

Finally, the first part of the report on Penhow, Monmouthshire (also to be in three parts), is concerned with a description of this small castle as well as the excavations in the courtyard (Wrathmell 1990), and the account of the short excavation in 1971 on the town defences of Chepstow, Monmouthshire, has just been published (Miles 1991). It was shown that the foundations for the wall were simply built on the natural ground surface, and that there was no ditch in front of the defences, simply a shallow depression.

Butler, L. (1989), 'Dolforwyn Castle, Montgomery, Powys. First report: the excavations 1981–1986', *Archaeol. Cambrensis* **138**: 78–98.
Butler, L. (1990), 'Dolforwyn Castle, Powys: the last castle of the last Welsh prince of North Wales', *Current Archaeol.* **10**, 13: 418–23.
Butler, L. (1991), 'Dolforwyn Castle and the Welsh castles of North Wales', *Fortress* **8**: 15–24.
Caple, C. (1990), 'The castle and lifestyle of a 13th century independent Welsh lord; excavations at Dryslwyn Castle 1980–1988', *Château Gaillard* **14**: 47–59.

Drage, C. (1989), 'Nottingham Castle: a place full royal', *Trans. Thoroton Soc., Nottinghamshire* **93**: whole issue.

Everson, P. (1988), 'What's in a name? 'Goltho', Goltho and Bullington', *Lincolnshire Hist. Archaeol.* **23**: 93–9.

Fulford, M. (1989), *The Silchester Amphitheatre: Excavations of 1979–85,* London.

Horsman, V. (1988), 'Eynsford castle: a reinterpretation of its early history in the light of recent excavations', *Archaeol. Cantiana* **105**: 39–57.

McNeill, T. E. (1987–8), 'Excavations at Tamworth Castle, 1972 and 1974', *Trans. S. Staffordshire Archaeol. Hist. Soc* **29**: whole issue.

Miles, T. J. (1991), 'Chepstow Port Wall excavations, 1971', *Monmouthshire Antiq,* **7**: 5–15.

Wrathmell, S. (1990), 'Penhow Castle, Gwent: survey and excavation, 1976–9: part one', *Monmouthshire Antiq.* **6**: 17–45.

John R. Kenyon
Llandaff, St David's Day 1991

List of figures

List of tables

Introduction

The growth in the interest in the archaeology of the medieval period is an important aspect of the post-war development of archaeology as an academic discipline, and in one field in particular this growth has borne remarkable fruit, namely castle studies. Many books and papers have been written on the subject, and a basic history of the chronological development of the castle is given by Avent (1983), Brown (1976; 1985) and Cruden (1963). However, this present volume has been written with an approach to the subject that differs in two ways from other books that have been written on castles.

First, it is a synthesis of the main results from archaeological excavations that have been undertaken in Britain since 1945, 'medieval' being interpreted as that period beginning with the Norman Conquest of 1066 and running through until the end of the fifteenth century. Naturally, a few of the important excavations, such as Castle Acre and Hen Domen, are mentioned in some recent books on castles, but there remained considerable scope for a much wider examination of the archaeology of castles in Britain.

Second, the arrangement of the book is thematic, thus enabling this writer to examine aspects of fortifications in greater detail than an outline chronological development would allow. Part 1 is concerned with castle defences, with the first chapter covering earth-and-timber castles, and the remainder with aspects of masonry defences. However, the student should always be aware of the fact that there were castles which were only partially built or rebuilt in stone, and which relied permanently on earth-and-timber for the outer defences. Also, some of the timber castles remained in their original form until well into the later middle ages, as is evident from both documentary sources and excavations.

Part 2 covers the other important aspect of castle building: the domestic structures such as halls, kitchens and chapels. The reader has to be aware of the danger in drawing too rigid a line between the military and domestic buildings of a castle, particularly as some structures such as the keep played dual roles. There is also a chapter on the artefacts discovered by excavation which have thrown light on life in castles.

Some of the chapters have been subdivided into several sections. The earth-and-timber motte-and-bailey is, therefore, discussed under various categories, and the analysis of one particular site may be found scattered over several pages, notable examples being the recently excavated Goltho and Hen Domen. This has allowed, for example, the evidence for the varied methods used in motte construction to be brought together in one section. The reader will be able to gain an overall picture of a particular site from the individual published reports given in the bibliography of this book, as well as from the entries in the index.

Town defences, a somewhat neglected subject, are treated in Part 3. There has been a large number of archaeological investigations of urban fortifications in recent years, although in many cases the excavation has simply been a case of a trench confirming the line of wall, bank or ditch. The more important of the published reports have been selected for discussion, virtually all the sites lying in England.

The fourth and final part looks at some of the evidence from excavations for the decline of various castles, and makes some suggestions for future research.

This book, therefore, is treating two very different types of fortification: private (the castle) and communal (the town). It will show how archaeological excavation has contributed to our knowledge of the physical form of these defences, as well as paying special attention to the domestic buildings and particulars of life in castles. Such aspects are often missing from, or summarily dismissed by, general castle studies.

The accepted definition of the term 'castle' which arose out of the Royal Archaeological Institute's project 'The origins of the castle in England' was that it was the fortified residence of a lord, a symbol of the feudal society in which it developed. The project, the findings of which were published in that Institute's *Archaeological Journal* (**134** (1977), 1–156), with a useful introduction by Saunders, cannot be said to have been a total success (Saunders 1977a). Financial resources were inadequate for further and long-term excavations which were needed, and only Roger of Montgomery's castle of Hen Domen, the subject of excavation since 1960, even before the Royal Archaeological Institute's project began, provides a detailed picture of how some of the first castles of earth and timber may have appeared. Even at this site half the bailey still awaits excavation, and work on the summit of the motte began only in 1988.

Although the overall shape of early Norman castles may have been superficially similar, whether motte-and-bailey, castle ringwork, or other forms, excavations have revealed just how varied each was in terms of construction methods and development (chapter 1). We are dependent upon excavation for our understanding of those castles where only earthworks survive; where there is upstanding masonry the architectural development is easier to assess although even with masonry castles archaeology can often lead to radical reappraisal, such as with Edward I's Aberystwyth. One of the most important contributions that archaeological excavation has made to castle studies has been the radical transformation of our knowledge of the earth-and-timber castle, its construction, defences and domestic buildings, much of the information coming from Hen Domen. Nevertheless, there have been over the past few years several important excavations at some of the main masonry castles in Britain, such as Castle Acre and Sandal. The evidence for the development of the Norman castle at Castle Acre from a lightly fortified country house to a great keep was a remarkable feature of the excavations. The value of the investigations at Sandal has been to present a picture of the development of an earth-and-timber motte-and-bailey into a masonry castle, and in addition the excavations have shed light on the alterations that were undertaken during the middle ages and through to the Civil War of the 1640s. However, these are but two excavations discussed in this book, for, as will be seen, the archaeology of numerous other masonry castles has thrown a considerable amount of light on the history of the castle in Britain.

Part 1 – The castle : defences

1 Earth-and-timber castles

Introduction

Since the pioneering work on castles in the second half of the nineteenth century by scholars such as G.T. Clark, there has been particular interest in the form and development of medieval earthwork defences. However, the original theories regarding the origins of castle mounds varied from Clark and E.A. Freeman favouring an Anglo-Saxon date to historians who viewed them as Norman in origin (e.g. Round 1902). It was the work of Round and also of Mrs Ella Armitage (1912; see also Counihan 1986) that finally brought about the general acceptance of the argument that these mounds or mottes were Norman.

Our understanding of these earthwork castles was minimal until recent years, for, as all that can now be seen are bare mounds and ramparts, only archaeological excavation can throw light on the form of the defences and internal buildings in their heyday. Excavations in the late nineteenth century and the first half of the twentieth century were not very informative, although there are a few exceptions. However, work since the end of World War II, coupled with the development of medieval archaeology as a discipline in its own right, has meant that we have learnt considerably more about the structures associated with these early castles. It is unfortunate that although documentary evidence does exist for many of Britain's first castles, some of which were built before the Conquest by Norman favourites of Edward the Confessor, archaeology has rarely provided us with the close-dating that is needed, leaving various questions unanswered. The problem of dating has been discussed with regard to the castles of Hen Domen, Montgomeryshire, and Okehampton, Devon (Higham 1982a), and in his conclusion Higham has stressed that 'Excavations specifically designed to discover the date of a site can be doomed to failure'. Nevertheless, one of the most important contributions that archaeological excavation has made to castle studies is in regard to the earth-and-timber castle.

The earthwork castles fall into two main types, mottes and ringworks. The former are usually associated with one or more baileys or courtyards, whilst a ringwork generally stands in isolation. The term 'enclosure' is preferred by some with regard to castle ringworks (Brown 1985: 21-2), but 'ringwork' is now an accepted term for this type of castle, whilst 'enclosure' could be applied to a major stone castle such as Conwy or Middleham as well as to an earth-and-timber ringwork. 'Enclosure' is also a term which is used widely in other archaeological contexts, hence its unsuitability as applied to castle studies.

A motte is an enditched mound, usually artificial, which supported the strongpoint of the motte-and-bailey castle, overshadowing the bailey or enclosed courtyard below it (figure 1.1). It is predominantly rounded in plan, but square or rectangular mottes are known, especially in Scotland (Talbot 1974: 50). The height of mottes varies greatly, the majority being under 5m, although a few of the sites built in the years immediately following the

Norman Conquest are well known for having some of the largest castle mounds in the country. King has divided English and Welsh mottes into three classes according to height, following a system devised elsewhere (King 1972: 101). Class I comprises mottes of 10m upwards; II, between 5m and 10m; III, under 5m. King has calculated that of the mottes in England and Wales, 7 per cent fall into class I, 24 per cent in class II, and 69 per cent in class III (King 1972: 101–2).

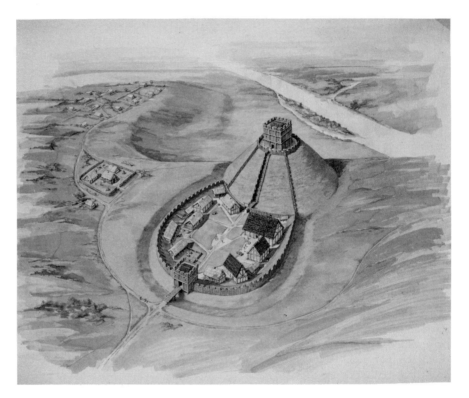

Figure 1.1 John Banbury's suggested reconstruction of the motte-and-bailey at Rhuddlan

A bailey could vary both in shape and size, and a castle could have more than one. At Windsor, for example, William the Conqueror's castle had a motte which stood between two baileys, a plan that is still evident today. There are, however, some mottes which never seem to have had an attached courtyard. We cannot be certain why this should be, but some mottes may have been built as fortified observation posts rather than for permanent occupation. Another reason might be that a motte without a bailey represents an unfinished castle.

The advantage of a motte is obvious, towering as it did in most cases above the surrounding terrain. That it was the key in the defences of this type of castle is emphasized in two contemporary accounts of attacks on two sites in

Wales. In 1075, two years after Rhuddlan Castle, Flintshire, had been built, the bailey was stormed and burnt by Gruffudd ap Cynan. Many Norman soldiers fell in the engagement, and only a few were able to reach the safety of the 'tower', a reference to the motte with a timber structure on its summit (Jones, A. 1910: 117). The second reference is to Llandovery Castle, Carmarthenshire, in 1116. Although the Welsh were successful in attacking and burning the 'outer castle' or bailey, the Normans on the motte caused enough casualties among their assailants for the attack to be withdrawn (Jones, T. 1973: 87). It is hardly surprising, therefore, that many of this type of castle were built; King (1983) records some 750 mottes in England and Wales, whilst around 300 are known to have existed in Scotland (Simpson and Webster 1985). The majority are of earth, but occasionally a boss of natural rock is scarped to form the motte, as at Launceston, Cornwall. At Cwm Prysor, Merioneth, the core of the remarkable motte of this native Welsh castle is a rock outcrop which was revetted with masonry.

The paper by King and Alcock (1969) is an essential introduction to the subject of castle ringworks. Ringworks could vary in form (King and Alcock 1969: 93, figure 1), but were generally circular earthworks, each consisting of a bank and ditch (figure 1.2), or they might be D-shaped where a natural scarp formed part of the defences as it did at Castle Neroche, Somerset, and Kidwelly, Carmarthenshire. A simple definition might be that a ringwork is a motte-and-bailey without the motte, and as its rampart could enclose a large area, these castles did not always have an additional bailey. The problem of this type of field monument is that it is not necessarily confined to the middle ages, particularly in Ireland. Here several thousand ringforts (or raths) date from the early Christian period (*c*. AD 500–1000). In Pembrokeshire Walesland Rath, which might just as easily have been taken to be a Norman earthwork because of its ringwork shape, has been dated to the late Iron Age (third to first centuries BC) (Wainwright 1971).

There are times, however, when a clear distinction cannot be drawn between mottes and ringworks, hence the unfortunate use of the term 'ring-motte' by some writers, a term to be avoided. Higham has emphasized the problem of distinguishing such sites in connection with the early castles in Devon, and he has suggested social reasons for the differences between flat-topped mottes and those with a more concave summit which have a superficial resemblance to ringworks. The former tend to be found in baronial castles, the latter lower down the social scale, such as a tenant of a barony (Higham 1982b: 109).

The ratio of mottes to ringworks in England and Wales is approximately 4:1 (*c*. 750 mottes and *c*. 190 ringworks), whilst in Scotland Simpson and Webster (1985) list a mere eighteen ringworks against 299 mottes (a ratio of 17:1), including doubtful/unproven sites, although others probably await identification. The reasons behind the choice of either motte or ringwork may never be fully understood. In some cases it might have been personal preference or the design of a lordship's castle influencing contemporary neighbouring sites, but in the Vale of Glamorgan there is convincing evidence that geology was the dominant influence (see p.24). In other instances a ringwork may have been viewed as the simplest method of defence for a site already occupied, and this has been seen particularly at Notre-Dame-de-Gravenchon in France (Le Maho 1987), and the ringwork at Sulgrave, Northamptonshire (Davison 1977). At

Figure 1.2   Terry Ball's suggested reconstruction of the ringwork at Penmaen

both these sites defences were thrown up to enclose earlier buildings, some of which were retained. In contrast, however, the Saxon fortified enclosure at Goltho, Lincolnshire, was succeeded in the late eleventh century by a small motte-and-bailey. Whatever conclusions can be drawn from this, it emphasizes the point that a Norman lord had his own ideas as to the form that his castle should take; he was not totally influenced by pre-existing defences. In the examples where the Normans placed their castles where there was already manorial occupation, it may have been done to ensure a stabilizing continuity of lordship in the area; it was certainly a symbolic move.

This reuse of sites by the Normans can also be seen in Ireland where mottes were first built following the arrival of the Normans in 1169–70. There seem to be, or have been, between 30–40,000 pre-Norman ringforts (Glasscock 1975: 96), and there is evidence that the Normans did make use of some of these, refurbishing the old defences or infilling and raising them to become mottes, an example of this infilling occurring in the early thirteenth century at Lismahon, Co. Down (Waterman 1959: 166–7). There are a large number of mottes in Ireland; the figure of about 340 (Glasscock 1975; McNeill 1975) is now considered to be a minimum, as much of the previous work in compiling a gazetteer was based on an examination of maps as opposed to being combined with fieldwork (Barry 1987: 38). The true figure may be, therefore, in the 400s, and it is possible that further excavation of Irish mottes will produce other examples of ringforts reused by the Normans.

For reasons of speed, it is not altogether surprising that several motte-and-baileys had ringwork forerunners (see below, p.29). It was often a feature where it was possible for a castle to make use of an existing defence such as a Roman fort or town wall, or a Saxon burh. Some calculations have been made in order to try and discover how long it might take for the raising of a castle mound. The motte at Lodsbridge, Sussex, which stands some 5-6m high, with a base diameter of *c.* 39.5m, was studied by Holden (1967: 116–17). He calculated that in fair weather fifty workmen working a ten-hour day would have taken forty-two days to build the motte. Davison has suggested that the motte at Castle Neroche, Somerset, added to an earlier ringwork, took between four and six months to construct (Davison 1971–2: 56–7), whilst at Bramber workmen may have been employed for about nine months in building the motte (Barton and Holden 1977: 69–70).

If these calculations are reasonably accurate, then one would expect to find that some of the first castles in England were of the ringwork type, particularly those which might be viewed as campaign castles. Excavations at the Tower of London in 1964 revealed this very sequence (Davison 1967: 40–3): a bank and ditch cut off the south-east corner of the Roman city wall, the White Tower being constructed within the Norman enclosure, although possibly at a slightly later date, from *c.* 1078. The same sequence occurred at Carisbrooke Castle (p.31). Another example is the period II earthworks at Castle Neroche (figure 1.15, p.30) which have been interpreted as the remains of a campaign castle built to suppress the 1067-9 uprising in the south-west (Davison 1971–2: 24). Here the Normans built a D-shaped ringwork within a hillfort, to be supplemented with an outer rampart which was never completed.

So in general, a ringwork must have been quicker and cheaper to throw up than a motte-and-bailey, and this factor undoubtedly accounts for such defences being built when some castles were first constructed in England and Wales. In cases where the Normans utilized earlier fortifications, such as Roman defences and Anglo-Saxon burhs or defended towns, in the immediate post-Conquest period, ringworks seem to have predominated. It cannot be a coincidence that when the Normans were endeavouring to extend their hold on south Wales in the early twelfth century, many of the castles were ringworks. Coity, Ogmore and Loughor in Glamorgan, Kidwelly, Llansteffan and probably Laugharne in Carmarthenshire are all good examples of this use of ringwork construction, the natural advantages of some of these sites also favouring this type of castle. Here the Normans, during their advance and occupation, were deliberately constructing what they considered to be a quick and effective form of castle. In contrast, it is worth noting that at the Roman town of Caerwent in Monmouthshire a motte straddles the south-east corner of the defences. However, it is not known whether this motte represents an early Norman castle or one built later in the twelfth century.

As they tend generally to be a prominent feature of the landscape, the number of known mottes is unlikely to increase appreciably, although ploughed-out examples have been found. The list might even decrease through excavations, as some mounds may prove to have been barrows or windmill platforms. An example of this was the discovery that the 'motte' known as

Deepweir Tump, Monmouthshire, was nothing more than a mound of modern builders' rubbish (Probert 1967). Elsewhere, at Middleton Stoney, Oxfordshire, excavations revealed that the castle was not a motte-and-bailey, for the 'motte' proved to be the collapsed remains of a stone keep whose destruction had been ordered in 1216 (Rahtz and Rowley 1984: 61). In contrast, excavations over the last few years have helped to enlarge the number of known ringworks, and no doubt will continue to do so, as other motte-and-baileys converted from ringworks probably exist. As will be seen below (p.28), some mottes have proved to be secondary features. In such instances a mound was either added to one side of an existing ringwork, the latter then being used as a bailey, or the original earthwork was infilled and raised to become the motte. However, there are occasions when the reinterpretation of an earthwork has led to a new site being added to the corpus of British castles. An example of this is Auldhill, Portencross in Ayrshire, where the site had previously been considered to be an Iron Age vitrified fort. Excavations have shown that Auldhill is a motte-and-bailey which was occupied in the twelfth and thirteenth centuries (Ewart 1987a).

Some sites do not fall easily into the above categories of mottes and ringwork castles, and no single term can be used conveniently to describe them. They range from the large rectangular platform of a castle such as Burwell in Cambridgeshire, begun and left unfinished in 1143–4 (RCHM 1972a: 41–2), to the small native Welsh site of Cae-castell, Rhyndwyclydach, Glamorgan, an 18.3 x 21.3m enclosure, which was partially banked and ditched (Spurgeon and Thomas 1980: 71, 73). However, the majority of excavations have been on either mottes or ringworks, and it is on these two main forms that the rest of the chapter will concentrate.

Most British mottes and ringworks date to the late eleventh and twelfth centuries, although some also show occupation in the thirteenth century onwards. The initial construction of some sites may, however, be later than the twelfth century (King 1972: 108), and the pottery evidence from the motte at Roberton, Lanarkshire, has revealed that the mound was raised no earlier than the end of the thirteenth century, possibly even during the early fourteenth century, as a product of the period of unrest during the Wars of Independence between England and Scotland (Haggarty and Tabraham 1982). On the continent examples of late medieval mottes are more common. In the Netherlands mottes date from the late twelfth century to the fourteenth century; although brick as a cheap source of building material led to the construction of new castles and the rebuilding of others there in the thirteenth century, it seems that some local landowners could only afford earth-and-timber castles because the small size of their properties did not make them wealthy enough to undertake more elaborate building projects. In other cases some thirteenth-century lords would only permit earthworks to be built on their lands, as these were regarded as being less of a threat to their authority. Such defences of earth and timber were presumably considered more vulnerable than walls of brick and stone (Besteman 1981: 42–3; 1985: 217–18). Several Danish mottes also date to the later middle ages. There is only one motte in Denmark that has been shown to be older than the late thirteenth century, whilst the excavation of another has produced evidence for a date of about the 1340s (Liebgott 1983: 196; Stiesdal 1969).

Mottes

The English motte — one might well say,
the motte wherever it is found — is a
Proteus, and the winning of its secrets
will not be achieved soon, or easily.'
(King 1972: 110)

Mottes – construction

Mottes vary from being totally man-made to having been scarped from the
natural terrain. The majority probably fall into the first category, with the
make-up coming from the surrounding ditch, but there are variations within
this theme. For example, the motte at Tre Oda, which once stood in the suburb

Figure 1.3   Aerial view of Sycharth Castle

of Whitchurch, Cardiff, had been built over a Bronze Age round barrow (Knight and Talbot 1968–70), and Tre Oda is by no means unique in this.

Tomen Llansantffraid, near Rhaeadr, Radnorshire, also had a preliminary mound within the motte, but it was part of the original construction of the motte. The builders had laid as a 'consolidating course' a thick layer of turf over the initial dump, and then the motte had been raised further with layers of clayey soil and gravel (Musson and Cain 1982). The use of turf to stabilize a motte during construction was also found during the excavations of the Peel of Lumphanan, Aberdeenshire. The mound at this castle is partly natural, and when the motte was raised a turf bank was used to stabilize the upcast from the ditch (Webster and Cherry 1976: 185–6). A similar method was used at Alstoe Mount, Rutland (Dunning 1936: 399) and at Lorrha, Co. Tipperary (Talbot 1972: 11), and may have been a feature of the castle at Framlingham, Suffolk (Coad 1971: 159).

A short excavation in 1979 and 1980 on the ploughed-out Bentley Castle, Hampshire, revealed that it had been a small, low motte-and-bailey, possibly built as a siege castle in 1147 by Henry of Blois, Bishop of Winchester, in order to regain his castle of *Lidelea*, (probably Barley Pound ringwork and baileys). As a siege castle it would not only have had a short life, but it would have needed to be built quickly if it were to fulfil its role as a defended outpost and watchtower. This explains the lack of height of the motte, originally only 1.2m above ground level, which was formed of turf and topsoil capped with clay from the ditch (Stamper 1984).

The motte of Sycharth Castle, Denbighshire (figure 1.3), stands on a glacial mound. Excavation revealed that a cairn of stones had been collected, and then covered with the soil and turf removed when the the limits of the motte ditch were marked out. The motte reached its final appearance with the addition of an outer ring of dumped clay (Hague and Warhurst 1966: 117).

The depiction of the motte at Hastings, Sussex, in the Bayeux Tapestry (figure 1.4), illustrates its supposed method of construction consisting of a

Figure 1.4   Hastings Castle as depicted on the Bayeux Tapestry

series of horizontal layers of soil. Baile Hill, one of the two mottes built by William I in York, has shown that mottes might be built in this manner; it consisted of several horizontal layers of clayey soil, and was surrounded by a ditch about 21m wide and 12m deep (Addyman and Priestley 1977: 124). A similar method of layering has been postulated for the small motte of Castle Hill, Bakewell, Derbyshire (Swanton 1972: 25), and was seen at Great Driffield, Yorkshire, where alternate deposits of gravel, clay and chalk were laid down over the initial turf stack (Eddy 1983). It is unfortunate that no evidence for this method of construction was found during the excavation of the Hastings motte itself (Barker and Barton 1977: 88).

Some mottes were also enlarged later in their history, particularly to provide greater support for masonry structures. The original mound at Hastings underwent this alteration in the fourteenth century, and a length of masonry curtain wall some 2m wide was built over it (Barker and Barton 1977: 88). When Thomas Hatfield, Bishop of Durham (1345–81), built the keep at Durham Castle it was necessary to encase the mound with a thick stabilizing layer of clay (Simpson and Hatley 1953: 58–9). Chalgrave, Bedfordshire, began as a small motte *c*. 1100, built close to the church and over an area which had been occupied by a manorial complex of uncertain date. Towards the end of the same century the motte was enlarged to take a long single-storey timber building, and the encircling ditch was recut; clearly the first castle was found to be too small to provide the facilities required by a new lord. However, in spite of this, the castle was abandoned for reasons unknown in the late twelfth or early thirteenth century in favour of another site close by (Pinder and Davison 1988).

A similar sequence was found at Goltho in Lincolnshire, where *c*. 1150 the small motte-and-bailey was converted into a large but low mound by the bailey being infilled with spoil from its rampart, as well as from the upper levels of the original motte built *c*. 1080 (figures 1.8 and 1.9, pp.16, 18). It is possible these alterations coincided with a change in ownership, when the conversion of a small and cramped motte-and-bailey into something more fitting might have seemed a logical step. The main building on the new mound was an aisled hall (see p.104) (Beresford 1987: 111-12).

The castle at Aldingham, Lancashire, went through several alterations in the twelfth and thirteenth centuries (see p.29), but the final phase was when the height of the motte was increased by 2m in the early thirteenth century (Davison 1969: 24). Evidence for a similar increase in the height of a motte was revealed during the excavations of 1959–61 at Rayleigh in Essex (Helliwell and Macleod 1981: 12), and it also occurred at Lodsbridge Mill, Sussex, in the thirteenth century (Holden 1967: 106). The sides of the Aldingham motte were revetted with timber set in a 2m deep foundation trench, whilst at Goltho timber, turf and stone were used to revet the small motte raised *c*. 1080. The revetment here consisted of a series of panels about 1.5m apart, and between the posts there were alternate layers of turf and stone (Beresford 1987: 100–2). A timber revetment was also used around a mound at Huntingdon, the site possibly being a siege castle of 1172 (Wilson and Hurst 1968: 175). The motte of Castlehill of Strachan, Kincardineshire, built around 1250, was surrounded by water and marsh, and so it had to be revetted with a low wall (figure 1.5), possibly 1m high, to enable consolidation to take place.

The wall subsequently collapsed into the surrounding ditch (Yeoman 1984: 340). At Bedford it was the inner scarp of the ditch which was revetted in masonry, as was the inner bailey ditch, while the motte had a turf revetment (Baker and Baker 1979: 13–17).

In some examples we can only surmise whether mottes were enlarged for social or military reasons. At Chalgrave it was clearly done to improve the domestic accommodation of the castle, with the construction of a long building, presumably a hall with a solar. The new works at Aldingham were a major refurbishment of the defences, but as is so often the case we have no idea of the reasons behind the refortification. It may have been because the original defences had decayed, or the result of some threat to the castle. The second phase at Rayleigh, which included the heightening of the motte and the improvement of the bailey defences, has been interpreted as coinciding with the years of civil war during the reign of King Stephen (1135–54).

Figure 1.5 The revetment surrounding the base of the motte, Castlehill of Strachan

Mottes — superstructures

The illustrations of buildings on mottes as depicted by the Bayeux Tapestry are well known, and they throw some light on the motte superstructures. Literary evidence also survives, for example the twelfth-century description of the building that stood on the motte of Durham Castle, as well as that on the motte of Ardres built *c.* 1117. Durham was described as a 'tumulus of rising earth' with the keep which rose 'into thin air, strong within and without, well fitted for its work, for within the ground rises higher by three cubits than without ... Above this, a stalwart house springs yet higher than the [shell] keep, glittering with splendid beauty in every part; four posts are plain, on which it rests, one post at each strong corner.' (Armitage 1912: 147–8). So on top of the motte there was a house surrounded by a palisade or curtain wall about the perimeter. The description of the keep at Ardres goes into far more detail. Arnold of Ardres had his 'great and lofty house' built by a carpenter, and he clearly was a great architect in timber, judging by the details that the chronicler has left us.

The building was

> an almost impenetrable labyrinth, piling storeroom upon storeroom, chamber upon chamber, room upon room, extending the larders and granaries into cellars and building the chapel in a convenient place ... He made it of three floors, the topmost storey supported by the second as though suspended in the air. The first storey was at ground level, and here were the cellars and granaries ... On the second floor were the residential apartments ... and the great chamber of the lord and his lady, where they slept ... On this floor also was the kitchen, which was on two levels ... On the top floor of the house there were small rooms in which, on one side, the sons of the lord slept when they wished to do so, and, on the other side, his daughters as they were obliged.

Mention was also made of the stairs and corridors that linked the floors, and the chapel, which was compared to the temple of Solomon (Brown 1984a: 22–3). Even allowing for the undoubted exaggeration of the decoration in the chapel, the keep at Ardres was obviously an impressive structure. However, until the classic excavation of a small motte at Abinger, Surrey, in 1949 (Hope-Taylor 1950) there was little archaeological evidence of buildings on mottes in Britain. Dunning (1936: 399) had found nothing at Alstoe Mount, Rutland, but Professor Gordon Childe did come across various features such as a postsocket on the motte at Doonmore, Co. Antrim, which was interpreted as a support for a wicker fence (Childe 1938). The Abinger excavations revealed a double row of postholes around the perimeter of the top of the motte, with larger postholes in the centre of the mound surface into which the timber supports for a small watchtower could have been sunk (figure 1.6). The position of the entrance to the motte top was marked by a gap in the palisade, with a posthole on each side for a large timber. These defences represented the second phase of fortification on the motte, probably constructed during the period of civil war in the reign of King Stephen (1135–54); the first phase of *c.* 1100 also had a wooden tower, and this may also have been enclosed by a palisade.

The postholes of the phase II palisade at Abinger were of two basic types. Those in the outer row were deep compared with the inner, and the latter were more widely spaced. The palisade, therefore, had a row of tall outer posts, with an inner series of short timbers linked to the palisade itself by cross-braces, presumably supporting a timber fighting platform or wall-walk.

The small size of the central tower is an indication that it was designed more for a sentinel post or look-out than a residential keep; it was also open at ground level, as it stood on what amounted to stilts. This is in marked contrast to one of the few other timber towers which have been excavated. This other example stood on the motte at Hoverberg in Germany, and was much larger (*c.* 6 x 5.5m) than the Abinger tower, although of the same construction; it may also have been stave-walled. The Hoverberg tower clearly represented the main residence of its lord, associated as it was with two smaller buildings and a well (Herrnbrodt 1958: 180, Abb. 76), whilst the Abinger structure did not.

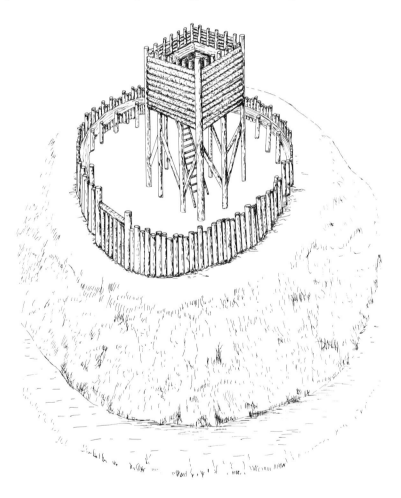

Figure 1.6 A reconstruction of the tower and palisade on the motte at Abinger (after Platt 1978)

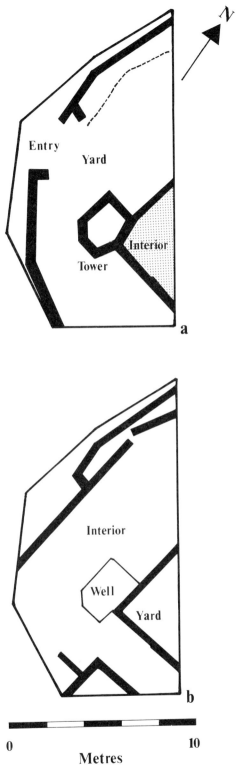

Figure 1.7 Two interpretations of the features on the summit of Baile Hill, York (after Addyman and Priestley 1977)

Further evidence for the method of construction of the timberwork at Abinger came from the postholes of two of the corner posts of the tower, for preserved in the sand were the shapes of the mortises or slots for horizontal timbers, possibly below ground level, intended to act as a secure foundation for the structure.

If there were a bailey attached to the motte, and there is no clear evidence for one, then the builder of the castle, Robert of Abinger or his son, may have resided in buildings there, but the possibility that the motte was primarily a

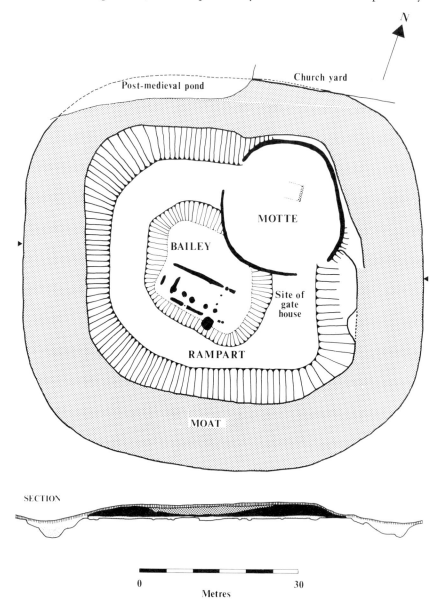

Figure 1.8 Goltho: plan of the motte-and-bailey *c.* 1080-1150 (after Beresford 1987)

military observation/warning post has to be considered, with Robert living elsewhere on his small estate.

The short lifespan of the castle may well have been typical of the many mottes in Britain. Some may never have been finished; some may have been destroyed at an early stage, especially in Wales and the Marches, or been abandoned for any number of reasons. At Bramber, Sussex, the motte was short-lived, and the ditch filled in when the main area of occupation was transferred to the stone gatehouse, itself converted soon afterwards into a keep (Barton and Holden 1977).

As part of the excavation of Baile Hill, one of William I's castles in York, a limited area on the summit of the motte was uncovered, revealing several phases of occupation, although the earliest levels were not reached. The small area excavated has made interpretation a problem, but the earliest structures discovered were dated late twelfth century or shortly after 1200, and two interpretations of the timber buildings have been suggested (figure 1.7). There may have been a rectangular building in the middle of the motte top, its foundation beams set in trenches, and small tower at one end, represented by pit 47, with its foundations deep within the motte. Between the central structure and the perimeter fence or palisade the surface of the motte was mortared. The second theory put forward by the excavators was that there were two ranges of timber buildings, and that the mortar surface was an internal floor, pit 47 in this scheme becoming a latrine or an internal well (Addyman and Priestley 1977: 126–32).

The total excavation of the castle of Goltho has produced remarkable results. An Anglo-Saxon defended enclosure first built *c.* 850 was replaced *c.* 1080 by a motte-and-bailey castle (figure 1.8), possibly reusing part of the existing defences which dictated the layout of the Norman castle. The castle was very small, and the massive rampart of the bailey, with the motte at one end, made the courtyard minute. There was only slight evidence for occupation on the motte itself due to the partial levelling in the twelfth century, but traces of the basement of a timber tower were revealed. The basement was 2.7m square, and may have been used for storage, or possibly as a water cistern. Its walls were lined with brick and stone, bonded with clay; the brick, which was contemporary with the construction of the castle, not reused Roman material, represents a very early use of this material in medieval Britain. In about 1150 the original motte-and-bailey was converted into a large platform by infilling the bailey with the upper part of the motte (figure 1.9). No traces of the defences survived due to the collapse of the platform, but defences there must have been, encircling the aisled hall and the other buildings, one of which may have been a timber watchtower or keep; this was situated in the north-east corner of the castle (Beresford 1987: 85-112).

Evidence for a number of timber buildings on motte summits has also been found in Scotland. An example was excavated on one of the largest mottes in Scotland, the Mote of Urr, Kirkcudbrightshire (Hope-Taylor 1950–1). A series of stone-packed postholes to take the timber uprights of a massive timber building were uncovered, together with a considerable quantity of large iron nails, seemingly used in the construction of the tower. The perimeter defences of the motte were interpreted provisionally as a timber palisade with a stone inner facing. Hope-Taylor suggested that there may have been a turret on the

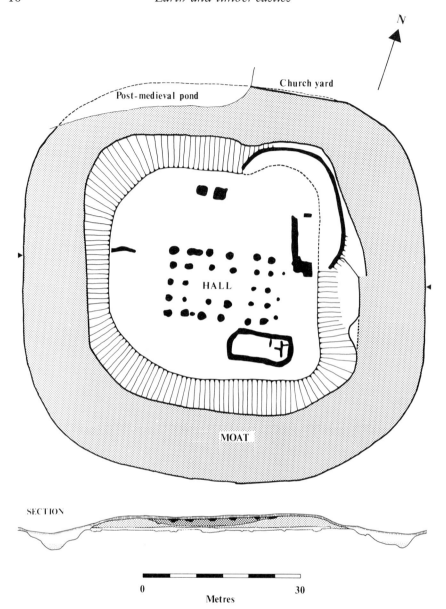

Figure 1.9 Goltho: plan of the castle mound *c.* 1150 (after Beresford 1987)

inside of the palisade, indicated by a shallow pit. However, a pit in this position might have been a 'weapon-pit' or protected emplacement for an archer by analogy with two mottes in Ireland, Clough and Lismahon, both in Co. Down (Waterman 1954: 119; 1959: 147).

The motte of Keir Knowe of Drum, Stirlingshire, was surveyed in 1957, and a small excavation was carried out by the RCAHM. A number of postholes in the centre of the motte summit could have originally held posts for a tower similar to the one suggested at Abinger. The evidence for a palisade around the

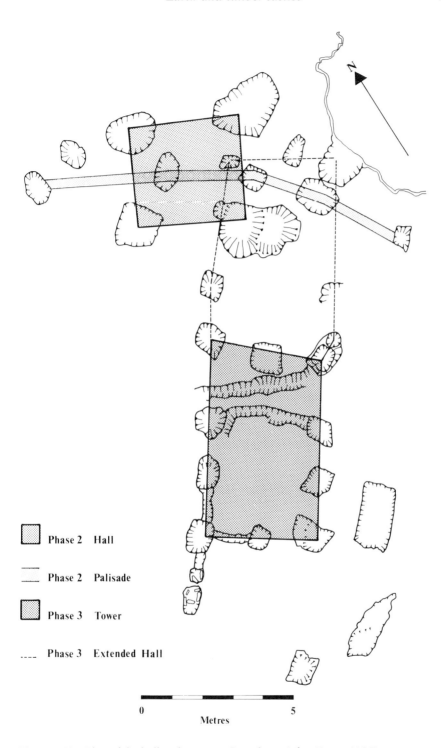

Phase 2   Hall

Phase 2   Palisade

Phase 3   Tower

Phase 3   Extended Hall

0   5
Metres

Figure 1.10   Plan of the hall and tower at Cruggleton (after Ewart 1985)

motte came from a series of stone-packed postholes, whilst on the north-west side a drystone wall formed either part of the perimeter defences or the remains of a building (RCAHM 1963: 176-8).

A drystone wall was found at one end of a mound scarped from rock at Barton Hill, Kinnaird, Perthshire, on the outside of which had lain a stockade which may have been bedded in turves and supported by internal stone facing as at Urr. A keep or tower-house of timber stood originally in the centre of the mound. The ditch around the mound had largely silted up by the fourteenth century, but, as with Keir Knowe, there was little indication of when the small castle was built. It is possible, however, that the site may be equated with the 'mansionem' in a charter of around 1209 (Stewart and Tabraham 1974).

At Cruggleton, Wigtown, a natural outcrop of shale, on which there had been a timber hall and palisade dating to some time after the mid eighth century, was enlarged to form a castle motte in the late twelfth century. A limited excavation discovered evidence for a timber tower, only 4m square, another example of the 'Abinger-type'. The hall on the motte may have been enlarged to form one unit with the tower (figure 1.10), and the excavator suggested that the tower may simply have been a solar (Ewart 1985: 18–22). A close parallel to this phase at Cruggleton is to be found across the sea to the west, in Co. Down. On the motte at Lismahon about the turn of the twelfth century a palisade enclosed a timber hall which was linked to a small tower half the size of the Cruggleton example (Waterman 1959).

When it was originally built the motte of Castlehill of Strachan, Kincardineshire (Yeoman 1984) stood like an island surrounded by watercourses and marsh, connected to drier terrain by a causeway (figure 1.11). It is a late example of a motte, seemingly built c. 1250, and occupied until the early fourteenth century. Its purpose may have been both to guard the ford across the river Feugh and to act as a hunting lodge.

Much of the summit of the mound of Castlehill had already been destroyed before excavation took place in 1980–1, but enough remained to provide a sequence of occupation. The natural mound was first scarped and levelled up, and a series of postpits for a palisade were then dug, about 4-5m apart, the spaces between probably being filled with horizontal wooden planks. The widely-spaced main palisade timbers here were also a feature of another Scottish motte, Roberton (Haggarty and Tabraham 1982: 54–5). Unlike other mottes where a timber tower was the main feature of the mound summit, Castlehill had a timber hall, like Cruggleton, although without the linked tower/solar. In the late thirteenth century the original palisade was replaced by one with a series of postholes c. 50cm apart, centre to centre, the posts being secured with stones packed about them. This later palisade was much stronger than its predecessor, and it has been suggested that there may have been a tower on the line of the perimeter.

The hall at Castlehill does not appear to have been a timber equivalent of Norman masonry buildings sometimes known as a hall-keeps; it simply provided accommodation, and will be discussed more fully in the chapter on halls in Part 2.

An excavation in 1977 on the surviving mound of Peebles, Peeblesshire, a castle of the Scottish kings, revealed two timber buildings dating to the twelfth century sealed by fourteenth-century occupation. One of the structures was

Figure 1.11   The motte, Castlehill of Strachan

clearly a tower, presumably a keep, but unusual in that it was circular, with an external diameter of *c.* 12m. A foundation gully had been dug for timber uprights, whilst postpits set in the outer edge of the trench may have been for supports for the tower (Murray and Ewart 1978–80). If the tower is indeed twelfth century, then it is a remarkable building, for circular keeps are not particularly common in Britain (see p.52). They are mainly found in South Wales and the Marches and built of stone, the majority dating from the late twelfth century to about the middle of the thirteenth century.

No other site has produced an exact parallel to the Peebles timber tower. It is worth noting, however, that on the west side of the bailey of Pleshey Castle, Essex, a circular foundation of chalk, clay and flint, dating to the later twelfth century, was uncovered in excavations; it was *c.* 5.2m wide and *c.* 0.3–0.6m deep and had a smaller foundation *c.* 2.4m wide adjacent to it. The main foundations probably supported a timber tower, with the other possibly supporting a circular staircase. The size of this supposed tower and its position argues against it having been a keep; it may not even have been military in purpose. Later buildings on the site were chapels, and it is possible that the foundation represents the tower of the first of them (Williams 1977: 37–50). Evidence for a circular timber building was found in the motte of Penwortham Castle, Lancashire, in 1856, although the date of the structure may be pre-Norman (Renn 1973: 276).

So far we have seen the results of motte excavations where the timber

Figure 1.12   An impression of the appearance of the motte at South Mimms in the twelfth century (after Davison 1986)

sequence has been within the eleventh to the thirteenth century, the peak period for timber construction on British mottes. In Wales an excavation of a small area of the summit of a motte took place at Sycharth Castle, Denbighshire, near the border with Shropshire, the castle being a motte-and-bailey which was probably constructed in the twelfth century (figure 1.3). The remains of the buildings that were uncovered did not relate to the earliest phases of the castle's history but to the last, for Sycharth was the home of Owain Glyndŵr in the late fourteenth century. It was burnt to the ground in the early years of the Glyndŵr uprising in 1403 by Prince Henry, the future King Henry V. The main structure found was a hall, to be discussed below; no masonry was uncovered, so the castle was one of a small group that remained as earth-and-timber constructions into the late middle ages. A series of stakeholes for a fence, as opposed to postholes for a palisade, showed that the site in the period after the Edwardian conquest of Wales was no longer the strong castle it would have been in the twelfth century; even on the Welsh border it was clearly felt that a massive palisade was no longer necessary (Hague and Warhurst 1966).

The excavations mentioned so far have all been of mottes with superstructures placed on the summits of the mounds. At South Mimms, Hertfordshire, excavations in the early 1960s revealed a very different story. The earthwork looked the typical motte-and-bailey before the excavations began, but on the natural ground surface a flint footing, about 10.5m square externally, had been laid for a timber tower on sleeper beams. The tower was set within the motte, and entrance to the castle was gained via a tunnel through the motte into the tower (figure 1.12). If this were not remarkable enough, the motte was revetted with timber shuttering so that most of the mound was not visible to the outside world (Kent 1968). The castle has been identified as the one Geoffrey de Mandeville, Earl of Essex, was permitted to build in 1141 (Renn 1957).

The construction of the tower at South Mimms can be paralleled at Totnes, Devon, where soon after the Conquest a baronial motte was raised upon the natural bedrock, within the late Saxon burh or defended town. While the motte was being built a large and deep rectangular foundation was laid down for what has been interpreted as a timber tower (Rigold 1954: 236–7, 242); such a foundation seems unnecessary for a wooden structure, and the tower's superstructure may have been of stone, although there is no other evidence for this. A similar feature was discovered at the Observatory Tower of Lincoln Castle (Reynolds 1975). Examples of masonry towers or keeps with their footings lying buried within the body of mottes are known from elsewhere in this country, and will be discussed below.

As we have seen from the above, the summits of several mottes have been investigated since Hope-Taylor's excavation at Abinger. Although a general picture can be built up, and one that is not totally surprising given the pictorial and documentary evidence, it is noteworthy how varied the finished products must have been. Certainly Abinger taught us from the outset that a motte might have carried nothing more than a simple watchtower; and that is all Abinger was, the military outpost of a small estate (Blair 1981). Many mottes of the castles of greater lords which might have had true timber keeps now support masonry buildings, so that evidence for the earlier phases has been lost; thus, the motte of Hen Domen, originally the castle of a great lord but unoccupied since the late thirteenth century, remains a site of great potential.

At Castlehill of Strachan the domestic occupation of the castle lay on the motte, with a hall taking the place of a tower. Even at Cruggleton where the motte had a bailey, the principal residence was on the motte, again a hall rather than a timber keep, linked to a solar or possibly a watchtower. In England the later phases of two castles, Chalgrave and Goltho, consisted of a large hall on an enlarged motte, presumably still enclosed by a palisade. Perhaps we have here examples of a greater emphasis on social and domestic functions rather than primarily defensive ones, for at both these sites alterations were carried out so that important new domestic buildings could be built.

Where there is evidence for large timber towers, the foundations were laid on the original ground surface. The advantage of this was twofold: the tower could be built while the motte was being raised, providing a residence and stronghold almost immediately, and a period of consolidation of the freshly built mound was not required as a building did not have to be constructed on the motte's summit. Excavations have served to emphasize just how varied motte superstructures were; it should not be assumed that all mottes carried the timber equivalents of the stone keeps that were being built at the same time.

Ringworks

Two counties in Wales emphasize the problem of the relationship between mottes and ringworks. Monmouthshire has five ringworks and twenty-nine mottes, whilst Glamorgan has twenty-seven ringworks and sixteen mottes. Furthermore, the five Monmouthshire ringworks are all in the medieval lordship of Usk; if one makes the dangerous assumption that these five were built at about the same time, then it is possible that one man's personal preference influenced the design of neighbouring castles (Spurgeon 1987a: 27). A possible example of this can be seen regarding the estate of Sulgrave in Northamptonshire, the tenure of which was held by three men at the end of the reign of William I. At Sulgrave itself there is a ringwork castle, and ringworks are also to be found on the other lands held by two of the three men (Davison 1977: 106).

In Glamorgan the geology seems to have influenced the distribution of ringworks. For example, in the Vale of Glamorgan, which lies to the south of the drift deposits of the southern limit of glaciation, the shallow layer of soil above the natural rock was more conducive to the construction of ringworks than of mottes. As the mottes required a greater quantity of soil to form the castle mounds, it is not surprising that mottes in Glamorgan are found in the north of the county, on the drift deposits (Spurgeon 1987a: 32–6; 1987b: 206–7).

The proximity of some ringworks to mottes or thirteenth-century masonry castles suggests that one may have been built as the successor to the other, and this has been proposed for Castell Madoc ringwork, Breconshire. The occupation of the castle was very brief, and the castle site may have been moved to where there is now a motte, some 122m downhill from the ringwork (Talbot and Field 1966–7).

The raising of a motte, even one less than 5m high (King's class III; see p.4), was a major undertaking, and an embanked enclosure would have been much quicker to build. The excavation of the ringwork at Chateau des Marais, Guernsey, built in the first half of the thirteenth century, made it possible to see how the encircling bank was constructed. The first activity in the building of the castle was to burn off the vegetation, and this was followed by marking out the line of the bank. The markers were apparently substantial stones placed to stand in the middle of the rampart. The next stage in the operations was the depositing of a bank of turves, over which the main clay rampart was heaped and strengthened by small lumps of granite (Barton 1980: 664, 666).

The use of ringworks as campaign castles (p.7) is illustrated further by the identification of some sites as siege castles, where once again speed in construction was vital. Examples of these castles are the ringwork-and-bailey known as 'The Rings', near Corfe Castle, Dorset, Panpudding Hill outside Bridgnorth, Shropshire, and Lyminster and Rackham Bank, Sussex (siege castles around Arundel). However, as with every rule there are exceptions. The castles of Bentley and Powderham were possibly built in 1147 as part of the siege of Barley Pound, Hampshire; both sites were low mottes (King and Renn 1971; Stamper 1984). If Alcock's interpretation of bank B of the South Banks at Dinas Powys, Glamorgan (a castle built for an unrecorded siege of the main ringwork) is correct, then this siegework is in the form of a *flèche*, that is an arrow-shaped construction with its salient projecting out into the field (Alcock 1963: 4, figure 3, 81–2).

One of the first ringworks to be excavated was Old Castle Camp, Bishopston, in the Gower, Glamorgan. The work was carried out by Colonel W.L. Morgan in 1898, and not only did he recognize the monument for what it was, a Norman earthwork, but his excavation revealed a perfect double line of postholes for the timber reinforcement of a clay wall which originally ran along the rampart (Morgan 1899: 254–5). Also in the nineteenth century,

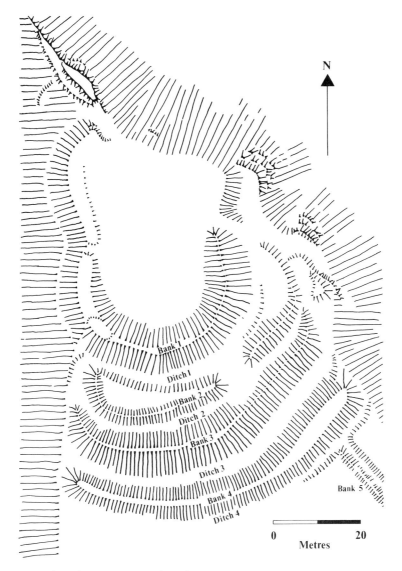

Figure 1.13 Plan of Dinas Powys (after Alcock 1963)

General Pitt-Rivers (1883) correctly identified part of Caesar's Camp, near Folkestone, Kent, as a Norman ringwork.

Excavations have not always been as successful as Morgan's in locating evidence for a palisade, as Talbot (1966) has stressed at Penmaen in the Gower where no traces of the presumed timber defences were found, perhaps because the rubbly make-up of the bank had not preserved the necessary evidence (Alcock 1966: 183). The same argument was suggested by Lewis following his excavation of another Glamorgan ringwork, Loughor (Lewis, J.M. 1975: 152). A bank and ditch would not have been a sufficient obstacle against a Welsh attack, so either evidence for a palisade has been lost, or the rampart may have consisted of a turf bank with a drystone wall, as opposed to a palisade. Erosion of a rampart since the abandonment of an earthwork castle may also have obliterated evidence for a palisade.

The excavations of 1954–8 at Dinas Powys succeeded in exposing the rampart defences. This multi-period site (figure 1.13) lies at the eastern end of the Vale of Glamorgan, one end of the hill having been fortified in the early Christian period by a bank and ditch (numbered II), dating from the fifth to the seventh century. In the Norman period a new bank and ditch (I) were added, bank II being obsolescent by this time. The scarp of the new bank was revetted in stone. Evidence for the revetment of ramparts has been found elsewhere, for example, at Tan-y-bwlch (Old Aberystwyth), Cardiganshire (Houlder 1957: 116), Rumney, near Cardiff (Lightfoot 1983: 2) and Hillesley, Gloucestershire (Williams, B. 1987: 152). In the first two examples timber was used, but at Hillesley the internal revetment was a low stone wall; Hathersage, a ringwork in Derbyshire, also had a masonry revetment (Hodges 1980: 28). Whether in wood or stone, the purpose of a revetment was to prevent a bank or mound of earth from collapsing, either into the ditch or the interior of an enclosure.

A double row of postholes at Dinas Powys indicated that the bank was surmounted by a palisade and fighting platform, and a widening at the south-west corner of bank I suggested that there may have been a timber tower at this point; a similar feature was revealed at Penmaen. The entrance at Dinas Powys was on the north-west side, with a timber gate at the end of the passage, whilst approaches to the entrance were covered by a small outwork (Alcock 1963: 73–9, 95, figure 13). This phase has been dated to the eleventh century, but the lack of firm evidence for occupation does not help with the interpretation of the defences and the question of who built them. Pottery suggests a late eleventh-century date for bank I but does not tell us whether it was a Norman or a Welshman who refortified the site. A little later Dinas Powys was radically strengthened with the the addition of banks and ditches III and IV (figure 1.13); it now formed a formidable stronghold, especially as the internal stone revetment of bank IV had a sheer drop of over 3m, which would have caused even the most determined attacker to pause before continuing the assault (Alcock 1963: 79–83).

Although this later phase cannot be dated precisely, it may have been built by the Normans as part of their general advance into south Wales in the early twelfth century, a period which is likely for another excavated ringwork in the Vale of Glamorgan, Llantrithyd (Charlton *et al.* 1977), and also the ringworks of Coity and Ogmore to the west.

The key to the defences of a motte-and-bailey was the motte; with the ringwork it was the gatehouse, or possibly a keep. At Penmaen a series of postholes marked the site of a gatehouse (Alcock 1966: 187). Cae Castell, Rumney, the subject of an intensive excavation, also produced evidence for a timber gatehouse in its first phase (figure 1.14) (Lightfoot 1983: 2); this was later blocked with clay and rubble, and a stone gatehouse was built elsewhere on the site.

Prudhoe in Northumberland as it stands today is a masonry castle of the twelfth century onwards, but excavations undertaken from 1972 to 1981 showed that an earth-and-timber ringwork was the first castle on the site, occupying an area where there had been a settlement which had consisted of

Figure 1.14 The site of the timber gateway, Rumney Castle

two timber buildings with hearths enclosed by a palisade, possibly dating to the mid eleventh century. The castle ringwork which replaced this settlement in the late eleventh century had a powerful clay and stone bank topped by a palisade. On the south-east side a structure, almost 6m square, had been totally robbed out to such an extent that it was not even possible to say whether the structure had been of timber or masonry, although the former would seem the most logical, as one would expect some remnants of stone and mortar to have survived the demolition of masonry. Unfortunately, safety prevented the full excavation of this building at Prudhoe, for the structure was over 6m deep, but enough was done to show that whatever stood in this position at the end of the eleventh century must have been either a gatehouse or a mural tower/keep (Keen 1983).

It is rare to find an early castle with multiple defences. One example with a double bank and ditch encircling the bailey can be found at Hen Domen in Montgomeryshire. A similar defensive arrangement is to be seen at Berkhamsted Castle, Hertfordshire, both castles having mottes. As we have seen, Dinas Powys ringwork also had a series of banks and ditches, whilst at Ludgershall in Wiltshire there is a remarkable double-banked double ringwork (or ringwork and bailey), although some of its original features have been obscured by subsequent developments of the castle.

Ludgershall was built on a site where there were no natural advantages which could have been incorporated into its defences, and this may account for the double banks. The main area of occupation was the northern half which may have been the earliest part of the castle. It was found that the earthworks were revetted by timber, and that there was a large timber tower supported on posts on padstones set deep in the ground, all this dating to *c.* 1100.

The first defences of the bailey to the south consisted of a palisade enclosing a rectangular area with an earth platform or mound at the corners which became incorporated into the later earthworks. When the bailey was built to replace the original palisade the defences were revetted with timber at the front and rear. Inside the defences the excavations uncovered a remarkable building. It consisted of a 'cellar' *c.* 8m × 6.4m in area dug more than 6m into the chalk, with internal posts and joistholes, and access gained apparently by a ladder and a short tunnel. The 'cellar' was at one end of a timber building which had its posts set into pits 1.9m deep. Whether this twelfth-century structure had a military function is not clear, but it is worth noting that there was a large twelfth-century masonry keep in the northern ringwork. This would imply that the timber building was not a keep, assuming that the two were contemporary (Addyman 1973).

We have seen (p.17) that the small motte-and-bailey at Goltho was built over an Anglo-Saxon manorial enclosure, an unusual circumstance, but not unique; the development at Prudhoe may have been similar. Intermittent excavations in the period 1960–76 were the first to produce such a sequence at a small yet powerful site, the ringwork at Sulgrave in Northamptonshire. Funding did not allow for the completion of the research programme, but in the six seasons of excavations enough was revealed to show that the ringwork overlay a Saxon manor with timber and stone buildings, possibly fortified in the early eleventh century. The massive Norman bank incorporated the lower storey of a Saxon masonry building which was used as the base for a timber tower on the bank. Although the rampart was later raised by 1.2m, and widened, no trace was found of the first Norman palisade, if one ever existed. The small timber keep or watchtower on the bank was repaired early in the twelfth century when a further layer of clay was added to heighten the defences, but by the middle of the twelfth century the ringwork was abandoned when the Sulgrave estate was given to the priory of St Andrew, Northampton (Davison 1977).

Castle Acre castle, Norfolk (to be discussed in more detail in the next chapter), is a castle of unparalleled development. Although its first phase, the late eleventh-century 'country house', was a stone building, it was surrounded by a very modest ringwork (figure 2.6). Apart from the house, it can hardly be seen as a strongly fortified site or castle, hence the term 'country house' used by the excavators, and such modest defences might be regarded more a feature of the later middle ages than the years immediately following the Norman Conquest. The first period, therefore, saw the raising of a low bank of chalk, possibly with a timber palisade along the crest. The original simple gateway, however, was soon replaced by a masonry gatehouse. This residence of the Warenne Earl of Surrey was thus in stark contrast to other early sites, and serves as a reminder that not every secular building built by a Norman magnate had to be a castle. William de Warenne did have castles elsewhere in England, for example, at Conisbrough in Yorkshire, but he clearly felt that a stronghold at Castle Acre was not necessary; that development was left to his successors. The early date for the 'country house' is implied in the record of the death of William's first wife in childbirth in 1085 at Castle Acre (Coad and Streeten 1982: 140, 178–9). A similar sequence may have also occurred at the de Clare castle of Bletchingley, Surrey, where re-excavation of this D-shaped ringwork has uncovered a similar Norman house, probably with a first floor hall (Turner, D.J. 1987: 253–4).

Mottes as secondary structures

South Mimms has shown that a motte need not have been the first feature of a castle to have been built, and this aspect will be illustrated further when masonry keeps are discussed. However, excavations have revealed that, unlike South Mimms where the motte and tower were contemporary, a castle mound might be also added to a castle several years after the date of the original construction.

During the initial Norman advance into the west country Castle Neroche, a strong earthwork castle of ringwork type (figure 1.15, a) was built on the edge of the Blackdown Hills, Somerset, commanding important routes to the south-west. It was, therefore, a campaign castle, and consisted of a bank and ditch enclosing a circular or subcircular area, and it would have been quick to construct. At some stage after the initial phase the castle was converted into a motte-and-bailey (figure 1.15, b). A motte, 6–7m high, was raised over part of the ringwork bank, whilst the remainder of the earlier earthwork became the bailey, a new earthwork dividing it into two unequal parts, the smaller inner bailey acting as a barbican or outer defence to the immediate approaches to the motte (Davison 1971–2). Clearly the new lord of the castle was not satisfied with the defences of the campaign fortress as a permanent strongpoint and residence. The motte and the division of the ringwork greatly strengthened the castle, and the large area on the motte, *c*. 36.5m in diameter, provided sufficient space for a large defended residence; the summit was later subdivided into a small enclosure or shell-keep, with the rest of the motte summit acting as a bailey.

Other examples where a motte was added to an existing ringwork, with the latter forming a bailey, include Bristol Castle, little of which now remains above ground (Ponsford n.d.: 8), and possibly Gloucester (Hurst, H.R. 1984: 76–81). In the second phase of 'The Castles', Barrow-upon-Humber, Lincolnshire, a ringwork was partially rebuilt to act as the first bailey of the motte which was raised over one side of the original earthwork (Atkins 1983).

A section through the mound at Aldingham, Lancashire, revealed that the motte, which was later heightened (p.11), was not the first castle. The original defences had been a 35m wide ringwork, and this had been infilled at a later date to become a motte (Davison 1969). The infilling of ringworks is known from other sites, and undoubtedly others await to be discovered. The motte of the small castle of More in Shropshire, near the Welsh border, was raised in this way (King and Alcock 1969: 120), and re-evaluation of the excavation at Burton-in-Lonsdale, Yorkshire, revealed a similar story (Moorhouse 1971). In Ireland, where raths and ringforts (ringworks) exist in profusion, it is not surprising that with the arrival of the Normans use was made of these earlier earthworks, as was found at Lismahon (Waterman 1959). In France a similar picture was revealed with the excavation of a small motte at Mirville, Normandy (Le Maho 1983; 1984; 1985).

A further cautionary tale in accepting a motte as a primary feature of a castle was learnt from the work undertaken in the bailey of Carisbrooke Castle on the Isle of Wight (Young 1983b). It has been shown that the large motte with its attendant bailey known as the Lower Enclosure belongs to a later phase of the castle's history, succeeding a castle ringwork of two phases. The first of these ringworks was probably first built by William fitz Osbern, Earl of Hereford (d. 1071), within the Lower Enclosure; this was originally considered to have been a Roman fort of the Saxon Shore (Rigold 1969), but is now viewed as part of the Anglo-Saxon burh system (Young 1983a). Fitz Osbern's

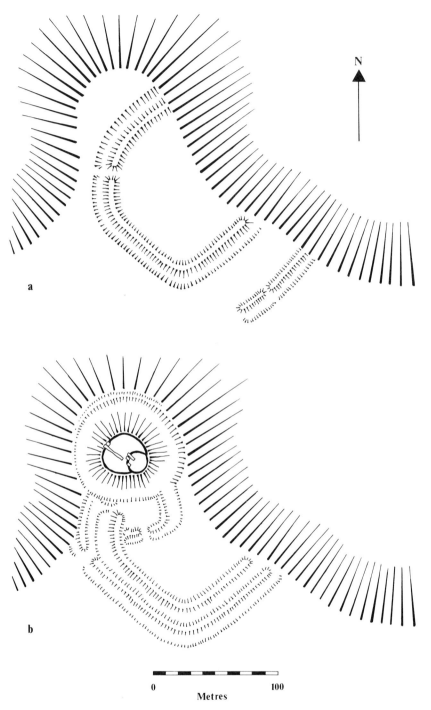

N

Figure 1.15   The development of Castle Neroche from ringwork to motte-and-bailey (after Davison 1971-2)

castle occupied an area of the Lower Enclosure cut off from the remainder by a bank and ditch, whilst the second phase of *c.* 1100 consisted of a more powerful bank and ditch enclosing a slightly smaller area than the first Norman defences. The first ditch was only 2m deep and 4m wide, the second twice the size. It has been suggested that the building of the motte-and-bailey, the third phase in the development of the castle, coincided with a change in ownership, when the lordship of the Isle of Wight was granted to Richard de Redvers by 1107.

The impressive series of excavations undertaken in Winchester in the 1960s and early 1970s included the northern area of the castle, little of which now stands above ground except for the Great Hall of Henry III. William I's castle of 1067 was constructed by enclosing an area in the south-west corner of the old Roman defences of the town by a bank and ditch which cut off a vast castle platform. It lay over Saxon occupation, an aspect of early Norman castle building known from both documentary evidence (e.g. Domesday Book entries for Wallingford and Shrewsbury) and other excavations such as at Oxford (Hassall 1976: 237–45; Jope 1952–3). The Winton Domesday of *c.* 1110 also records the loss of a street at Winchester when it was 'destroyed when the king had his ditch made' (Biddle 1976: 47).

The excavation at the north end of Winchester Castle discovered that after the building of the initial platform in 1067, a motte was raised at the extreme northern end of the site *c.* 1071–2, where the castle's eastern rampart met the Roman town walls. The motte had a timber revetment, to be replaced by a stone wall *c.* 1075, but subsequent development in the twelfth century destroyed evidence of the defences on the motte (Biddle 1970: 291; 1975: 104–5). The Conqueror's original earthwork castle was impressive enough not to require a motte as part of its defences; however, the reason for its construction may have been the need to build a platform to command the approaches to the city's West Gate which lay about 100m to the north of the castle.

In conclusion, a cautionary tale regarding secondary mottes relates to the excavations at Loughor in Glamorgan. Here it was shown that although the motte-like appearance of the castle was due to the infilling of a ringwork, this had not been a deliberate development. Instead the build-up of occupation debris over the interior of the ringwork from the early twelfth century to the late thirteenth century gave it its present appearance (Lewis, J.M. 1975: 149, 152).

The bailey defences

Not all mottes had baileys, but where they are present we have learnt something about several of them from excavation, but generally only small areas have been studied apart from the classic site of Hen Domen. Where work has been carried out it has usually concentrated on only a very limited area, and that usually the defences.

Therfield Castle, Hertfordshire, was possibly built during the Anarchy of the reign of King Stephen. The excavator suggested that the small size of the motte and the lack of any evidence for a building on the mound were indications that

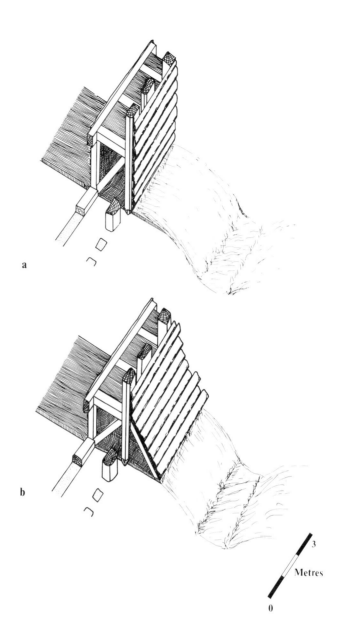

a

b

3
Metres
0

Figure 1.16 Two impressions of how the bailey defences at Therfield may have appeared (after Biddle 1964)

the castle was unfinished, although the area of the bailey defences which was excavated did reveal evidence for a palisade. The rampart consisted of a clay bank together with a timber revetment of the type which has already been seen at the mottes of South Mimms and Aldingham. The vertical timbers at the rear of the bank were set into sillbeams, but as figure 1.16 shows it was not clear what form the front of the palisade took (Biddle 1964: 58–63). Whatever the external appearance, the shallow postholes (*c.* 30cm deep) are an indication that Therfield's defences were hastily erected and somewhat vulnerable, especially as the encircling ditch was less than a metre deep, and approximately 4m wide.

Other bailey defences have been excavated at Launceston, Cornwall, and Tamworth, Staffordshire. The bailey at Launceston is now encircled by a mid thirteenth-century curtain wall, but before the masonry defences were added to the rampart the bank evolved over four distinct phases, dating to the late eleventh and twelfth centuries. The first rampart was more than 12m wide at the base, but any evidence for a timber revetment at the front had been removed by road improvements in the nineteenth century. However, there were traces of a slight turf-capped bank which was probably used for marking out the line of the bailey defences. In the second phase the rampart was raised on a secure foundation of large stones behind the crest of the earlier line. The revetment consisted of vertical timbers set into sillbeams, and secured by posts, 30cm thick, running through the bank. A row of postholes marked the line of

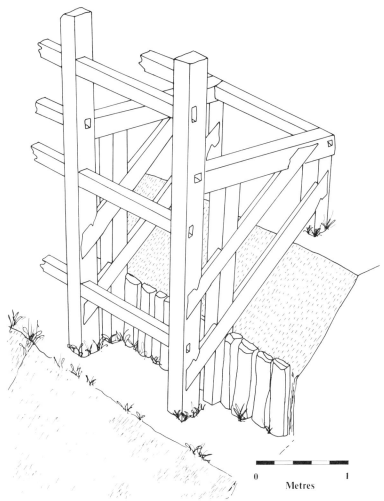

Figure 1.17 A hypothetical reconstruction of the bailey defences at Tamworth (after Meeson 1978-9)

the inner revetment. The third and fourth phases consisted of the heightening of the bank, using the same revetment, although it is probable that some of the timbering would have had to have been replaced over the years (Saunders 1970: 90–1).

In the south-west corner of Launceston's bailey the remains of a stone-lined pit, *c.* 3m square, were found set behind the rampart; it had been destroyed in the thirteenth century. Its function is unclear, but it would not appear to have been a garderobe pit as it was not associated with any building. However, its proximity to the rampart suggests that it may be the remains of an early mural tower, either all of masonry or a masonry foundation supporting a timber superstructure. A similar feature was discovered beneath the later north gate of the castle (Saunders 1977b: 133–4). The features, if they were defensive, throw an interesting light on the beginnings of the transformation of an earth-and-timber castle to one of stone, although earth-and-timber and masonry defences did exist side by side in several cases. Evidence for small towers set just within the line of the defences can be seen at another Cornish castle, Restormel (Radford 1986: 7), and also at Newcastle-upon-Tyne (Harbottle 1982: 410). In connection with these examples, one of the features uncovered at the small Normandy castle of Mirville was a rectangular stone foundation for an eleventh-century timber tower (Le Maho 1984: 16, 24).

Some of the existing stonework at Tamworth, both on the motte and in the bailey, dates to the Norman period. An earlier Norman phase was revealed when excavations carried out in 1977 discovered evidence for the original timber defences of the bailey. As at the above English sites, a timber revetment indicated by a single row of postholes ran along the rear of the rampart, whilst at the front a double row was excavated. The interpretation favoured by the excavator (figure 1.17) was of a timber-framed construction revetting the front and the rear of the rampart and supporting a wall-walk or fighting platform around the bailey, with bracing posts securing this heavy timber construction (Meeson 1978–9). The pitfalls of interpreting this type of structure solely from posthole evidence are obvious. One can never be certain about the superstructure when there is only evidence for the timber uprights, and such reconstructions should be approached with caution. The outer line of postholes indicated the nature of the defences; positioned close to the ditch as the Tamworth revetment was, this timber-framed construction, where the front posts were apparently tied in with those at the rear, would have been the logical step to have taken to prevent the defences from slumping. There may have been a similar revetment around the bailey of Barnstaple Castle, Devon (Miles 1986: 72), whilst at Eaton Socon, Bedfordshire, the sides of the bank and ditch seems to have had a revetment of planks reinforced with posts (Addyman 1965: 48).

The motte-and-bailey at Goltho had very strong defences for its size, leaving a small area for the bailey interior, much of which was filled by a timber hall. The moat about the castle was *c.* 12m wide and had an average depth of 4m, whilst the rampart was *c.* 15–18m thick, and originally *c.* 4m high. The immediate approach to the castle lay on the east, with the motte dominating a ramp which led to the presumed gatehouse into the bailey. The construction of the later castle on the same site resulted in the loss of evidence for the nature of the defences on the bailey bank, but the rampart itself had been faced with turf to prevent subsidence, the turves being held in position with willow stakes (Beresford 1977b: 54; 1987: 87–90).

The most significant excavation of a castle earthwork is that of the motte-and-bailey near Montgomery known by its Welsh name Hen Domen (Old Mound), significant because few other early European castle excavations can match Barker and Higham's work for thoroughness. The first season of excavation was in 1960, and it still (1988) continues. It is, therefore, a site to which the student of castle studies should pay special attention, particularly with regard to the internal buildings (pp.126–8). In the two centuries of the castle's existence, *c.* 1071–1300, the buildings of this first castle of Montgomery were of earth and timber, and a feature of the excavation was the evidence for a great variety of buildings and construction techniques. The first volume, on the excavations up to 1979, has been published (Barker and Higham 1982), and contains detailed plans of all the phases; a forthcoming report will cover the reconstruction of the buildings in more detail. A summary report covers the excavations from 1960 to 1988 (Barker and Higham 1988).

Hen Domen (figure 1.18) is considered to have been the castle of Roger of Montgomery, Earl of Shrewsbury (1071/4–94). It was built in a key area of the border between England and Wales, overlooking the strategic ford of Rhydwhiman, and close to the site of the Roman fort of Forden Gaer. The land on which it was situated had been part of a ploughed field which had reverted to scrub, and it is interesting to note that plough-land was also discovered beneath the bailey bank of Sandal Castle, Yorkshire (Mayes and Butler 1983: 70–2). The motte stands on the west side of the bailey, the latter having the unusual feature of being surrounded by a double rampart and ditch. The original bailey bank was a turf-capped clay bank, whilst the timber defences were, as postulated at Tamworth, a timber-framed palisade and wall-walk, the posts standing on clay pads (figures 1.19, 5.1, p.99). Although there was no firm evidence for timber mural towers on the line of the palisade, an area at the north-west corner of the rampart had been raised to create a platform which may have formed the base of a tower; building LVI at the entrance on the east side may also have been a tower.

A few decades later, possibly even as a result of the Welsh attack on the castle in 1095 in which the garrison was killed, the defences were rebuilt. The carpentry of the new defences was apparently less sophisticated, post-built and without a framework of interlocking timbers, but with a fighting platform or wall-walk and a tower at the north-west corner of the bailey, overlooking the bailey and motte ditches (tower XX). The excavators have commented on the use of massive timbers in Roger of Montgomery's castle, impressive especially when they are compared to those of the later phases. They have suggested that the change in ownership after 1102, from the powerful Montgomerys to the socially less important de Boulers family, might have been a reason for the change in building techniques evident from the excavation. It may have been that the de Boulers employed craftsmen inferior to those who built Earl Roger's castle.

The next phase of the bailey defences dates from the middle of the twelfth century (see frontispiece and figure 5.2, p.100), and emphasizes how varied the structures of a timber castle could be. The palisade tower in the north-west corner was rebuilt (tower XVI), and the initial section of palisading to the east

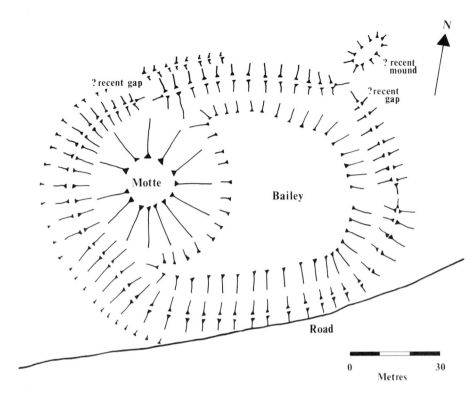

Figure 1.18 Plan of Hen Domen (after Barker and Higham 1988)

Figure 1.19 The first defences of the bailey at Hen Domen, with the ranging rods marking the clay pads on which stood the timber uprights of the palisade and fighting platform

was set back from the bailey bank, presumably to allow the tower to flank the defences, one of the prime functions of any mural tower. The remainder of the palisade on the north side of the bailey was much narrower than the section of platform to the west, whilst on the north-east the defences were marked by large, deep postholes. The entrance to the bailey was overlooked by another timber tower, and the area of packed stones and boulders by the entrance may mark the site of a guardchamber belonging to the gatehouse which may have stood here.

There was little evidence for the penultimate phase of the defences of Hen Domen in the late twelfth and early thirteenth century (see figure 5.3, p.102), but from what could be ascertained they were no longer built of timber set in postholes, but were probably of sillbeam construction; two lengths of beams were uncovered in the outer ditch. An angular D-shaped tower was built at the north-west corner (tower IV), in the same position as its predecessors, confirming the need to renew earlier timberwork constantly. It was destroyed by fire, and the evidence from the conflagration suggests that the tower was a substantial building; only the destruction by fire of a major structure could have caused the clay to turn so red. Assuming that tower IV was of one period, then its method of construction entailed the use of both sillbeams and posts set in holes in the ground. The other mural tower, overlooking the eastern entrance, was renewed in this same phase, its main timbers set in postholes.

The final occupation of the motte-and-bailey is dated *c*. 1223–*c*. 1300, a period when the castle coexisted with the new castle of Montgomery to the south-east, built by the king from 1223. King Henry's castle may have initiated renewed life for the old castle, for the view into Wales from New Montgomery is obscured by the hill occupied by the Iron Age hillfort of Ffridd Faldwyn. Hen Domen, therefore, remained as an observation post for the royal castle during the thirteenth century, until the Edwardian conquest of north Wales made it redundant. The nature of the defences in this period is uncertain, although tower IV may have still been standing, and there were traces of a rectangular tower (XXXVII) guarding the bailey entrance, so a palisade between the two is likely.

A wooden palisade was also a feature of the outer defences in the later period; only a small area has been excavated, and that just below the turf, so earlier periods have yet to be exposed. A series of post- and stakeholes, with slots for a fence, suggest that these defences consisted of a rampart strengthened with a wattle fence on the crest, with a fighting platform behind (Barker and Higham 1985). The method of construction of the outer defences can be paralleled elsewhere in the bailey, especially building XXII of the mid twelfth century. These defences as a whole serve to confirm the potential strength of Hen Domen as a fortress, however susceptible to fire it may have been, a problem faced by other such castles.

The examples of bailey defences cited above, particularly those at Tamworth and Hen Domen, were sophisticated structures. However, not all castles had such elaborate palisading. An example of a more basic design is the single line of timbers which formed the palisade at Hen Blas, Flintshire (Leach 1960: 19).

The majority of earthwork castles fall into the above types, mottes and ringworks, with or without baileys. There are, of course, some castles which do not conform to these two categories. Lochmaben, Dumfriesshire, is an example of this. Here two adjacent platforms form the castle or 'peel' which was constructed during Edward I's campaign in Scotland. Its timber palisade and associated wooden buildings remained a feature of the castle's main platform until the 1360s (Macdonald and Laing 1974-5).

Excavations of mottes have stressed just how apt is David King's use of the term 'Proteus' (p.9). Many castle mounds have produced buildings and palisades on their summits, but such discoveries are to be expected given the purpose for which the mottes were intended. Nevertheless, the results from excavations of sites such as South Mimms, Aldingham, Castle Neroche and Goltho have shown that it is dangerous to accept the motte at face value. It need not have been a primary feature of a castle, but only excavation can tell us this. The problem of how a motte fits into the sequence of development of a particular castle is one that will recur in the next chapter.

Excavations have not only enlightened our knowledge of motte superstructure, but also of the physical construction of these earthworks. Nevertheless, it could be argued that too much attention has been paid to mottes to the detriment of detailed examination of the baileys, although the thorough examination of the latter requires a considerable amount of money and time for the work to be of any significance. Thus, one tends to refer constantly to the work at Hen Domen where it has been seen that long-term occupation of a motte-and-bailey made it necessary for the timber defences, as well as the internal buildings, to be repaired or replaced frequently due to the elements and the Welsh, as well as just general wear and tear.

Although the ringwork has been recognized as a Norman monument since Pitt-Rivers excavated at Caesar's Camp, Folkestone, and Morgan's excavations in the Gower, it is only since the 1960s, with work at castles such as Penmaen and Sulgrave, and the publication of King and Alcock's seminal paper (1969), that this type of earthwork castle has found a permanent place in castle literature. Davison's work at Castle Neroche and Young's at Carisbrooke have shown that this type of castle was often used by the Normans as a campaign fortress. This fact can also be confirmed by an examination of some of the first castles built in South Wales that lie on the coast or within the immediate hinterland; a large number began as earth-and-timber ringworks.

2 Masonry castles – keeps

The keep as an element of a castle is a theme which runs through the middle ages, from William fitz Osbern's building at Chepstow of *c.* 1067–71 to the polygonal Yellow Tower of Gwent, the keep of fifteenth-century Raglan, both Monmouthshire castles. The later medieval tower-houses of northern England and Scotland, which are basically in the 'keep' tradition, also continue to be built well into the post-medieval period, particularly in Scotland. The square or rectangular keep is a dominant feature of the Norman period (Renn 1973), whilst in the thirteenth century many of the main towers built *de novo* were circular (Renn 1961); few were rectangular. Whereas the majority of the greater keeps still stand, and have been the subject of much study, excavations have brought to light several smaller examples, in most cases keeps that have been lost to sight for generations. The grassed-over remains of some of these towers have even led to some of them being interpreted as mottes.

A castle mound would have needed a very large summit to take a stone keep; a substantial square or rectangular keep would have been too heavy to have been supported by a motte, Norwich being a notable exception. A solution was found at Clun in Shropshire, where the keep was built into and down the side of the motte. At Bristol Castle it was presumably considered more convenient to demolish the motte when the keep was constructed in the twelfth century (Ponsford n.d.: 8; 1987: 147). A circular keep was a different matter; because it was less massive in build and smaller in area, it could be comfortably supported by most large mottes, as shown by several castles in the southern Welsh Marches, such as Bronllys, Breconshire, and Longtown, Herefordshire. There are, of course, a few mottes which consist wholly or partially of natural outcrops of rock; such mottes could provide firm foundations for keeps.

An event that took place at the castle of Athlone in Co. Westmeath illustrates the problems that could occur when building a stone keep on a man-made mound. It is recorded that £129 12s. 0d. was spent on the construction of a stone tower in 1211–12, and that it collapsed the following year killing nine men (Hillaby 1985: 220). The sum of money clearly represents a tower of some size. As a comparison the keep of Peveril Castle, Derbyshire, built in 1175–7, cost Henry II £184. It is about 12m square and 18m tall. However, it is not known whether the Athlone Tower was round or square in plan; the remains visible today are of a decagonal keep, with the mound revetted in stone, presumably to prevent a repetition of collapse. Nevertheless, round or square, the Athlone incident is a reminder of the vulnerability of a large masonry building on a motte, although it is conceivable that the cause of the collapse was due to the motte being of recent construction and not fully consolidated.

There are a few castles where small square or rectangular keeps were built on mottes. At Okehampton, Devon, a castle which is mentioned in Domesday Book, a small and narrow rectangular keep stands on a large motte; excavation and analysis of the standing remains have shown that the western half is an addition to an earlier tower built when the domestic arrangements were radically improved *c.* 1300 (Higham 1984: 10–11). As the motte was

constructed of shale over a natural rock outcrop, it was able to support what
was an early stone keep, albeit small in area. The excavations revealed that the
deep foundations of the keep were laid down and built up at the same time as
the upper levels of the motte. In contrast to this, the later medieval addition to
the west was simply built directly on the summit of the mound. The earliest
part of the keep, the width of which measures *c.* 10.8m externally and 6.4m
internally, has been interpreted as the work of the sheriff of Devon, Baldwin de
Brionne, in the reign of William I (Higham 1977).

A comparison between Okehampton and other castles in Devon and
elsewhere does not lead to any obvious parallels, except perhaps the
contemporary rectangular gatehouse of Exeter Castle, a royal stronghold built
on the instructions of the king *c.* 1068, with the work being supervised by de
Brionne. The gate at Exeter (Blaylock 1985) is in marked contrast to the
remains of the Norman keep at Okehampton, but they are both interesting
examples of very early castles, for masonry is a rare feature of the first Norman
castles. The most notable stone building in a castle built from the years
immediately following the Norman victory at Hastings is the keep of 1067–71
at Chepstow.

Small Norman keeps are still a feature of the landscape. For example, the
one at Oxford, St George's Tower, which is possibly a contemporary of de
Brionne's building at Okehampton. South Wales has several examples, notably
Usk in Monmouthshire, a mid twelfth-century trapezoidal tower *c.* 9.5 ×
10.5m, placed on the line of the defences to flank the gate, as was possibly the
twelfth-century keep at White Castle in the same county, of which only the
foundations remain. The fragments of a small late twelfth-century keep which
was also built on the line of the defences was uncovered during excavations at
Rumney Castle, Cardiff (Lightfoot 1983: 2, 4). The building could not be fully
excavated, but it was about 13 × 11.5m, and overlooked the original entrance
to the ringwork. Very little of the walls remained, but there was enough of the
interior to show that it had been floored with slabs of sandstone and limestone.

A keep of a similar size to those above was excavated in 1946–7 at Ascot
Doilly, Oxfordshire, and was dated to the second quarter of the twelfth
century. Before the excavation, the castle had all the appearances of a small
motte-and-bailey, but what was revealed was a 10.7m square keep (figure 2.1).
The castle mound had been added against the keep, and its construction kept
pace with the building of the lower courses of the tower as high as a slight
offset. The motte was not an impressive earthwork compared to other
examples, and its function may have been simply to provide additional
protection for the keep foundations. The basement floor of the keep consisted
of a layer of mortar, and it was evident that its internal walling had been
plastered, a feature still to be seen in parts of most masonry castles that survive
today. Another feature of the keep was a masonry abutment added to one
corner, interpreted as the base for a timber staircase which would have led to
the first floor entrance (Jope and Threlfall 1959). This twelfth-century keep
was deliberately demolished, but the date when this event occurred is
uncertain. It may have been destroyed on the orders of Henry II on his
accession in 1154 after the civil war of Stephen's reign, although Jope and
Threlfall also suggest that the keep may have been one of the victims of a series
of demolitions of castles undertaken in the 1170s. An example of this policy is

the castle of Benington in Hertfordshire; in 1176–7 one hundred picks were bought in order to demolish the keep. Another castle which was ordered to be demolished was Middleton Stoney in the year 1216 on the instructions of King John. The excavations at this Oxfordshire castle showed that the 'motte' was the remains of a Norman keep. Only a small area was excavated, including the staircase which would have led up to the first floor entrance; like the abutment at Ascot Doilly the steps were not bonded into the adjacent keep (Rahtz and Rowley 1984: 50, 57–61, 63). It is possible that the staircase at Middleton Stoney was originally wooden, but was later replaced by stone steps; hence it was easier to abut the new steps against the keep than bond them into it.

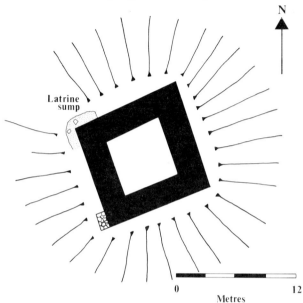

Figure 2.1 Plan of the keep, Ascot Doilly (after Jope and Threlfall 1959)

As well as adding further examples to the number of Anglo-Norman keeps, Ascot Doilly and Middleton Stoney serve as a warning not to assume that what looks like a typical motte is one. In 1958 a trench was dug across the 'keep' of Farnham Castle, Surrey, a motte revetted by a late twelfth-century shell-keep with rectangular turrets. In the centre of the mound a *c.* 15m square stone foundation was uncovered, set within the motte, with a central well-shaft *c.* 4m square (figure 2.2). This proved to be the remains of a keep with a chalk flange around it, and the whole structure was set in a mound or motte of marl. The motte, therefore, acted as a massive buttress to support the keep; the flange provided greater stability, enabling the keep to be bigger than otherwise would have been possible on a less secure foundation. Just how much the motte was intended to act as a deterrent to the undermining of the keep is open to question, but it naturally provided a further strongpoint from which the castle could be defended.

At Farnham the foundations beneath the flange were 7.3m high and 11.9m square; the keep itself may have been about 14m square, and possibly towered 18–21m above the motte. The workmanship of the foundations suggested to

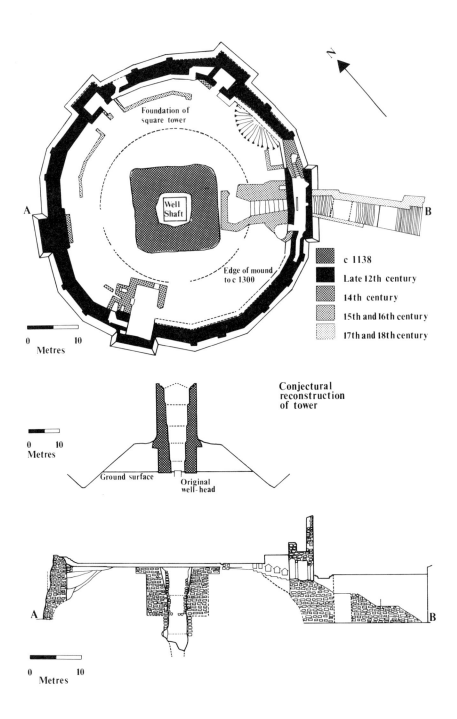

Foundation of
square tower

Well
Shaft

A

B

Edge of mound
to c 1300

c 1138

Late 12th century

14th century

15th and 16th century

17th and 18th century

0   10
Metres

Conjectural
reconstruction
of tower

0   10
Metres

Ground surface   Original
well-head

A

B

0   10
Metres

Figure 2.2   The keep and motte at Farnham Castle (after Thompson 1967)

the excavator that the original intention had been to build a free-standing keep; if this were the case, the change in plan was decided upon during construction. The tower, built by Henry of Blois, Bishop of Winchester (1129–71) and begun in 1138, must have been a daunting sight, but it was not to stand for long, for its destruction was ordered by Henry II in 1155 (Thompson 1960). The subsequent rebuilding saw the construction of the shell-keep, and in the thirteenth century the area between the motte and this new enclosure wall was filled in to form a level interior. A similar revetment of a motte in stone can also be seen at Whittington, Shropshire, where a wall with rounded mural towers and a gatehouse were added in the thirteenth century. Interestingly, excavations here also uncovered a rectangular keep in the middle of the motte. Unfortunately the depth of the foundations within the mound is not known (Wilson and Moorhouse 1971: 148), so at present there can be no direct comparison between the two sites.

Another Norman keep, like Farnham with its own internal well, was excavated at Tote Copse, Aldingbourne, in Sussex (Brewster 1969). Its existence had been known for some years, as in modern times it has been used as a convenient source of building stone, but excavation uncovered evidence that this *c.* 12m square building had been enclosed within a motte of clay and rock. Repairs to the keep whilst it was a free-standing building were carried out on part of the chamfered plinth. This indicated that the motte was a later addition, not raised as the courses of masonry were being laid down, as at Ascot Doilly. The high quality of the dressed stone was further proof that the motte was an afterthought, but as the plinth showed very little sign of weathering the mound must have followed soon after the initial building. This was confirmed by layers of mortar within the make-up of the motte which suggest that work on the upper levels of the keep was still proceeding when the motte was raised. The repairs to the plinth, therefore, must have been undertaken before the keep was finished, although it is surprising that such work needed to be done so soon. Both motte and keep were encircled by a masonry curtain wall. The date of the castle is uncertain; the design of the keep itself suggests that it must be twelfth century, although the interpretation of the pottery evidence has been called into question (Barton 1979: 1).

The quality of the stone plinth of the Aldingbourne keep is a reminder that few of the keeps that have been excavated are notable for the fineness of their masonry. It is the more important, and thus generally the grander, examples that still stand today. However, the remains of the keep of Brandon Castle, Warwickshire, possibly built by about 1150, had a fine plinth and string-course (Chatwin 1955).

Bungay in Suffolk had a similar story (Braun 1935: 205), and also Wareham, Dorset, where the lower courses of the keep were buried to a depth of 1.5m within a gravel mound (Renn 1960: 56); this may also have been the case at Caerleon, Monmouthshire (Knight 1963). Lincoln, one of only two castles possessing two mottes, the other being Lewes in Sussex, may have had a tower rising from a foundation within the mound known as the Observatory Tower; but there are some uncertainties here as to the form of the earlier keep, or even if it were a stone building (Reynolds 1975). At Lydford in Devon there is a further variant on this theme.

An important aspect of the original tower at Lydford is its description in the

Pipe Rolls of 1195 as a 'domus firme ad custodiendos prisones' when £74 was spent on this 'strong house' (Saunders 1980: 127, 153). Its function was a prison as opposed to a castle in the strict sense, and it continued in this role until the seventeenth century, for it formed part of the administration of the tin industry, being the prison for the Devon Stannaries. It was not until 1957, when consolidation of the tower began, that the discovery of an infilled basement within the body of the motte showed that the history of this castle was more complicated than it first seemed. Until this discovery Lydford had been seen as one of the few examples of a square keep on the summit of a motte, a successor to the small Norman ringwork at the end of the promontory on which the settlement is situated.

In its initial phase the castle was a free-standing tower of at least two storeys, with walls just over 3m thick, and probably built in the late twelfth century. It remained standing for about a century before undergoing a radical alteration with the demolition of the upper part of the tower, leaving only about 4m standing, with the surviving windows being deliberately blocked. A thinner-walled two-storey tower was then built on the surviving walls of the Norman tower, and at the same time a powerful motte *c.* 5m high was raised around the older building (figure 2.3), encircled by a ditch, and with a bailey added on the western side. The ground floor was largely filled in about the same time, although there was some evidence which indicated that the original plan in the thirteenth century had been to keep it as an unlit basement; however, one small area was retained as a 'cellar' (Saunders 1980).

What brought about this drastic change in the tower which was both a prison as well as the residence of its keeper? Evidence for a fire was found during the course of the excavations, but it was not clear whether the fire resulted in the rebuilding or was simply part of the demolition work. The fact that the tower was a prison and courthouse rather than a castle suggests that whatever the purpose of the 'motte', it was not military. It may have been to give Lydford the illusion of being a castle — 'The conversion of the prison to a castle-like appearance with the creation of a motte and miniature bailey was perhaps a deliberate anachronistic conceit intended to give visual confirmation of the title Lydford Castle while at the time manifesting the power and authority of the Earl of Cornwall and his control of the Stannaries.' (Saunders 1980: 162). Certainly thirteenth-century Lydford Castle must have looked more impressive than the Norman tower on its own.

The earliest known example of the enclosing of a keep within a later motte was found in France during the excavations at Doué-la-Fontaine. The castle began as an undefended ground floor hall *c.* 900, but in the middle of the tenth century it was transformed into one of the first European castles, possibly by the Count of Blois, with the conversion of the hall into a small keep by the addition of an upper storey. The ground floor door was blocked, and the new entrance was on the first floor. In a subsequent phase, *c.* 1000, the small keep had a motte raised against it (de Boüard 1973–4). The function of the Doué motte might have been defensive. Nevertheless, the addition of an upper storey to the original hall might have resulted in serious structural weaknesses appearing in the keep at the turn of the tenth century, hence the change to a keep 'emmoté', a building enveloped by a mound. Despite this example, most instances of this aspect of castle building are known from England, but as

Figure 2.3   The keep or prison tower at Lydford

castles continue to be excavated other cases may well appear.

The early development of Eynsford Castle is difficult to parallel (Rigold 1971). It was primarily a masonry castle from its foundation in the 1080s, at least as far as its curtain wall was concerned. However, the main building within the enclosure was a timber keep, with the area between the tower and the curtain mounded up to enclose the keep, leaving only a sunken courtyard around it; a timber revetment prevented the motte from slipping into the yard. An idea of how Eynsford may have looked in the eleventh century is included in the report by Rigold on the excavations (Rigold 1971: 140). Originally the enclosure in which the keep stood was designed to protect the 11m square keep or watchtower and to provide a refuge in time of need, for it does not seem to have enclosed any domestic buildings; these were possibly located in the outer enclosure where a Tudor house now stands, an area which has yet to be excavated.

An important castle, particularly one with a long history of royal ownership, was rarely static in terms of the development of its defences and domestic buildings. Increasingly sophisticated defences were added, such as mural towers and strong gatehouses, whilst greater domestic comfort was sought through improved lodgings, halls and service areas. Winchester is a good example of a castle continually undergoing change. The establishment of the Conqueror's castle and the raising of the motte at the northern end of the site shortly afterwards were mentioned in chapter 1. At some stage in the reign of Henry I (1100–35) the motte was levelled and replaced by a square keep (Biddle 1970: 291) (figure 2.4). The keep was but the second stage in the development of the northern defences of the castle; after standing for about a century it was levelled to below the top of its foundations and replaced by a large round tower.

Figure 2.4   The remains of the Norman keep at Winchester

Biddle has stressed that the Winchester keep cannot be regarded as the main tower of the Norman castle, for the inner ward lay at the southern end of the castle platform, and it would be here that one would expect to find such a tower. It was, however, a major tower, its 4.6m wide foundations implying that it had at least two upper storeys (Biddle 1969: 300), and it fulfilled the same function as the motte by overlooking the approaches to the West Gate. What may have been part of the gateway leading to the keep was uncovered in 1984. For a short period it served as part of the entrance porch to Henry III's new hall, the building of which commenced in 1222 (Youngs *et al.* 1985: 183).

Evidence for the various covered entrances or forebuildings of another Hampshire keep, a close contemporary to the Winchester example, has been revealed in a series of excavations at Portchester. The fourth volume of the published results (Cunliffe and Munby 1985), which is devoted to the inner bailey of the castle, includes a thorough architectural study of the standing remains (Munby and Renn 1985). The keep may have started as a single-storey hall in the late eleventh century, with a subsequent conversion to a two-storey tower in the early twelfth century. Its walls were then thickened, and open steps leading up to a first floor entrance added, as at Ascot Doilly and Middleton Stoney. Later the same century the keep was heightened, and a series of forebuildings added to the east side; these underwent considerable alteration and expansion, particularly in the fourteenth century. Not only did these forebuildings provide additional accommodation and a covered passage to the keep and the adjacent ranges, but would have proved somewhat confusing to an attacker endeavouring to discover the entrance to the keep itself. A forebuilding was a feature of many of the great Norman keeps, such as Rochester and Dover in Kent, but few can have matched the complexity of the Portchester examples. An understanding of the development of the buildings attached to the keep during the middle ages is helped considerably by the reconstructions illustrated in the report.

So far we have looked at examples of rectangular/square keeps that are of Norman date and build. However, it is not only Norman buildings that have been the subject of recent research. In Wales, excavations at Dolforwyn, Montgomeryshire, began in 1981, and are planned to continue into the 1990s (Butler 1985). The castle was one of the last to have been built by the native Welsh princes; in this case it is the work of Llywelyn ap Gruffudd, Prince of Wales, some time between the Treaty of Montgomery in 1267 and the first of Edward I's wars in Wales (1276–7), but probably after 1273. It was captured after a short siege early in 1277, and was in the hands of the Crown for a period in the fourteenth century before falling into disuse. This rectangular castle crowns a ridge along the Severn valley, and was obviously designed to act as a sentinel over Llywelyn's south-eastern frontier.

Excavations at the south-western end of the castle uncovered a rectangular keep 9m x 19m (figure 2.5), the largest of all the native Welsh towers. The keep, which survives to a height of 3m, underwent a series of alterations during its short history, many of which must have been undertaken after its capture. The main ward lay between the keep and a round tower at the opposite end of the castle, but the keep was set in a small 'courtyard' on to which the main entrance opened. The building seems to have had the usual first floor entrance most keeps have for reasons of security, but with a ground floor door added later. The very poor quality of the main stonework (shale) may have been the cause of the various repairs to the fabric, particularly characterized by the use of a higher quality mortar. Evidence was also uncovered to show that the tower was rendered. The poor quality of the building material suggests that this form of weatherproofing was a feature of the castle as built by Llywelyn.

The irregularity of plan of the native Welsh castles (see illustrations in Avent 1983) has often been commented upon, the terrain in which they were built being an obvious influence. Several of the thirteenth-century Welsh castles lack the systematic arrangement of carefully planned and distributed mural towers

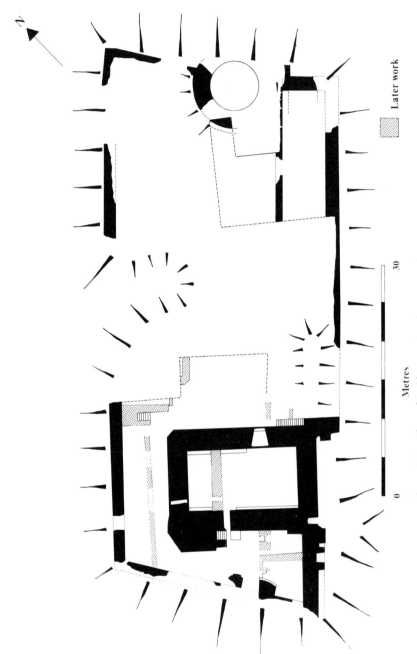

Figure 2.5 Plan of Dolforwyn Castle, 1988 (after Butler)

Metres

0   30

Later work

and gatehouses found in English castles of the same date. Dolforwyn falls into this native Welsh tradition, for there is no gatehouse, simply a gate protected by the keep, admittedly an arrangement also found in Norman castles in south Wales. There is also only one certain mural tower. A rectangular keep is also an unusual feature for a late thirteenth-century castle in Britain. The Welsh castle of Dinas Brân, situated on a hill above Llangollen, Denbighshire, and possibly built in the 1260s, is very similar in plan to Dolforwyn. It also has a rectangular keep, although the entrance which it overlooks takes the form of a twin-towered gatehouse.

Other rectangular keeps have been discovered at several castle ringworks. At Ludgershall there was a tower with foundations at least 5.4m deep, possibly dating from the first half of the twelfth century. It was demolished later the same century and replaced by a smaller structure, a mural tower (Addyman 1973: 9–10). At Pontesbury in Shropshire the *c.* 4m wide foundations of a building were an indication of a square tower of considerable proportions built on the line of the ringwork defences (Barker 1964). The tower may have been a gatehouse, but its size suggests a keep, presumably with the entrance to the castle adjacent to it. A similar arrangement can still be seen at the castles of Coity and Ogmore, Glamorgan.

When the circular earthwork known as 'The Mound' at Church Norton, Sussex, was first excavated in 1911, the defences and the masonry structures were interpreted as fortifications of the sixteenth century. A re-examination of the pottery of both the 1911 and 1965 excavations showed that 'The Mound' was a Norman ringwork (Aldsworth and Garnett 1981). The 1965 season rediscovered the masonry buildings revealed in 1911; one was about 9.5m square, whilst the other just 1m to the east was a small building of post-castle date. The main tower was clearly a Norman keep associated with the ringwork, and built within the defences.

The development of the main building within the upper enclosure at Castle Acre (figures 2.6 and 2.7) was one of the most remarkable archaeological discoveries of the 1970s (Coad and Streeten 1982). It has already been seen (chapter 1) that the late eleventh-century building consisted of a large mansion or country house surrounded by a weak ringwork. The conversion of the first-phase building into what was intended to be a massive keep dates from the 1140s, but with major modifications in the 1150s. The scheme involved strengthening the walls by doubling their thickness; such a technique was found at Dolforwyn, but there it was presumably part of the English reinforcement of the Welsh build. An even closer parallel to the development at Castle Acre has been argued for the initial phase of the keep at Portchester (Munby and Renn 1985: 75–6). The additional walling at Castle Acre was built inside the country house, and the interior of the house was raised. This resulted in the blocking of the main entrance and spine-wall door.

Evidence from the southern half of the building suggested that the original plan of converting the whole house into a keep was not implemented. The lining wall on the south side had all the appearance of being unfinished, and this, coupled with the fact that the wall added to the south side of the spine-wall was later than the rest of the thickening of the walls of the house, implies a change in plan. The keep, therefore, rose up from only the northern half, and when completed would have been at least 13m tall. The masonry

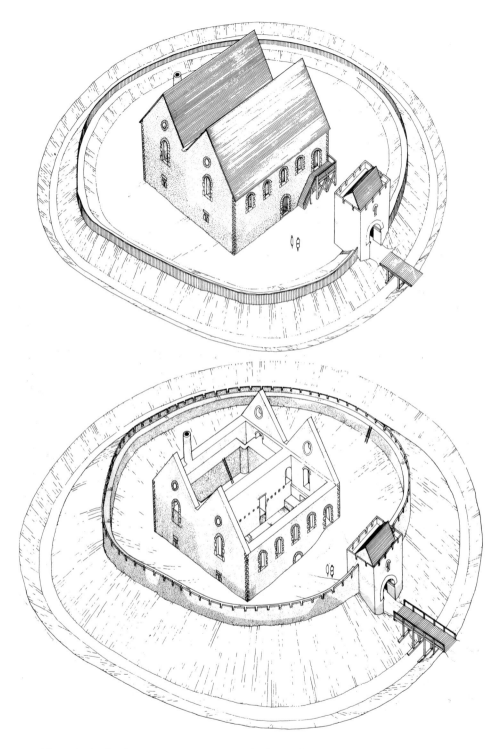

Figure 2.6 Castle Acre: reconstruction of (above) the country house, and (below) the conversion from house to keep

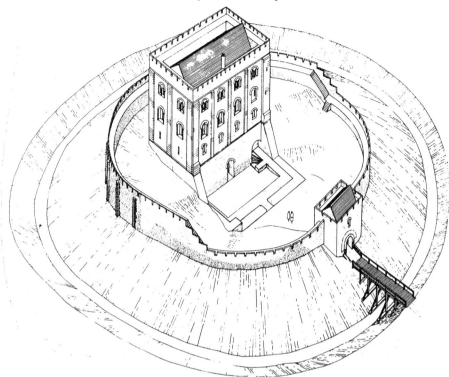

Figure 2.7　Castle Acre; hypothetical reconstruction of the keep

curtain on the ringwork bank was built while the house was being converted, but when the keep was reduced in area a new curtain wall was built on top of the original wall for the greater part of its circuit.

As the conversion of the Castle Acre house dates to the 1140s and 1150s, the keep falls into the period of instability of the reign of Stephen. William de Warenne III who succeeded to the earldom of Surrey in 1138 may, therefore, have been the man responsible for the building work, and his death in 1147, which marked the end of his family's male line, may have led to the alteration in the design that he had originally envisaged. Certainly the occupation of the upper ward had ceased by the end of the twelfth century. The limited excavations that have taken place in the lower ward together with the prominent outlines of buildings below the turf, including a probable hall, suggest that the later occupation was concentrated in this area.

At Castle Neroche part of the summit of the motte was included in the archaeological investigation of the site as masonry had been recorded there in 1854 and 1903. The top of the motte, *c.* 36.5m in diameter, had been encircled by a stone curtain wall to form what is known as a shell-keep, but this was only one aspect of the motte's defences. On one side of the motte there was a smaller mound about 12m wide, but under 1m high. This additional stronghold also had a shell-keep, for the mound was revetted by a stone wall *c.* 1.3m thick. These twelfth-century improvements to the castle overlie the original occupation levels on the motte, and although the 1963 excavation was selective, enough evidence was produced to give credence to this unusual development where an entire motte itself seems to have become a keep-and-bailey (Davison 1971–2: 39).

Excavations on the tops of mottes have provided few examples of shell-keeps other than the Castle Neroche example. However, archaeology has provided several additions to the corpus of circular and polygonal stone keeps. Whereas the square or rectangular keep is a specific feature of the twelfth century, the change in emphasis to a more rounded or purely circular form is apparent during the closing years of that century, and is particularly characteristic of new keeps of the first half of the thirteenth century. It is worth noting that the majority of these towers, mainly of Anglo-Norman build, are clustered in south Wales and the Marches (Renn 1961). Many coincide with the resurgence of the Welsh under Llywelyn ab Iorwerth (d. 1240), but later thirteenth-century examples are also found, such as Flint in north Wales built by Edward I. There are Scottish examples at Bothwell and Kildrummy in Lanarkshire and Aberdeenshire respectively; nor should one forget the twelfth-century keeps at Conisbrough, Yorkshire (*c.* 1180), and Orford, Suffolk (*c.* 1167). A cylindrical keep, with its potential for all-round vision from its battlements, was a much more effective structure to add to an existing motte-and-bailey than was a square keep. These round towers were built at a time of increasing sophistication in military architecture, with the addition of mural towers and arrowslits from the late twelfth century, developments admirably described in castles in Wales by Knight (1987). Since Renn produced his list (1961) other rounded keeps have come to light, the first of which to be discovered was the polygonal example at Richard's Castle, Herefordshire.

Prior to the excavations of the early 1960s, the most noteworthy aspect of Richard's Castle was the height of the motte, almost 14m tall, but with a summit diameter of only *c.* 6m. However, excavation showed that the motte was *c.* 9m high and 20–21m across the top when a stone keep was added to it in the late twelfth century (figure 2.8). The collapsed remains of this tower gave the motte its apparent height. The castle has been associated with one of the few pre-Conquest castles built in the 1050s by Normans brought over by Edward the Confessor, but the construction of the keep in the twelfth century must have destroyed any evidence for the earliest occupation on the motte, so its unusually early origin is unlikely ever to be confirmed archaeologically.

The tower at Richard's Castle was octagonal within and without and about 13.4m wide externally, with a series of pilaster buttresses at each angle, although these were removed at a later date, perhaps during the alterations undertaken in the thirteenth century. As the walls were *c.* 3.65m thick, the chambers inside the tower were small, about 6.1m wide. A lack of space was a particular disadvantage of rounded keeps confined by the size of their mottes. A ditch originally separated the motte of Richard's Castle from its bailey, but the two were linked by wing-walls running from the bailey curtain up the sides of the motte. In the thirteenth century an apsidal building of unknown purpose projecting down the slope of the motte was added to the keep, and in the same century there began to be problems with the stability of the tower. They were solved by burying the bottom of the outside of the keep in a mass of mortared rubble (Curnow and Thompson 1969).

Other excavations in Wales and the Marches have revealed round keeps not

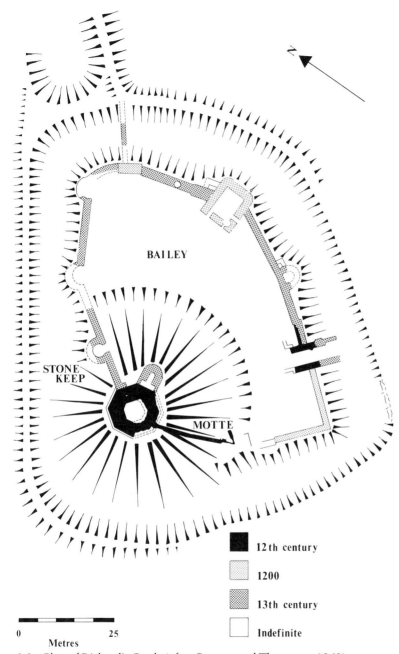

Figure 2.8 Plan of Richard's Castle (after Curnow and Thompson 1969)

associated with mottes. In several castles cylindrical keeps stood in an independent position within an enclosure, as witness the examples which still stand, including the finest of them all, William Marshall's great tower at Pembroke, Dyfed, and the native Welsh towers at Dinefwr, Carmarthenshire, and Dolbadarn in Caernarfonshire. Castell Bryn Amlwg, Shropshire (figure 3.6) (Alcock *et al.* 1967–8), stands on the top of a hill, as its name implies ('castle on the prominent hill'), at a point which marked the westernmost point of the lordship of Clun in the middle ages. Standing in the Welshry of that lordship, its purpose must have been to act as an outpost for the lords of Clun, looking west into Wales. The original castle, possibly the one mentioned in 1160, was a ringwork, presumably with timber defences, although no evidence was found for these during the excavations; not only was the excavation on a small scale, but the later masonry defences must have removed any evidence for a palisade.

It may have been John Fitzalan I, lord of Clun (d. 1241), who began to build the masonry defences of Castell Bryn Amlwg. The earliest building was the circular keep at one end, forming one with the curtain wall when it was added soon afterwards, although the walls do not bond with the keep. The size of the tower, *c.* 11m across, compares favourably with keeps in the Marches to the south, such as the Breconshire towers of Bronllys and Tretower (figure 2.9), and these keeps generally consisted of a basement and three upper storeys.

Figure 2.9   Tretower Castle

One of Llywelyn ab Iorwerth's own castles was Degannwy, built on the twin crags at the mouth of the river Conwy, Caernarfonshire. The castle suffered various vicissitudes (Alcock 1967: 196) before Henry III rebuilt it in 1245–54; it was soon afterwards razed to the ground by Llywelyn ap Gruffudd in 1263, destroying what contemporaries regarded as one of the strongest castles in the land (Colvin 1963: 626). The core of the castle was on the westernmost of the two hills, referred to as the 'donjon' in the building accounts, the surviving fragments consisting of stretches of curtain wall and rounded towers, and a rectangular hall. The 'donjon' was in effect the upper bailey, and at its south-eastern corner stood a circular keep *c.* 12m wide, overlooking the entrance to the castle with its twin-towered gatehouse. The offensive position of the keep emphasizes its military function, but it still fulfilled a domestic role by being attached to the hall to its west; the upper chambers in the tower may have acted as the solar to the hall. A similar arrangement can be seen at Barnard Castle.

Certain aspects of the castles of the Welsh princes can be seen to have particularly native characteristics, for example the large apsidal-ended towers (Avent 1983: 11, 13) as at Castell-y-Bere, Merioneth. However, Anglo-Norman influences obviously stimulated Welsh castle building, from the motte-and-bailey of Tomen-y-Rhodwydd, Denbighshire, to the gatehouse at Criccieth, Caernarfonshire. The round keeps at Dolbadarn and Dinefwr have already been mentioned, and a third native Welsh example has been excavated at Dryslwyn (figure 2.10). This castle was the westernmost of a line of three in Carmarthenshire, Dinefwr lying to the east of Dryslwyn, and Carreg Cennen beyond that to the south-east. Dryslwyn stands in a superb position on a hill commanding the Tywi valley, and excavations have preceded the consolidation of the inner ward (Webster 1987). Apart from two large sections of upstanding masonry, all that could be seen before the excavations were the grass-covered mounds of the collapsed stonework. Although considerable rebuilding of the castle by the English followed its capture in 1287, it seems certain that not only was the keep of Welsh build, but one of the first buildings on the site. Its remains are fragmentary, but it was originally similar in size to

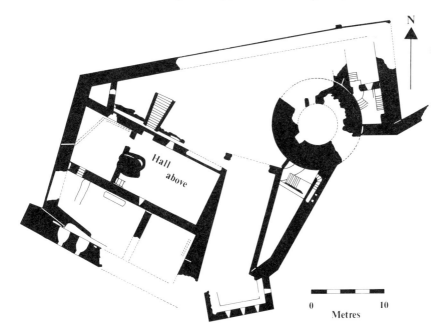

Figure 2.10   Plan of the inner ward of Dryslwyn Castle (after Webster 1987)

English keeps, with an external diameter of _c._ 12.25m. Although it had a first floor entrance it had the unusual feature of a door at basement level leading into the courtyard of the ward.

Before leaving the subject of round keeps in Wales, mention should be made of the small round tower at Llansteffan, as it has been interpreted by some as a keep. The present writer has preferred to assign it to the section on mural towers (p.73).

Not all excavations on circular keeps have been restricted to Wales and the Marches. The six-acre site of Sandal Castle, Yorkshire, was fully excavated from 1964 until 1973, revealing the development of the earth-and-timber motte-and-bailey from around the year 1100 through to the siege of 1645 and its subsequent slighting (Mayes and Butler 1983). The conversion of Sandal from a timber to a stone stronghold by its owners, the Warenne earls of Surrey, took place in the midthirteenth century, _c._ 1240–70. A circular keep with four small turrets was built on the motte. One of the turrets enclosed a well and was rebuilt in polygonal form in 1484–5; a further two flanked the entrance to the keep (figures 2.11 and 4.1, p.80). However, the Civil War slighting and subsequent robbing of the keep for its stone have resulted in the survival of only the lowest courses of masonry.

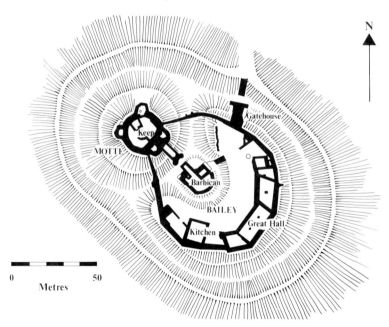

Figure 2.11 Plan of Sandal Castle (after Mayes and Butler 1983)

The Sandal keep was substantially built, its _c._ 3.9m thick walls enclosing an area with a diameter of 17m. On either side of two of the towers wing-walls were built down the side of the motte, as at Richard's Castle, to become part of the defensive circuit around the bailey, and a walled passage ran up the motte to the keep from a pair of drum towers (figure 4.1, p.80). As will be seen in chapter 3, the early thirteenth century marked the beginning of the use of strategically placed mural towers, with main entrances being flanked by a pair of closely placed rounded towers to form gatehouses as opposed to gatetowers. Much of the building at Sandal in the thirteenth century was the work of John de Warenne, seventh Earl of Surrey (1240–1304), a castle builder of some renown (Butler 1987), but the keep may have been started by his father, the sixth earl (1202–40).

Some idea of the keep's appearance can be obtained from an Elizabethan survey made in 1565–6. All the towers which formed part of the keep were four storeys high, but it is not clear how the main body of the keep was designed; it was either completely roofed, or it had an open courtyard, as implied by the discovery of paving in the centre. Butler favours a roofed keep of two or three storeys; the accommodation requirements for a castle of Sandal's standing would suggest this. The private chambers would have been situated in the small towers, while the Warenne hall must have occupied one of the central floors. A similar arrangement can be seen in the keep built at Orford by Henry II, where a polygonal tower, but circular internally, had three turrets which housed kitchens, chambers, and the main staircase (Brown 1964).

Excavations have served to confirm the pattern of development of the masonry keep as outlined in works such as Brown (1976), and have increased the number of cylindrical keeps known from the Welsh Marches. We can also see the Welsh as builders of both round and rectangular keeps in the thirteenth century, with Dryslwyn and Dolforwyn. The most interesting results from excavations have been the examples where a rectangular keep has either been built in association with a motte or had an earth mound added to it at a later date. The researches have thrown light on this hitherto unknown aspect of Norman castle building. The reasons behind this phenomenon are still unclear. The mound at Farnham was clearly designed to give greater stability to the keep, but it is not possible to be so certain about other castles. Was the motte at Ascot Doilly a piece of deliberate symbolism, as has been suggested for the thirteenth-century rebuilding at Lydford? We do not know, nor is it likely that we ever will. This is just one aspect of castle studies where archaeological and historical research cannot help in the solution to problems. It may be that the Ascot Doilly mound was raised simply to protect the foundations of the keep, not necessarily from undermining. Certainly the purpose of the 'motte' at Skenfrith, Monmouthshire, cannot have been 'military'. The round keep in the centre of its bailey had always been regarded as standing on the truncated remains of the motte from the twelfth-century castle of Skenfrith. However, a trench across the castle revealed that the motte-like appearance of the ground about the tower was the result of the deliberate build-up of material laid down to protect the foundations during the construction of the keep (Craster 1967: 142). It was the burying of the foundations that made the mound, and the heightening of the level of the courtyard before the keep was built also added to the effect of a tower on a motte.

3 Masonry Castles – Gateways and Mural Towers

Gateways

Professor R.A. Brown has reminded us (1984b) that there are three types of castle gateway: the simple entrance through a curtain wall; what is basically a mural tower with a passage running through it (gatetower); and the more sophisticated gatehouse with twin towers that develops in the thirteenth century. Some of the variations upon these themes can be seen in a recent typology (Salamagne 1988). Numerous examples of all three types still stand in castles throughout Britain, from the simple entrance at Usk in Monmouthshire, the early gatetower at Exeter, and the great gatehouses of Edwardian Harlech and Beaumaris in north Wales, to one of the last major gatehouses to have been built in the middle ages at Raglan Castle, Monmouthshire. Excavations have brought to light examples of all three types, although the majority have been of the twin-towered gatehouse variety, of thirteenth- and fourteenth-century date. Although the simple entrance is a more characteristic feature of Norman castles than those built later, it will be seen from the sites reviewed here that it is not possible to assign one particular type to a narrow chronology.

Deddington Castle in Oxfordshire (Ivens 1983; 1984) was founded in the late eleventh century as a motte with a large bailey lying over the remains of late Saxon buildings, and may have been built by Odo of Bayeux as the centre of his estates in Oxfordshire. In the first half of the twelfth century its timber defences were replaced by a stone curtain wall, with possibly a tower at the northern end of the castle. This rebuilding has been assigned to William de Chesney who held the manor in 1157, although it is likely that it was in his hands some years previously. An adherent to the cause of King Stephen, he was military governor of the Oxford area, with various castles under his control. He is also known to have been responsible for undertaking new works at a number of castles.

The entrance to the Deddington enclosure was originally just a simple break in the curtain wall (figure 3.1, IV), without any sophisticated arrangements, but this was to change within a few years. By the end of the century the gate arrangement consisted of a new entrance passage just to the north of the old one, flanked by a gatehouse tower (figure 3.1, V). This lasted until the late thirteenth century when the castle fell into disuse. There may have been a similar arrangement at Loughor, Glamorgan, in the later twelfth century (Lewis, J.M. 1975: 154). The example excavated at Dolforwyn is extremely simple (an arched entrance in the curtain wall), although as an additional defence it is overlooked by the keep (see figure 2.5, p.48) (Butler 1986: figure 2). The entrance at Castell-y-Bere, Merioneth (figure 8.4, p.158), a castle built in the 1220s by Llywelyn ab Iorwerth, is also overlooked by a tower, but in this case it is a circular tower. The simple entrance is protected by an elaborate barbican, but there is some doubt as to whether it was built by Llywelyn or when the castle was in the hands of the English after its capture in 1283 (p.81).

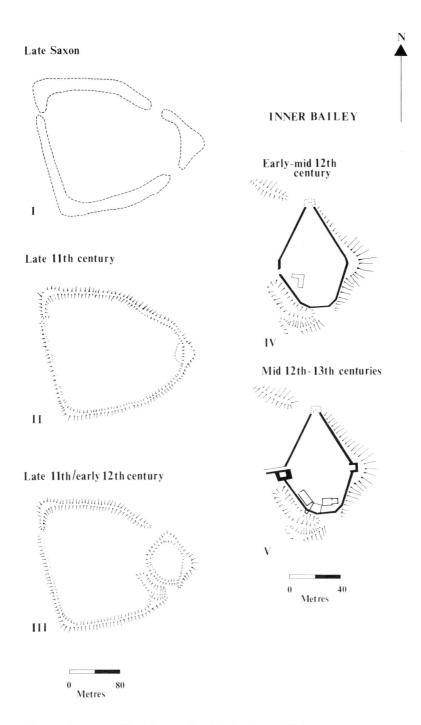

Late Saxon

I

Late 11th century

II

Late 11th/early 12th century

III

0   80
Metres

INNER BAILEY

N

Early-mid 12th century

IV

Mid 12th-13th centuries

V

0   40
Metres

Figure 3.1   The development of Deddington Castle (after Ivens 1984)

The most primitive form of entrance to a castle, a simple doorway set in a curtain wall adjacent to a mural tower, is not confined to the Norman period, where one of the best examples, William Marshall's gate of *c.* 1200, is the

entrance to what is now the middle bailey of Chepstow Castle. Besides
Castell-y-Bere, this type is also to be found later in the middle ages, at Barnard
Castle, for example. At the same time as the fourteenth-century gatetower was
built at the entrance from the town ward to the middle ward at Barnard Castle,
Co. Durham, the defences of the inner ward were improved by the building of
a new method of entry (Austin 1980: 80–1). The approach to the bridge and
the gateway was protected both by a D-shaped tower which was built over the
abutment of the earlier bridge of the first masonry castle, and the Headlam
Tower in the south angle of the bailey (figure 3.2). Once the bridge had been
crossed, however, there was a more sophisticated arrangement than that at the
Marshall's gate at Chepstow. Those entering the castle had to make two
right-angle turns before they could pass into the ward itself, and the passage
was further defended at its inner end by the construction of a guardroom set
into the back of an earlier tower.

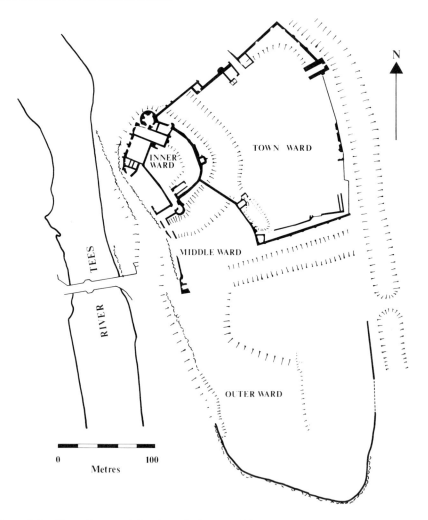

Figure 3.2   Plan of Barnard Castle in the later middle ages (after Austin 1980)

Just as some early castles, such as the first phase of the ringwork at Penmaen, had entrances through timber gatetowers, others had similar arrangements in stone. Before the country house at Castle Acre was converted into a keep, the original timber gateway was replaced by a stone gatetower forming an integral part of the slight ringwork (figure 2.6, p.50). However, it has been stressed that the gate with its wide passageway was designed more for show than for serious defence, especially as the ringwork defences remained unaltered. In the subsequent building campaign the ringwork bank was raised to support a masonry curtain wall set back from the line of the original palisade so that the gatetower projected further from the ramparts, and soon afterwards the gate's defences were improved by narrowing the archway at the rear (Coad and Streeten 1982: 178–80). This tightening of the castle's fortifications was all part of the programme of works undertaken in the first half of the twelfth century, as outlined in the previous chapter. At another ringwork site, Rumney Castle, Cardiff, there was a similar sequence of a timber gatetower being replaced by one of stone in the early thirteenth century, although here the later gate was in a new position (Lightfoot 1983: 4).

There was also a gatetower at Castle Acre on the line of the curtain wall on the east side of the lower ward, near its junction with the upper ward. Its purpose was to connect the outworks or barbican with the main body of the castle. It cannot be closely dated, but there seems little doubt that it was standing in the mid twelfth century, and that it was probably contemporary with the gatetower into the upper ward. It was not a strong building; it only had one door, and that was secured by a drawbar, the horizontal slot for which still survives. The only subsequent addition made to the gate was the blocking of the outer portal, but it is not known whether that was partial or total. Nor is it known when this development took place, but the excavators favoured the idea of the gate being completely blocked, implying that the defences on the east side were abandoned at the same time (Coad *et al.* 1987: 271–3). The subsequent use of the outer or lower ward as the main area of occupation resulted in the construction of a new gateway on the west side of the ward, which was in a different style to that on the east, but this will be discussed below.

Part of the gatetower of Richard's Castle still stands, enough to show that there was originally a chamber on its first floor. The earliest masonry is twelfth century, forming a tower about 7m square (figure 2.8, p.53), but this building was improved in the thirteenth century as part of the refurbishment of the bailey defences. The gate was extended forward towards the ditch, the new work being bonded with the Norman work for strength and stability, except in the lower courses. A feature of the new gate was the provision of a small chamber on the northern side, presumably for the porter, whilst a latrine chute served the upper floor and possibly the roof. The porter's lodge seems to have had its own external door, or it may be that the door was for pedestrian access to the gate, separate from the main passage (Curnow and Thompson 1969: 115–16). A similar arrangement may have been present in the gatehouse at Ludlow before it was converted into a keep (Renn 1987) and can also be seen in the outer bay of the gatehouse to the inner bailey at Portchester Castle, although this was a much later alteration, probably late in the sixteenth century.

Clearance, survey and limited excavation of the West Gate of the castle at Lincoln showed that the entrance was originally a timber building on stone foundations. This gate was replaced in the late eleventh or early twelfth century by a rectangular stone tower, and repairs to this gate in 1233–4 virtually amounted to a rebuilding. The stone gate originally consisted of a vaulted entrance passage with chambers above, with an open extension forming a barbican or outer defence at the edge of the ditch. The alterations in the thirteenth century removed the vaulting which may have been replaced by a timber ceiling. At the same time, an arch was added next to the original Norman arch at the entrance to the gate, possibly to create a channel for a portcullis (Elliott and Stocker 1984: 25–7; Stocker 1983).

The two phases at Penmaen cannot be closely dated, but the ringwork with its timber gateway is accepted as being Norman (figure 1.2, p.6). At some stage the gate was destroyed by fire, although whether this was through a Welsh attack or domestic mishap will never be known. However, it was replaced by a drystone-walled gatetower (Alcock 1966: 184), which could have been Norman, or, equally possible, a rebuilding by a Welsh lord, Rhys Gryg ap Rhys, who had destroyed all the castles in the Gower in 1217. A structure with drystone walls was more likely to have been Welsh in origin; it was uncharacteristic for the Normans to build in this fashion. The problem will be discussed further in connection with the halls at Penmaen and another Glamorgan ringwork, Llantrithyd (p.116).

The approaches to the middle ward from the town ward were refortified as part of the fourteenth-century transformation of the domestic and defensive arrangements of the great northern stronghold of Barnard Castle (figure 3.2, p. 60) by the earls of Warwick (Austin 1979). In this Warwick period the defence of the castle seems to have been concentrated on the inner ward, utilizing the middle ward as the outer defence. The reasons behind the new defences were probably a combination of the threat of Scottish raids and the claims to ownership of Barnard by the bishops of Durham in the fourteenth century. A strong base was required for the new northern Warwick estates centred on Barnard, although the castle does not seem to have been lived in by the earls themselves. The new works were designed to provide this secure base, and at the same time the other two wards, outer and town, were emptied of most of their buildings. The eastern side of the middle ward with its early thirteenth-century curtain wall was protected in the fourteenth century by a wet ditch. Evidence was found here, in the form of a sluice with its timbering, for a dam to control the level of the water of the moat, and the moat was crossed by a drawbridge leading to the rectangular entrance of the middle ward. This entrance was the same basic type of gatetower as discussed above (p.61) but, unlike the extension to the gate at Richard's Castle which was bonded on to the earlier gate, the new Barnard gate was just butted against the two buttresses which remained from the first gate. It may have been considered quicker and cheaper to build in this way, for bonding it with the existing stonework would have been a laborious task.

The uncertainties of the political situation in the north of England in the later middle ages, especially in those areas close to the border with Scotland, led to the building of numerous strong houses and towers, or the incorporation of unfortified houses within defensive circuits with fortified gates. A good example of this has been excavated at Edlingham Castle in Northumberland (Fairclough 1982; 1984) where a late thirteenth-century unfortified hall-house was built by William de Felton, a man who had served his king well at home and abroad. It was left to Felton's son, another William, to convert Edlingham into a small castle, possibly around 1340, with a curtain wall surrounding the hall, and a solar tower linked to the hall on the southern side. On the far side of the courtyard, opposite the hall, a gatetower was built at the same time to defend the entrance (figure 3.3). This was a small tower but with a drawbridge, and a passage defended by wooden doors and a portcullis, together with a vaulted chamber on one side. The presence of a portcullis necessitates a first floor chamber above the passage to hold the winding mechanism, as does the existence of a garderobe chute; the room was probably reached via an external stair. The gatetower was enlarged later in the century to take a newel stair leading to the upper chamber, and at the same time the gate was extended outwards, creating a passage twice as long as the original one of *c.* 1340, and with a second drawbridge. The excavator has suggested that as well as providing an adequate defensive structure at the entrance to this small castle, the gate, especially in its later fourteenth-century form, was equally a status symbol, reflecting the social position of the Felton family. It may even have been decorated with heraldic devices, as a stone shield was found nearby. Such ornate treatment of later medieval castles can be found not only elsewhere in the north, as at Hylton Castle, Co. Durham (Morley 1976), but also on the outside of the state apartments of Raglan Castle, Monmouthshire (Kenyon 1988), and the gatehouse at Bodiam Castle, Sussex (Curzon 1926).

The original design for Bothwell in Lanarkshire in the late thirteenth century was for a castle on a grand scale, with mural towers, a large circular keep, and a twin-towered gatehouse. In the event the main feature that was constructed before work was brought to an end for a period was the keep, although foundations for other buildings were laid. It was not until the late fourteenth and early fifteenth century that the Black Douglas family completed the enclosure to the east of the keep, the latter having been partially demolished in 1337 (Simpson 1985). In 1981 excavations against the north curtain wall of the Douglas castle located what seems to have been the gate of the later medieval castle (Lewis, J.H. 1984). The gate was a rectangular building; its narrow east wall gives the appearance of the entrance having been on the east side, with a right-angle turn into the castle interior. Examples of this type of entrance are rare but not unknown in Britain, for example, Caldicot in Monmouthshire. However, Lewis dismisses it as impractical at Bothwell, and the plan would seem to corroborate this, for such an arrangement would have made it difficult to manoeuvre such items as heavy goods through it. An engraving of Bothwell dated 1693 suggests that the entrance was in fact a typical gatetower, with a passage leading directly from the outside into the enclosure.

A feature of those thirteenth-century and later castles built *de novo* or radically rebuilt was the twin-towered gatehouse, usually with rounded gatetowers. Such gateways, together with mural towers, had been built in the 1180s by Henry II at Dover Castle (the rectangular Palace Gate and the King's Gate which opened onto the inner bailey). From the 1220s both rounded gatehouses and mural towers, with their advantages over the square or

Figure 3.3   General view of Edlingham Castle, with the gatehouse in the foreground

rectangular form, including better fields of vision with no dead areas at the corners, began to be constructed by the king and his leading magnates. A development from the gatetower towards the fully-fledged gatehouse can be seen at a few castles where the towers themselves take the form of solid rounded buttresses as opposed to towers with chambers. This was the type of gate built in the late twelfth century at the de Warenne castle of Conisbrough in Yorkshire, although the towers were refronted in the fourteenth century (Johnson 1980: 60–5; 1984). A similar gate has been excavated at Castle Acre, another de Warenne castle. This particular gatehouse, possibly replacing an earlier entrance, gave access to the lower ward from the defended town to the west, and has been dated to around the year 1200 (Coad 1984: 15). It is remarkably similar in plan to the north gate of the town which still stands, both having solid drum towers and entrance passages defended by two sets of doors, and with a portcullis apiece. The castle's gatehouse had a chamber butting on either side of the passage, the southern one being simply a small vaulted unlit chamber cut into the bailey bank, possibly used for storage. The rectangular north chamber was constructed in the angle between the gatehouse and the stone curtain or wing-wall which ran down from the defences of the upper ward to meet the gate, and the presence of a garderobe chute implies that there was an upper room to this chamber block, which remained in use until the fourteenth century. The only surviving evidence for access to the upper levels of the gatehouse was the flight of steps added slightly later to the rear of the gate at the south-east corner. Presumably the steps led up the bank to the chamber from which the portcullis would have been operated, and it may have been possible to reach the northern chamber from this room also (Coad and Streeten 1982).

At Montgomery in 1223 the young King Henry III was shown 'a place where a most impregnable castle might be built' (quoted in Knight 1983: 170), and from 1224 until about 1235 work proceeded on enclosing an inner ward in masonry. The gatehouse occupies the whole of the southern end of the ward (figure 3.4), and was one of the first of its type to be built. It was reached by crossing over a massive rock-cut ditch, the entrance passage being defended by portcullis and gates. The towers are solid at their lowest levels, and there is a chamber behind each one, neither of which was originally entered from the gate passage. The west room, which lacked any form of lighting slit, may have been a prison as it could only be reached from the first floor by a ladder, although later in the thirteenth century a door was inserted giving access from the gate passage. The east chamber had a ground floor entrance in its north wall, and presumably was the porter's lodge or guardchamber, although its only source of natural light was an arrowslit in its east wall; it was from this room that the drawbar was operated for securing the outer gate. The later alteration in the method of entry to the west room, probably undertaken in the 1280s, is not altogether surprising as most later gatehouses had direct access from the passages to their ground floor side-chambers. Entrance to the upper chambers of the gate was by an external wooden staircase at the back of the building (Lloyd and Knight 1981: 19–21). This arrangement is unusual but not unique, and was used at Beaumaris Castle, Anglesey, the last of Edward I's castles in north Wales. A smaller gatehouse with less prominently rounded towers was built at Montgomery in the mid thirteenth century at the entrance to the middle ward, but very little of this survives.

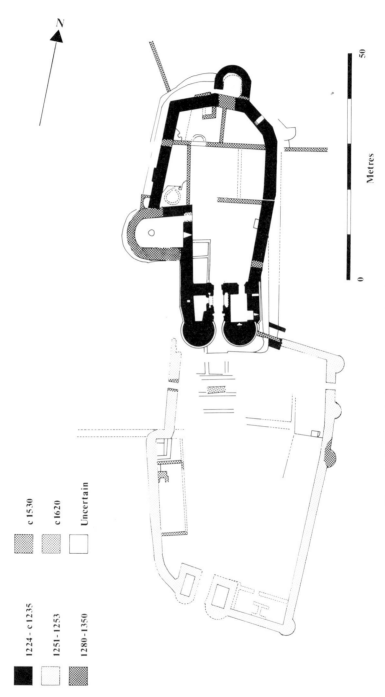

N

c 1530

c 1620

Uncertain

1224 - c 1235

1251 - 1253

1280 - 1350

Metres

0

50

Figure 3.4   Plan of Montgomery Castle (after Knight 1983)

A contemporary of the king's new castle of Montgomery is Beeston Castle, Cheshire, begun in 1225 by Ranulf de Blundeville, Earl of Chester. Perched on its rock, dominating the Cheshire Plain, the entrance to its inner and outer wards was through twin-towered gatehouses, and a similar gate was found at Bolingbroke Castle, Lincolnshire, a polygonal castle which was also built by the Earl of Chester about the same time (figures 3.5 and 5.8, p.110). Little of Bolingbroke now stands, but enough has survived and been revealed by excavation to give the ground plan (Thompson 1966; 1969; 1974). The towers of the gatehouse are D-shaped, with a lodge or guardchamber in the east tower communicating with the entrance passage, whilst beneath the inner half of the passage there was a small chamber reached by a flight of steps leading down from a door in the west tower of the gatehouse. The purpose of this room is uncertain, but the excavator has suggested that it may have been a prison; its position is unusual, and it was nothing to do with the workings of the drawbridge whose pit was further forward. Examples are known in a few castles in south Wales where a postern or sallyport leads out from under a gatehouse; this can be seen at Caldicot, and such a postern has recently come to light at Laugharne, and there may have been a similar arrangement at Neath

Figure 3.5   Aerial view of Bolingbroke Castle

in Glamorgan. In mid Wales, there was a similar arrangement on the north-west side of Edward I's castle at Aberystwyth. However, there was apparently no evidence at Bolingbroke for such a feature.

Unfortunately, due to reconstruction in the Civil War and the subsequent slighting of the castle, it is not possible to be completely certain of the form of the main gatehouse at Banbury Castle, Oxfordshire (Rodwell 1976). The castle was rebuilt in concentric form, with a pentagonal inner ward, and as such had been assigned to the late thirteenth century, or even the early fourteenth century, in common with other concentric castles, Harlech and Beaumaris, for example. However, as a result of the pottery analysis a date of *c*. 1225–50 has been proposed (Fasham 1983: 79, 117). If we are to be guided by the study of the pottery, then Banbury is remarkable for its early concentric shape, although Henry II's Dover was partially concentric. The Banbury gatehouse into the outer ward may have had completely circular towers, unlike those at Montgomery, Bolingbroke and Beeston, but at some stage, possibly in the seventeenth century, the gate towers were refronted and generally altered to make them rectangular in shape. If the towers were originally fully rounded, a virtually unique form of gatehouse, then this may be best assigned to the early thirteenth century, as proposed on the pottery evidence, rather than later in the century; the Banbury gate would be an even more unusual design if it belonged to the Edwardian period. Admittedly, circular towers flanked the entrances to the castles of Conwy and Holt in north Wales, both built in the 1280s, but the gate arrangements at these two sites are not comparable to the true twin-towered gatehouses to be seen at Edward I's Harlech or Beaumaris.

A gatehouse of the later thirteenth century which in plan resembles those of some of the finest castles of that period was uncovered at Castell Bryn Amlwg, Shropshire (Alcock *et al.* 1967–8), but it represented a rebuilding of the original entrance. Although the excavations were limited to a series of small trenches in only one season, enough was uncovered to suggest how the castle evolved (figure 3.6), and its cylindrical keep was mentioned in the last chapter. The gatehouse as uncovered belongs to the later phases of the castle's history; originally the entrance was merely flanked by two D-shaped towers, the backs of the towers being continuations of the curtain wall. Its conversion into a gatehouse of a more developed form followed soon after when rectangular chambers were added behind the towers, thus forming a long entrance passage. The poorly preserved condition of the castle meant that no evidence was found for the passage gates, nor for a portcullis, but the entrance to the western chamber or guardroom was uncovered. A date in the first half of the thirteenth century for the earlier of the two gates should not be dismissed. However, in the report it was suggested that it may have been the work of Llywelyn ap Gruffudd in the years following the Treaty of Montgomery (1267), a time when the prince was in a powerful position on the borders of the lordship of Clun, but before 1276 when Roger Mortimer wrested control from him. If this theory is correct, then it would be only natural for the castle to have been strengthened once it was back in English hands, hence the reconstruction of the gatehouse, and a date before the final overthrow of Llywelyn in the Welsh war of 1282–3 is conceivable.

The suggestion that Llywelyn ap Gruffudd may have been the builder of the earlier of the two gatehouses discovered at Castell Bryn Amlwg is an intriguing

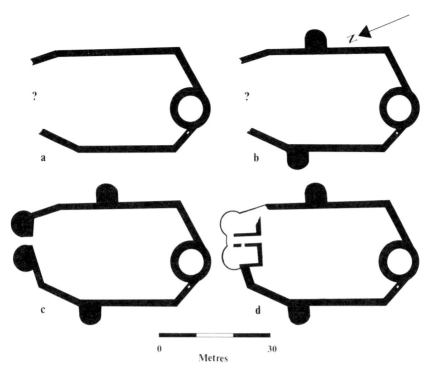

Figure 3.6 Conjectural reconstruction of the development of Castell Bryn Amlwg (after Alcock *et al.* 1967-8)

one, and one that has not been pursued further in Welsh castle studies. The construction of gatehouses in the 'English' style by the Welsh is not a common feature; there is a peculiarly long and narrow gate with rounded towers at Castell Dinas Brân, above Llangollen in Denbighshire, probably built in the 1260s, and an earlier and better example at Criccieth, Caernarfonshire. The twin-towered gatehouse at Criccieth is now generally accepted as having been built by Llywelyn ab Iorwerth, grandfather to Llywelyn ap Gruffudd, some time in the 1230s (Avent 1987), although later heightened, and as with the earlier of the two gates at Castell Bryn Amlwg the rear walls of the Criccieth gate are on the line of the curtain wall.

The remains of strong late thirteenth-century gatehouses are to be seen at the Scottish castles of Bothwell, Lanarkshire, and Kildrummy, Aberdeenshire (figure 3.7). Also, the hitherto unknown remains of another gatehouse with two rounded towers were brought to light during excavations in 1987 at Dundonald Castle, Ayrshire; the gate had been slighted some time in the fourteenth century (Ewart 1987b). Bothwell was probably built from around the year 1250; certainly there was a castle by 1278 at the latest (Simpson 1985). As excavations have shown, the original design was never completed, for the northern half of the castle consists of foundations only, and even these are non-existent along parts of the planned circuit. However, enough of the gatehouse remains to show that it was twin-towered, with a drawbridge pit before it. The remains of the slightly later gatehouse at Kildrummy are more substantial. The castle was built or begun in the second quarter of the thirteenth century, but the existing gate is English in build, probably constructed on the orders of Edward I, and dating to the year 1303. Much of the gate was uncovered before 1927, with further work on the castle undertaken in 1952–62 (Apted 1962–3), and its appearance is certainly Edwardian in style; in its finished state it must have been one of the finest gatehouses to have been built in Scotland. Its similarity in plan with the great gate built at Harlech in the 1280s has often been commented on, and the architect of Harlech and the other castles of Edward I in north Wales, Master James of St George, was himself present in Scotland at this time. All that remains of the Kildrummy gate is a few courses of walling surrounding the chambers on the ground floor, some of which is a modern rebuild, but enough has remained to show that the gate at this level was divided into four chambers, the main rooms being separated from those in the round towers by cross-walls. The western rear chamber was equipped with a large fireplace, and the implication is that this room was the porter's lodge (Tabraham 1986).

Figure 3.7   Kildrummy Castle, with the gatehouse in the foreground

In the late fourteenth century, when Lochmaben Castle, Dumfriesshire, was once again in the hands of the English, the timber castle which had been built by Edward I as a result of the Scottish campaign of 1298 was refortified with stone. Some building seems to have been undertaken in 1365, with further works in 1375. Excavations in front of the castle revealed three phases, although it seems certain that they represent one building operation. The original intention seems for there to have been a gatehouse with rectangular towers, although the only evidence for this were the remains of the platforms which were to support the towers. The platforms were then abandoned, with the parallel walls of the barbican extending over and out from them, and soon after that a new curtain wall was built fronting the barbican (Macdonald and Laing 1974–5: 135–9). From the fourteenth century there is a greater variety in the form of gatehouses; for example, the rectangular gatehouse at Bodiam in Sussex and the half-hexagonal Great Gate of Raglan, Monmouthshire. However, the late fourteenth-century new entrance to Carisbrooke serves as a reminder that the gatehouse with twin rounded towers was not merely a thirteenth-century phenomenon. Also, contemporary with the Carisbrooke gatehouse, the east gate of Southampton Castle was strengthened by the addition of two rounded towers which flanked the entrance passage (Aberg 1975: 182–4).

A further type of entrance of which little mention has been made so far is the postern or sallyport. This is a small gate, usually in the curtain wall, which could allow a garrison to leave a castle to make a surprise attack on a besieging force, or permit men or goods to enter the castle without having to lower the drawbridge and raise the portcullis of the main gatehouse. The majority are simple narrow doorways, like the one at Bolingbroke, but occasionally more complicated arrangements are to be found. At Bristol Castle a postern was found in the form of a tunnel 16m in length and 2m square, leading down to an opening near the bottom of the encircling ditch (Wilson and Moorhouse 1971: 146). It is uncertain how this postern was secured, although evidence for one door was uncovered. The winding tunnel arrangement at Denbigh Castle, for example, originally had doors, a portcullis, the grooves for which remain, as well as two murder-holes. Similar tunnels or passages are a feature of Henry III's great round tower at the north end of Winchester Castle; this had two sallyport passages leading from its basement out under the ditches, one opening within the city, whilst the other led to the suburb on the west side (Biddle 1969: 300). Another postern which had a portcullis, midway along its 27.5m course, was first uncovered in 1926 at Knaresborough Castle, Yorkshire, and further revealed in excavations in 1961 (Le Patourel 1966). In one of the wing-walls which connected the motte to the bailey at Sandal Castle, the excavators uncovered a postern where the western wall crossed the motte ditch (figure 4.1, p.80) (Mayes and Butler 1983: 44). At Montgomery, the walls which blocked each end of the rock-cut ditch between the middle and inner wards also had posterns (Lloyd and Knight 1981: 18–19).

The final excavation of a gatehouse which merits a mention here is that of the inner gatehouse of Aberystwyth Castle, begun in 1277. It was built on the grand Edwardian scale that we associate with his other castles such as Harlech. The south tower of the gate has recently been cleared and excavated, and has produced a highly unusual feature. Running across the tower from front to back are piers to support a cross-wall at the first floor level, dividing the floor into two unequal areas (Davis 1986). The arrangement is strange, to say the least, especially when compared with the other great gatehouses of the period, and not just in Wales. However, further archaeological work is needed, and hopefully will be undertaken, before we can find a solution to the problem.

Mural towers

There is nothing surprising about the widespread use of mural towers in castles from the early thirteenth century onwards, associated with the increasing sophistication of gatehouses; it was all part of the greater emphasis on the defence of the castle at the curtain rather than at a keep within. What is surprising is that it took so long for the idea of mural towers to develop, when one considers that several Norman castles were placed in Roman forts, such as Pevensey and Portchester, which had such towers or bastions. There are examples of the early use of mural towers, for example, those built in the late eleventh century at Ludlow, but these were designed for defence from the wall-walks, as they did not contain any arrowslits; most mural towers would have been used by archers below wall-walk level. Other rectangular towers were built at Framlingham *c.* 1175, by Henry II at Orford in the 1160s and Dover in the 1180s, whilst at the Tower of London, the Bell Tower, built in the late twelfth century, is octagonal in plan up to the level of the second floor, and then circular for the remainder of its height. It is the circular or D-shaped tower which is the dominant form of the thirteenth century, although square, rectangular or polygonal forms were also used in later medieval castles.

An unusual form of tower was associated with the twelfth-century defences of the bailey of Launceston Castle, and was mentioned in chapter 1. Two were excavated, and they resembled stone-lined pits, yet seem to have acted as small mural towers (p.34). Whether they were constructed totally in masonry is open to question; they may have been stone bases for timber superstructures. The tower to the west of the South Gate was dug into the inner slope of the rampart, and from the pottery evidence it was suggested that it had been destroyed in the thirteenth century, presumably as part of the refurbishment of the defences (Saunders 1977b: 133–4). A tower of the same date and similar to those at Launceston has also been excavated at the castle of Newcastle-upon-Tyne, Northumberland (Harbottle 1982: 410). Rochester in Kent has square mural towers dating to the fourteenth century, but one of the towers sits on an earlier structure which may be a rectangular tower built to flank the walls of the inner bailey. It could be assigned to the early twelfth century and associated with work undertaken *c.* 1127, or equally it may belong to building works of the later Norman period (Flight and Harrison 1978: 32–4).

As part of the refurbishment of the inner bailey defences of Deddington in Oxfordshire in the late twelfth or early thirteenth century, which included the gatetower mentioned above, a rectangular tower was inserted into the motte on the line of the existing curtain wall (figure 3.1, V, p.59). The tower was evidently open at the back, as there was no indication of an inner masonry wall. However, the rear wall may have been timber-framed, like the tower in the barbican at Chepstow, because slots which originally housed horizontal timbers were uncovered (Ivens 1983: 37). The positioning of the tower would have enabled archers to flank the lengths of curtain wall running from it, but one mural tower does not make a sophisticated defence, and the southern end of the castle was very vulnerable. A more systematic use of small square towers is to be found at Hadleigh Castle, Essex, although some of these were replaced by rounded towers later in the thirteenth and in the fourteenth century. The bailey at Hadleigh is enclosed by a polygonal curtain wall, with towers placed strategically at some of the angles (Drewett 1975). The castle was built by Hubert de Burgh, justiciar of England, in the 1230s, with much alteration in the fourteenth century, but what is surprising, assuming that the phasing of the castle is correct, is the shape of the towers for a castle of the 1230s, particularly when one considers the building record of de Burgh in Wales prior to the construction of Hadleigh. His Monmouthshire castles of Skenfrith and Grosmont both have rounded mural towers, work which dates primarily from the 1220s. However, de Burgh fell from power in 1232 and lost Hadleigh to the Crown in 1239, and these events may have some bearing on the final design of the thirteenth-century castle.

Two square towers on each side of a pair of narrow chambers or passages have been uncovered recently on the north side of the inner bailey of Eye Castle, Suffolk. It has been suggested that they were built in the late twelfth century, and thus contemporary with the towers at another Suffolk castle, Framlingham (Anon. 1987).

The development of the rounded mural tower, along with the gatehouse, is the major feature of the European castle in the thirteenth century. Ranulf de Blundeville's castle of Bolingbroke has five towers besides those of the gatehouse (figures 3.5, p.67 and 5.8, p.110), all rounded or D-shaped in plan, except for the south-west tower which was rebuilt in polygonal form in the middle of the fifteenth century. With walls about 4m thick, and the short lengths of curtain, from 13.7m to 32m, flanked by large mural towers, Bolingbroke presents a picture of great strength, and displays all the advantages of building a castle on a new site. Because of the present condition of the castle, one can only assume that the towers were equipped with arrowslits, especially as Ranulf's castle of Beeston has them. There were two methods of entry into the towers; a flight of steps led down into the basement, whilst external timber stairs took one up to the first floor and the battlements (Thompson 1974: 315–16).

Thought even went into the planning or positioning of the two towers added to the curtain of the small fortress of Castell Bryn Amlwg (figure 3.6, p.69). The longest stretch of curtain, the western, had a single tower near its centre, whilst the tower on the eastern side stands at the junction of two sides of the castle, enabling the tower to flank both (Alcock *et al.* 1967-8). A single circular tower was built, probably early in the thirteenth century, on the line of the original ringwork defences of what became the inner or upper ward of Llansteffan Castle, Carmarthenshire. It has been interpreted as a round keep (Guilbert 1974: 38), for it may predate the stone curtain wall, but the tower is small when compared with true keeps, having an external diameter of only 7.25m, the walls being 2m thick. When mural towers were added later in the thirteenth century, they were on the line of the curtain enclosing the lower-lying outer ward.

The round tower of the upper ward at Llansteffan is probably earlier than the outer defences, and could cover the northern approaches to the entrance to the upper ward. It is not known when the tower was levelled, but assuming it was still standing in the late thirteenth century it was in an ideal position to cover the lower ward should an enemy have ever gained a foothold there. Solitary rounded towers have been excavated at other sites where hilly topography has influenced a somewhat irregular plan, such as at Dolforwyn and Montgomery, where in each case a tower stands at one end of a ridge, commanding the ground below it. However, at de Blundeville's Beeston, contemporary with and on a site at least as impressive as Montgomery, several D-shaped towers were built. This example serves as an apt reminder that not all castle plans are the same; each follow the dictates of both builder and location.

Until recently Edward I's Aberystwyth was thought to have been a concentric castle from the beginning, lozenge-shaped in plan. At the east angle of both the inner and outer wards stood a gatehouse, whilst at all the others there was a mural tower. However, excavations in the area between the inner and outer southern mural towers have shown that the plan of the castle as we know it today was the result of two phases of construction (figure 3.8). Originally the southern inner curtain running from the main gatehouse did not end in a mural tower but continued to meet the outer defences. This means that Aberystwyth was only concentric on three sides. It became fully concentric when a tower, designed to be circular in plan before a change made it D-shaped, was built midway along the wall, the remainder of the curtain being demolished. Presumably the same development occurred at what became the west angle of the inner ward, and the two new mural towers were linked by the new line of curtain, with a further tower in the centre (Davis 1985). That this new curtain was a later development is shown by the fact that it partly overlay a limekiln used in the construction of the initial phase (Spurgeon 1977; personal communication). It is possible that this change in Aberystwyth's defences was a direct result of the capture and partial destruction of the castle in March 1282, with Master James of St George, the architect of the king's Welsh castles, being the man responsible for the new works.

In the fourteenth century and later, mural towers tended to vary in plan as much as gatehouses, with rectangular and rounded forms being built, often in the same castle. The two almost circular towers built by Edward III on the east side of the bailey of Hadleigh, still a prominent feature of this Essex castle, were originally matched by the 'High Tower'. This tower overlooked the new entrance built by the king, and apparently replaced one of the earlier towers built by Hubert de Burgh. At Barnard Castle, the fourteenth-century strengthening by the Earl of Warwick of the defences included a mural tower in the south-west corner of the town ward which was designed to flank the approaches to the new gate into the middle ward. The square plan of the tower, however, was dictated by the existing defences, for it lay in the corner where the southern wall of the ward met the western defences. The tower was built at the edge of the moat, but in the late fifteenth century its base was strengthened by the addition of a thick masonry batter which ran down into the moat. It may have been the original intention to have the new tower permanently manned by sentinels, for just to the north was a pair of latrines which may be dated to the Warwick period (Austin 1979: 68–71).

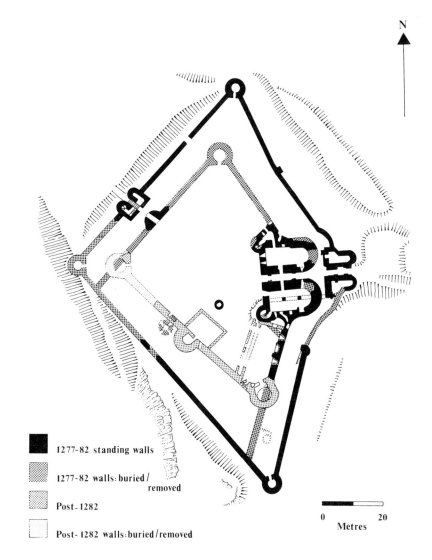

0   20
Metres

Figure 3.8 Provisional plan of the two phases in the building of Aberystwyth Castle (after Spurgeon)

The significance of the fifteenth-century defences surrounding the late fourteenth-century tower-house of Threave, Kirkcudbrightshire, is that they may represent the earliest purpose-built artillery fortifications to have been erected in Scotland (Good and Tabraham 1981; Tabraham and Good 1981). This island stronghold of the Black Douglas originally relied on its watery isolation for its outer defence, but in the late 1440s a masonry curtain wall and a rock-cut moat were added, surrounding all but the northern side of the tower-house. At the same time two buildings in the outer enclosure were demolished, as they would have obscured the field of fire on the eastern front. A dendrochronological study of oak timbers discovered during the excavations provided a date of the winter of 1446–7 for the felling of the trees, suggesting that the outer defences were under construction, using unseasoned timber, in

1447, a date supported by the associated coins and jettons. The new curtain wall on the east and south (landward) sides included three round towers, of which only one stands complete, but the lower courses of the remaining two were excavated. It is clear from the gunloops in the surviving south-east tower that all three towers were designed to take small pieces of ordnance or handguns, whilst bows would have been used behind the slits in the curtain.

The role of the south-west tower at Threave was to protect the small harbour to the west of the tower-house (figure 3.9); it was further defended by a curtain wall which was weaker than the artillery curtain. This length of wall ran along the edge of the river, and then returned to meet the north-west corner of the tower-house, leaving only a turf rampart to cover the north side of the castle. The excavations were unable to confirm that the harbour wall was built at the same time as the artillery work, for a garderobe chute added to the south-west tower in the seventeenth century had led to the destruction of the original walling where it met the tower. However, it seems probable that both the main work, which protected the more vulnerable side of the castle, and the west wall were contemporary.

Figure 3.9   Mural tower and harbour, Threave Castle

This chapter has been concerned with those castles where excavations have provided the relevant evidence for gates and mural towers. The variety in the form of castle gateways revealed by archaeology has served to confirm and increase what is known from extant remains. However, whereas all castles had entrances of some kind, it is important to note that not all had mural towers; the standing remains of a castle such as Okehampton are proof of this. The excavations at Sandal Castle have shown different priorities for the refortification of the castle in stone (figure 2.11, p.56). The bailey was enclosed within a masonry curtain but no mural towers were added to the line of the original earth-and-timber defences, although there may have been turrets, and the outer gatehouse was a very weak affair. This would seem to have been deliberate, as the de Warennes were prodigious castle builders. An examination of that part of the castle adjacent to the bailey shows that it was here that the main strength of Sandal lay, with the keep on its motte discussed in chapter 2, and the great barbican at the foot of the motte. One precaution that was taken with the bailey curtain at Sandal, however, was that it was made deliberately narrow nearer the motte; this was to make it more difficult for assailants to gain access to the keep along the wing-walls.

Barbicans and bridges, an essential part of the study of castle entrances, form the subject of the next chapter.

4 Masonry castles – barbicans and bridges

This chapter is basically a continuation of the first part of the previous one, the section on gatehouses, for both a barbican, where present, and a bridge naturally form an integral part of the entrance arrangement of a castle. The section on bridges covers structures found at both earth-and-timber and masonry castles. This is because excavated examples are few in number, and also because the form of framing is often the same whether at a timber or stone castle.

Barbicans

A barbican is an outer defence to the main entrance of a castle, with its own gateway, and often standing within its own ditch. Extant examples are not numerous in Britain; a twelfth-century barbican survives at Dover, enclosing an area north of the King's Gate which opens on to the inner bailey, and a similar enclosure, but with a powerful mural tower, was added at the west end of Chepstow in the first half of the following century. The remains of a large D-shaped or half-moon structure of the later thirteenth century can be seen at Goodrich, Herefordshire, and the Tower of London had a similar arrangement. At Alnwick in Northumberland a more basic form was built in the early fourteenth century, consisting of two parallel walls running out from the gate to the outer bailey, a device to be seen at Walmgate Bar, one of the gates of the city defences at York. Excavations have also shown how varied these outworks were, but they all served one purpose: to keep the enemy away from the entrance, that most vulnerable part of a castle, by not only providing a physical obstacle, but also another platform from which the garrison could harass the opposition. A barbican could also supplement inadequate defences, as at Beaumaris on Anglesey where the south gatehouse was still incomplete in 1306, and lacked its portcullises, so a small rectangular barbican was added, butting against the gatehouse.

In addition to the north barbican at Dover which has already been mentioned, there was also a south barbican to the inner ward surrounding Henry II's great keep. Unfortunately this was almost totally destroyed in the eighteenth and nineteenth centuries, although excavations undertaken in the 1960s did reveal something of its original form (Rigold 1967). It was different in design from its northern counterpart as it had a gatetower, Arthur's Gate, as opposed to a simple gateway. Two mural towers also made it an altogether stronger work. One (Well Tower) was a square building, the other (Armourer's Tower) was open at the back. It may be assumed from this that the south gate into the inner ward was regarded as the main entrance to the castle in the time of Henry II. The excavations also discovered that Arthur's Gate was not the first gatetower on the site, for it clearly partly overlay another, and stronger, tower. It has been suggested that this earlier tower formed part of the original work at Dover built by the king in the period 1168–74, later largely swept away by the works of the 1180s.

At the West Gate of Lincoln Castle the small barbican projecting from the gate was modified at the end of the twelfth or the beginning of the thirteenth century, possibly to take stone-throwing artillery (Elliott and Stocker 1984: 27). The northern of the two parallel wing walls which formed the barbican had a rectangular platform added to it on the north side (Stocker 1983: 23, figure 8, 25–6), with its west wall on a stone foundation above the ditch, and the east side cut into the existing bank. Although the excavation was unable to provide evidence for the exact form of this later work, it seems that the structure was a platform rather than a tower. If this was the case, then such an addition might have formed a position for a catapult rather than the base of a watchtower. However, the size of the platform was less than 0.5m wide and 1m long; not only is this too small an area to mount an effective weapon, but it would not have left much working space for the operators.

One of the discoveries resulting from the excavations undertaken at Oxford in the 1960s and 1970s was evidence for the east barbican of the castle (Hassall 1976: 243–54). Oxford was under siege by the barons in 1216 when it was relieved by a royal army, and as a result the castle's defences were strengthened on the east side where the church of St Budoc stood, encroaching upon the castle's ditch. This entailed the destruction of the church which was subsequently rebuilt on another site. The removal of this twelfth-century church made sound military sense, for if it had ever fallen into enemy hands it might have been used against the castle as a siege castle. Not only would it have provided assailants with a safe refuge, but it would have also given cover for attacks on the castle itself. It was not possible to excavate the barbican building itself, but the ditch was located, and it seems to have surrounded a large D-shaped platform. The ditch was certainly substantial; before modern building could begin on the site it had to be totally excavated by the contractors, and then filled with concrete. The only other feature of note was that it had been revetted with clay because of the gravelly nature of the scarps.

In spite of our limited knowledge of the Oxford barbican, this outer defence was clearly different in form from the two at Dover but more comparable with the D-shaped structure added as part of the refurbishment of the defences of the motte-and-bailey at Sandal (Mayes and Butler 1983: 47–8, 77–8). A considerable portion of the bailey was lost with the building of the Sandal barbican in the thirteenth century, for this large tower also stood surrounded by its own ditch (figure 4.1). It is unusual in being an internal barbican, lying between the motte and the bailey; most barbicans lie in front of the outer gate. The Sandal barbican was built on an outcrop of sandstone, to which a sloping revetment of very superior ashlar or dressed stone was soon added. This masonry survived unweathered because the ditch was never cleansed of the rubbish which accumulated in it, burying the lowest courses of the barbican's revetment. The tower was linked to the motte and the bailey by bridges, and when the importance of the tower declined in the later middle ages a further bridge was built to connect it directly with the kitchen area. There was also a postern reached by a flight of steps opening on to the ditch between the barbican and the motte. This postern or sallyport must have been intended to form a link with a similar gateway in that section of the bailey curtain wall which crossed the motte ditch, linking the bailey wall itself with the curtain which ran down the side of the motte (figure 4.1).

Figure 4.1   The barbican, motte and postern, Sandal

Although only the lowest courses of masonry survived from the Sandal barbican, the discovery of a latrine serving a guardroom implies that the tower was designed to be permanently manned, with accommodation on an upper floor. It was a fortified island capable of independent defence and, like its parallels in the D-shaped barbicans at the Tower of London and Goodrich, it constituted a major obstacle to an enemy trying to reach the main part of the castle. Not only was the entrance from the bailey over a drawbridge, but the passage may have been further protected by a door with a portcullis. Once this had been reached, a right-angle bend in the passage would have needed to be negotiated, leading to another door, perhaps with portcullis, before the bridge linking the tower to the motte was reached. One of the main differences between the Sandal barbican and its contemporaries at the Tower of London and Goodrich is that the one at Sandal was a tower, whilst the larger examples at the other two consisted of a curtain surrounding an open yard, but possibly with lean-to buildings within. A second difference is the positioning of the barbican tower at Sandal. The barbicans at the Tower of London and Goodrich represented the outermost defences of these castles; at Sandal, the placing of the tower between the motte, with its keep, and the bailey suggests that the Warennes were concentrating their strength in this limited area to the detriment of the bailey. It was emphasized in the previous chapter that the bailey at Sandal did not have the sophisticated defences associated with most thirteenth-century castles. Sandal lacks a strong outer gatehouse and mural towers, although it seems to have had turrets. This contrasts markedly with the castle built by John de Warenne, seventh Earl of Surrey, at Holt in Denbighshire in the 1280s (Butler 1987), but he had a virgin site on which to build. Very little of Holt remains, but it was pentagonal in plan, with a circular tower at each corner.

A final thirteenth-century example comes from Castell-y-Bere, a castle founded in 1221, where, as mentioned in the previous chapter, the main entrance was a doorway through the curtain wall in the lee of a round tower. An elaborate barbican fronted by a wide and deep rock-cut ditch was built at an unknown date in the thirteenth century (see below). The outer stage of the ditch would have been crossed by a fixed wooden bridge, whilst the inner section could only have been negotiated by means of a drawbridge, or rather a turning-bridge. This type of bridge pivoted on a central axle, and when it was in the 'up' position the inner section sank into a deep pit. A passage led from the barbican entrance to a second turning-bridge in front of the main entrance. The passage itself was overlooked by a square tower, whilst the whole unit was commanded by the round tower beside the main entrance and the middle tower or keep on its rocky platform above the barbican (figure 8.4, p.158).

Plans of the castle show the barbican as being of Welsh build (Avent 1983: 28; Butler 1974: figure 1, upon which figure 8.4 is based). However, a recent visit to the site by this writer, coupled with some points expressed by Avent (personal communication), has resulted in some doubts as to this attribution. If the barbican is Welsh, then it is surprising to find such a sophisticated barbican with its two turning-bridges, seemingly the earliest examples of this type of bridge; they are more commonly found in later English castles. However, if the barbican was added by the English following the capture of the castle in 1283, it is strange that no straight joints are apparent where the English masonry meets the Welsh fabric; in other parts of the castle these joints are plain to see.

Edward III's major improvements at Hadleigh in the period 1360–70 included the destruction of the original entrance on the east side, and the construction of a new gate with barbican on the north front (figure 4.2). The work required a break of some 3m in the original thirteenth-century curtain wall; the sides of the new gateway were then refaced with blocks of stone, and a groove for a portcullis added at the same time. The barbican walls projected northwards from this gate, and ended at an outer doorway, to either side of which were solid towers or turrets. These defences were soon to be improved with the addition of a drawbridge, of which more below. The defences of the barbican also included the 'High Tower' of the building accounts, mentioned in the previous chapter. This mural tower, which stood immediately to the west of the barbican, covered the approaches to what must be viewed as a relatively unsophisticated entrance for a royal castle (Drewett 1975: 94–101).

Figure 4.2   The barbican, Hadleigh Castle

A similar basic barbican was added to the front of the gatehouse of Kildrummy Castle, probably in the fifteenth century. It had, like Hadleigh, two parallel walls with a pit for a turning-bridge occupying most of the passage area (figure 3.7, p.70). Access to the room above the passage was from a staircase in the west wall of the barbican, whilst in the east wall there is a postern positioned close to one of the gatehouse towers (Tabraham 1986: 23).

Bridges

Archaeological evidence for castle bridges is not quite as limited as that for barbicans, but there are not many examples. However, Britain has produced the best range of structures in western Europe, for excavated bridges from the Continent are very few, although traces were uncovered at the Husterknupp, a motte-and-bailey in Germany (Herrnbrodt 1958: 58–65); the papers by Bauer (1981) and Hertz (1982) provide useful parallels. Several of the bridges uncovered in Britain have never been fully published, or are to be the subject of forthcoming reports, but the bridge arrangements that have been revealed fall into four categories: horizontal and vertical timbers from the remains of bridges across moats, masonry supports for timber superstructures, stone ramps, and drawbridge pits.

The evidence for medieval timber bridges was gathered in a corpus by S.E. Rigold (1975), to which there was a later addendum (Rigold 1976). The corpus concentrated primarily on minor bridges, that is to say short bridges which crossed moats around individual structures such as castles and moated sites, as opposed to major river crossings. Since the publication of Rigold's researches, further information has become available on some of the castles which he considered, and other examples of bridges have been excavated with which comparisons may be made, although not all the recent discoveries have been at castles. Rigold divided the archaeological evidence into three main types, based on the means of support for the bridges. Only the footings and the lower sections of the verticals have survived, and this makes reconstructions of the superstructures difficult.

The first of Rigold's types comprises those bridges supported on timber piles, an unusual form for castles and moated sites, although a good example comes from the late eleventh-century castle at Goltho. The second type was based on transverse timber soleplates, examples existing with and without transverse bracing (Rigold 1975: 57, figure 17, x and y). The basic form of this type of bridge is one that can be found throughout the middle ages, from the Norman period to the end of the sixteenth century. Rigold's type III was based on soleplates laid in both directions, and in various forms (Rigold 1975: 57, figure 17, IIIa–c).

Excavations between the motte and the bailey of Hen Domen uncovered the remains of five successive bridges dating from the 1070s until the thirteenth century (Barker and Higham 1982: 51–9). The first four bridge structures accord with Rigold's type II, whilst the last was altogether of a weaker build and supported on posts set into the ground. The evidence for the first bridge is the most interesting, for the waterlogged conditions at the bottom of the motte ditch had resulted in the preservation of the sillbeam with two mortise holes for vertical posts (figure 4.3); further foundations were represented by slots in the ground for other timbers. Postholes, slots and trenches provided the evidence for the succession of bridges which followed the substantial, earlier bridge. The excavation of the motte may provide the necessary evidence for the structures at the upper end of the various bridges, although gullies have already been located which may well represent trenches for timber footings of some form of entrance from the bridge.

Figure 4.3   Sillbeam of the first timber bridge in the motte ditch, Hen Domen

The excavators of Hen Domen have stressed that the powerful earlier bridges seemed to have been unnecessarily wide and strong for access to and from the motte. The suggestion is that they were specifically designed to be massive, to support the weight of the timbers needed to build, or rebuild, the tower and palisade. Obviously the bridge would then have remained in use for ordinary traffic after the motte superstructures had been constructed. In the case of the final bridge, which was weaker than its predecessors, either rebuilding on the motte was with less substantial timbering, or it may have been that the bridge alone required replacing. Only the excavation of the motte summit can help to confirm this hypothesis.

Evidence for at least three successive small bridges dating to *c.* 1080–1150 was found at the entrance to the motte-and-bailey at Goltho (Beresford 1987: 89–93). There was no bridge to the motte, which was not separated from the bailey by a moat, so access here was presumably via the wall-walks of the bailey defences. The three bridges were all of a similar design, supported by a line of timber uprights set in a trench in the middle of the moat. The width of the final bridge was the only one which could be ascertained (3.6m), but all were *c.* 11.1m in length. The replacement of the original bridge led to the second being placed just to the north of the first; the third bridge lay to the south, and was partially superimposed over the footings of the original bridge. Although the posts of the bridges had been removed, timbering was located in the moat and this represented the remains of a timber revetment consisting of horizontal posts held in position by wooden uprights (figure 4.4). The revetment had been added to support the base of the inner bank of the moat, for the construction of the successive bridges had weakened the footings of the bank. The bridges may have led to a small gatetower, although there was no positive evidence for one. It seems that the actual approach, once the bridge had been negotiated, was up a ramp, but it is impossible to tell whether there was some form of lifting-bridge immediately in front of the gate.

Thus, the Goltho excavations have shown us how the typical bridge to a small castle would have looked; obviously such bridges do not compare with the contemporary bridges which ran up the motte at Hen Domen, for these were of a much stronger build. A more direct comparison between the bridges of the two sites will only be possible when the area outside the main entrance of Hen Domen, on the east side of the bailey, has been excavated.

The evidence for bridges at other motte-and-bailey castles is slight, but there are a few other sites where some traces of a bridge have been found. At Abinger a causeway of natural sandstone in the moat probably supported a timber superstructure (Hope-Taylor 1950: 25). The reconstruction of this site depicts a flight of steps running up the side of the motte as the most likely means of access to the summit. At Baile Hill, one of York's two mottes, slots seem to have held the horizontal timber footings for the bridge across the ditch, and here there was definite evidence for a flight of steps, probably timber-lined, running up the mound (Addyman and Priestley 1977: 124). The ditch seems to have been about 21m wide, so the bridge would have required a series of supports rising from the bottom of the ditch and from the steeply sloping sides. At Okehampton, one or more paths with steps up the face of the motte were the main means of access from the bailey up to the keep; no evidence has been found for a bridge (Higham 1977: 27).

A series of steps was also located at Great Driffield, Yorkshire, dug into both the motte and the side of the ditch. In this example the steps were cut for the timber footings of a succession of bridges (Eddy 1983: 46). In common with Baile Hill, the ditch was not fully excavated, but here also the bridge would

Figure 4.4   Timber revetment for the footings of the bridge at Goltho

have required vertical timbering rising from the ditch bottom. At Castle Hill, Bakewell, no timbering was revealed in the trench across the motte ditch, but a line of river-worn boulders, which must have been brought up from the valley below specifically for the purpose, was used to revet the base of the motte. The excavator suggested that the weight of the original bridge at this point had weakened the scarp (Swanton 1972: 21, 23), or the building of a replacement had involved a certain amount of damage to the motte. A second trench across the ditch and into the bailey also found evidence for a bridge.

The surviving brick bridge at Pleshey is dated to the late fourteenth or early fifteenth century. A timber predecessor may have been built *c.* 1200; one side of it was set on flint footings on a ledge cut into the slope above the ditch on the bailey side (Webster and Cherry 1978: 169; Youngs and Clark 1981: 200). Traces of bridges found at other motte-and-baileys include South Mimms, Hertfordshire (Kent 1968: 2), and references to other sites, including earlier excavations, are listed in Rigold (1975).

At Castle Acre traces of four timber bridges, all dating to before the mid twelfth century, were uncovered during the excavations carried out between 1975 and 1982 (Coad *et al.* 1987). Two successive structures originally connected the lower ward to the gatetower of the upper ward, whilst the other two lay before the east gatetower that connected the lower ward with the outworks. The evidence for the first bridge to the upper ward consisted of the the remains of a trench 3.2m long for a timber soleplate, and this would have acted as the base for the main pier of the bridge. The bridge, which may have consisted of three 4m spans, was replaced by another, possibly about 1135–50 when the upper ward was being refortified. The main posts were set in sockets, of which two pairs remained. Bridge two may have been a longer structure as the piers were set further apart (three 5m spans), but it was narrower. It has been suggested that the reason for this narrowing was the reduction in width of the upper gateway passage.

The original bridge at Castle Acre which led from the east gate to the outworks was similar in design to the first bridge that linked the two wards. Not long after it was built the approach to the gate was altered by creating a solid causeway cut by a ditch; this may have been part of the refortification of the castle which took place *c.* 1135–40. The masonry which formed the causeway incorporated the timbers of the first bridge, and the excavators uncovered the voids in the walling left by the lower sections of some of the horizontal, vertical, and diagonal timbers for both the main and the secondary piers. The bridge must have been an impressive work; the soleplate of the main pier was 0.5m square and at least 8m long. The posts which it supported were 0.35m square, the same size as those which formed the secondary pier, although the soleplate for this was smaller. The later encapsulation of the bridge in masonry has resulted in one of the few instances where it has been possible to reconstruct the form of an original bridge with a high degree of accuracy, although naturally the form of the superstructure can only be an educated supposition.

In the light of the carpentry of the first bridge at the east gate of Castle Acre, it is surprising that there was felt to be a need for the masonry causeway. In the words of the excavators, the approach to the gate does indeed 'bear the distinct hallmarks of short-term expediency', perhaps due to the lack of a drawbridge, and the desire to have a more fireproof structure. It may be that the second bridge did include a section which could be removed or lifted. In terms of defence the approaches to the east and upper ward gates lack the sophistication to be found at the later gatehouse built as the western entrance to the lower ward, but they were on a par with contemporary arrangements elsewhere.

The main entrance to Eynsford Castle from the twelfth century was through a gatetower added against the late eleventh-century curtain wall. Examination

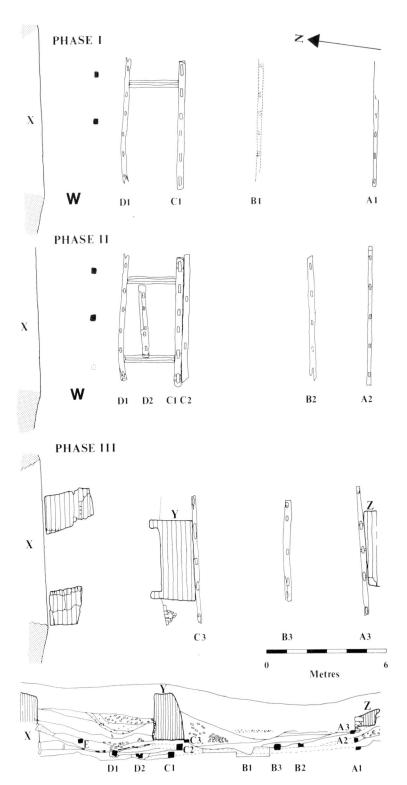

Figure 4.5 The three phases of the bridge at Eynsford (after Rigold 1973)

of the ditch at this point by Rigold revealed the remains of a bridge 17m long (Rigold and Fleming 1973; summary in Rigold 1973: 185–6, and 1975: 62–4). The bridge was of three phases (figure 4.5), the first two of which were five-bay structures. The innermost timbering consisted of a line of vertical posts, interpreted as 'shock-absorbers' for the drawbridge (figure 4.5, W), the outer lip of which rested on a rigid pier (figure 4.5, C–D). As a means of strengthening this pier it was enclosed on three sides by vertical planks, and horizontal boards on the fourth. The outer two bays of the first two bridges formed the fixed sections (figure 4.5, A–C). These outer bays in the third bridge were set between two masonry abutments (figure 4.5, Z, Y), and presumably the bridge spanning the gap between abutment Y and the two piers in front of the gateway would have been mobile.

The dating of the bridges at Eynsford is only approximate. It was possible to submit one of the timbers from the first phase for dendrochronological analysis. The results provided minimal support for the period favoured by Rigold on archaeological grounds, the excavator suggesting a mid twelfth-century date for the first bridge (Rigold 1975: 90–1). Dendrochronology was not able to serve Eynsford as well as it did Caerlaverock, as will be seen below. If we accept Rigold's chronology, the second phase amounted to a repair of the original bridge in the late twelfth century, and towards the end of the following century the third and final bridge was built.

During the course of the excavations of the late thirteenth-century castle of Caerlaverock, Dumfriesshire, the timbers of a bridge were found in the moat (figure 4.6). The best account to date is in Rigold (1975: 71–4). The bridge was 30m long, and had undergone various repairs during its history before it was heavily modified in 1593 as part of the refurbishment of the defences. The original structure consisted of five bays, and was represented by massive timbers; in the later middle ages, when repairs and alterations were carried out, the bridge was of four bays. The dating of the three medieval phases was *c.* 1290, second quarter of the fourteenth century, and fifteenth century. However, the timbers of the bridges had been replaced in the moat after the excavation, and in 1977 the moat was drained to enable the wood to be the subject of dendrochronological analysis (Baillie 1982: 160–3). The results showed that the first bridge was built about 1277, the felling date of the original timbers. The findings relating to the second bridge revealed that although it was dated *c.* 1371, it included wood that had been felled originally in 1333 for some unknown purpose. Baillie was not successful, however, in dating the third phase, although a fifteenth-century date is the most likely. The date of the construction of this second castle of Caerlaverock has always been uncertain. It was the scene of a famous siege in 1300 by King Edward I, and it has been assumed that it was built in the last decade of the thirteenth century. The successful analysis by Baillie has shown it to be a contemporary of the castles built by Edward I in north Wales.

Contemporary with the first bridge at Caerlaverock was the example excavated, together with the outer gatehouse, at Edward I's castle of Flint. The castle was begun in 1277, and when the moat surrounding the outer ward was dug, a rock causeway was left *in situ* to support the footings of the bridge which connected the castle with the town; when the moat was filled with water the causeway would then have been covered. This bridge at Flint underwent

Figure 4.6   The remains of the bridge timbers, Caerlaverock

two main phases. The first structure was supported on timber trestles, and some of the timbers discovered must have been the soleplates into which other parts of the framework would have been jointed. It was not possible to examine the remains of this bridge in detail because much of it lay beneath the later example. Within a short period of time the bridge had been rebuilt, and it was associated with a stone outer gatehouse which had a turning-bridge (figure 4.7). The difference between the new bridge and its predecessor is that the vertical timbers of the new structure were now set on a series of masonry piers. The building accounts reveal that carpenters were working on a bridge between the castle and the town in 1286 (Colvin 1963: 316; Taylor 1986b: 24), so it would seem that the first structure was very short-lived. However, it may never have been intended that it should last for several decades, but was thrown up quickly as soon as the moat had been dug once work had begun on this castle, one of the earliest that Edward I established in north Wales.[1]

[1] The report on the excavations at Flint by T.J. Miles in 1971–4 has yet to be published, but there is a detailed archival report with illustrations held by Cadw: Welsh Historic Monuments, Cardiff.

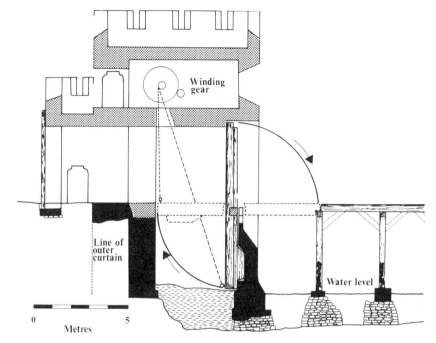

Figure 4.7 Conjectural reconstruction of the bridge and outer gatehouse at Flint Castle (after Miles)

The final bridges where considerable timbering has survived are at the late fourteenth-century castle of Bodiam in Sussex. The bridges were first examined by Lord Curzon during his repairs to the castle earlier this century (Curzon 1926), but the draining of the moat in 1970 enabled a further and more detailed study to be made (Martin 1973). There were two long bridges, one on the south side of the castle crossing the moat to the postern gateway, whilst the other led from the north-west side of the moat to an octagonal platform. Access to the main gatehouse was then gained by passing through a barbican, on each side of which were either fixed or mobile bridges. The only timbering that remained were the soleplates of the main bridge, although the positions for the plates for the postern bridge were uncovered. None of the upper timbers was discovered, and it was apparent that at some date both bridges had been systematically removed. The postern bridge was the shorter of the two, having six supports on plates, whilst the other had nine. A further soleplate at the entrance end of the main bridge seemingly supported timbers for a drawbridge linking the bridge to the outer bank.

Although little or nothing may have survived of most bridges, particularly where there was no water-filled ditch, other forms of evidence do remain, as at Montgomery. The rock-cut ditch between the middle and inner wards of the castle was filled in as part of slighting carried out by Parliament in 1649. The excavations, a full report of which is forthcoming, revealed that it was 6.1m deep and 13.7m wide. The masonry piers of a series of four timber bridges were uncovered in the bottom of the ditch (Knight 1983; Lloyd and Knight 1981).

The approach to the inner gatehouse of Beeston Castle took a different form altogether in its second phase. As originally constructed in the 1220s, it consisted of a timber bridge which was supported on a pillar of sandstone, left isolated when the rock-cut ditch was quarried. The pillar stands 4m high, but it seems likely that it was taller than this originally. In 1303–4 the entrance arrangements were radically altered. The documentary accounts reveal that a stone ramp or causeway was built, which was 34 feet (10.35m) high, 7 feet (2.13m) wide and 20 feet (6.1m) long, and which led up to a new drawbridge; the remains of this causeway still stand. Excavations in 1975–7 revealed much of the extent of the ditch, and showed that the ramp consisted of a rubble core faced with sandstone ashlar (Hough 1978). However, one unresolved problem is that the original dimensions of the ramp based on the remains do not accord with those given in the accounts of the chamberlains of Cheshire. It seems unlikely that a clerk would have made major errors in all three measurements, but this appears to be the only conclusion that can be drawn, unless the remains of the ramp evident today are not those of the one built in 1303–4.

It has been seen from the above that archaeological evidence for movable bridges is slender, although the remains of certain timbers at both Eynsford and Bodiam suggest there once were drawbridges there. The stone-lined pits for turning-bridges which pivoted on a central axle or trunnion are a common feature of masonry castles of the later thirteenth century onwards, and have been found at some of the recent excavations; those at Castell-y-Bere have been mentioned already in connection with the castle's barbican (p.81). At Sandal Castle the barbican was approached over a bridge from the bailey, the footings for which remain, as do those for the bridge from the barbican to the motte. Within the barbican was a pit which was 3.8m long, 3.2m wide and at least 3m deep, built to receive the inner half of a turning-bridge when it was in the 'up' position. The outer half of the pit formed, therefore, a major obstacle to an assault on the entrance. A further, but smaller, drawbridge pit was excavated in the main gatehouse on the north side of the bailey (Mayes and Butler 1983: 47–52). These improvements at Sandal represent part of the thirteenth-century transformation of the castle from timber to stone.

At the same time as Sandal was being rebuilt, a new entrance, the Black Gate, was added to the castle of Newcastle-upon-Tyne by Henry III in 1247–50. A turning-bridge formed part of the defensive arrangements, with the counterweights housed in two slots in a pit. A similar bridge was a feature of the passage or barbican which connected the Black Gate with the twelfth-century North Gate (Harbottle and Ellison 1981: 80–5).

The fourteenth-century gatetower which linked the town ward to the middle ward at Barnard Castle was provided with a turning-bridge, the basement of the tower forming the pit (Austin 1979: 67–8). The barbican which was a feature of Edward III's refurbishment of the defences of Hadleigh in the 1360s also included a turning bridge. The pit (figure 4.2, p.82) was 6.75m long, 2.2–2.5m wide, and 2.5m deep, and both sockets for the bridge axle were located, one in a robber trench, the other *in situ* (figure 4.8). A further pit can be seen in the fifteenth-century barbican at Kildrummy (figure 3.7, p.70).

The peak of British castle design was realized in the buildings of the late thirteenth and fourteenth centuries. This achievement is symbolized in particular by the castles of Edward I in north Wales. However, one should also

Figure 4.8   Axle socket for the drawbridge in the barbican at Hadleigh

be aware of the works carried out, for example, at Warwick Castle, to name but one stronghold where important military buildings were added to an existing castle in the fourteenth century. The growing sophistication of castles from the 1220s, with rounded mural towers and twin-towered gatehouses, is well reflected in the below-ground archaeology, as has been seen in chapter 3. It was the concern of the medieval kings and magnates for the potentially most vulnerable part of a castle, the entrance, that gave rise to the powerful gatehouses, as well as the small number of barbicans that we know about. More importantly, however, the vulnerability of the gateway was further alleviated by the inclusion of more elaborate drawbridge arrangements. The move from the simple lifting-bridge, hinged at the inner end, to a turning-bridge which pivoted on a central axle is a feature of the gatehouses and barbicans of the mid thirteenth century and later. A particular advantage of the turning-bridge was the deep pit required to take the inner half when the bridge was raised; such pits also acted as formidable obstacles.

Part 2 – The castle : domestic

5 Halls

The hall was just one of a whole range of buildings that could be expected to have been found within the courtyard of a castle. Few sites have had their interiors opened up to a large degree, excavation being limited in area, and often undertaken in advance of consolidation of a particular monument. A notable exception is the work at Hen Domen where about half the bailey has been excavated to reveal a profusion, or confusion, of buildings built and rebuilt from the late eleventh century.

The role of the hall within a castle was varied, its main functions often depending on the nature of the castle itself. One tends to think that the hall would form the domestic focus of life within the walls, and certainly this may have been the case in smaller castles, such as Goltho and Sycharth. However, in the major castles of the land, those held by the king and his senior magnates, the main hall was probably not intended for everyday use but formed the centre of the administration of estates and of justice. Naturally, it would also be used for great occasions; for example, when the castle's lord was present, for few magnates, whether king or lord, could spend time in every stronghold that formed the centre of their estates. Also many castles had separate private lodgings for either the owner or the castle's constable or steward; here might be found a small hall for informal, family use. In cases where more than one family or household lived within the same walls, accommodation for both would necessitate a series of apartments. This might result, in the larger castles, in the provision of more than one hall. This is a particular feature of the later medieval castles (Faulkner 1963) such as Bolton, Yorkshire, but by no means common to all (Morley 1981).

The halls formed part of a collection of buildings distributed about castle baileys and have rarely remained in the generally good state of preservation in which the defences stand. The same applies equally to the other domestic ranges. Although stone defences are just as prone to dilapidation, they were generally more solidly built so that they have survived in a better state. Also, castle walls and towers tended not to be rebuilt during the middle ages, whereas domestic ranges were often improved, as will be seen below. However, some early domestic buildings do still stand in a good state of preservation, and one thinks in particular of the late twelfth-century aisled hall at Oakham in the old county of Rutland, and the magnificent hall, also aisled, built by Henry III in his castle at Winchester, the construction of which is well documented (Colvin 1971: 89–187). It is no coincidence that the Winchester hall was taken over by the county at the beginning of the seventeenth century for the administration of the law; this had been one of its functions from the beginning (Biddle and Clayre 1983: 29). The study of the remains of those ecclesiastical and secular medieval halls which still stand in almost their original form has helped in the interpretation of the more meagre remains which have been uncovered by excavation. Also, the relationship between these halls and adjacent buildings such as private apartments and service ranges enables one to interpret the function of these excavated buildings as a whole with some confidence.

One feature of medieval vernacular buildings is the adoption of aisled halls in the thirteenth and fourteenth centuries. They are rarely preserved from the Norman period, nor are they common in sixteenth-century houses (Sandall 1986), although the use of the aisled framework continues well into the post-medieval period in agricultural buildings such as barns. However, excavations have revealed several examples of the late eleventh and twelfth centuries, and although one at least may have been an elaborate building reflecting the high social status of its owner (Goltho *c.* 1150), others were not. Certainly Mercer's statement that 'The farther back that the aisled hall is traced the higher the standing of its occupants is found to be' (Mercer 1975: 9), then citing such Norman halls as Oakham, Leicester Castle and the Bishop's Palace, Hereford, is one that no longer holds true.

Examples of very early Norman halls are rare. The development of a castle through the middle ages, both of its defences as well as the buildings within its walls, has often led to the destruction of the original halls. However, excavation has revealed both timber and masonry buildings that date to before 1100. Their survival has been due in most cases either to an early abandonment of the sites or to their having been succeeded by further timber buildings which have not completely removed traces of the original ranges. For the sake of convenience this chapter has been divided into timber and masonry halls, although the division is not clear at times, as will be seen below. The division is based on the material with which the walls of a hall were built, whether it was timber with clay, wattle-and-daub or some other infilling, or masonry.

Timber halls

The building which must have dominated the bailey of Hen Domen, following its construction in the 1070s, was a structure at the western end, close to the motte ditch (figure 5.1). It seems to have been a forebuilding through which the bridge to the motte was reached, but its dimensions have not been fully recovered. It has been suggested that the building was at least two storeys high, and possibly three, for although the sillbeams had not survived, the large trenches in which they had been bedded were uncovered. As we have already seen in the section on the bridges at Hen Domen (p.83), Roger of Montgomery's castle was constructed of very large timbers, possibly prefabricated in comparative safety a few miles further east in England. The excavators' provisional interpretation of this structure (building XVII, renumbered LIa in Barker and Higham 1988) is that above the undercroft of the forebuilding lay the main hall of the castle (Barker and Higham 1982: 89). It might also be argued that the function of the forebuilding was to protect the approaches to the motte from the east; in effect, a barbican. However, whether such a building would have required such massive timbers is open to question. The excavators emphasize that its foundations would not have disgraced the supports for a building such as a 'wing of an Elizabethan mansion'.

A similar building, possibly with a portico, stood in the same position in the mid twelfth century (building LI, or LIb as it appears in Barker and Higham 1988), and presumably had the same function (see frontispiece and figure 5.2).

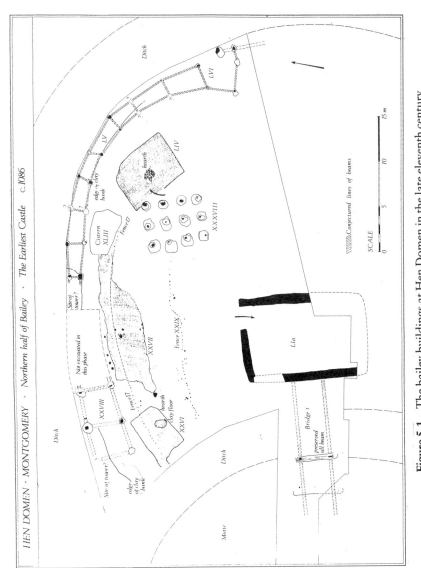

HEN DOMEN · MONTGOMERY · Northern half of Bailey · The Earliest Castle c.1086

Ditch

Site of tower?

edge of clay bank

XXVIII

Fence 17

hearth

clay floor

XXVI

Ditch

Motte

Not excavated in this phase

Site of tower?

XXVII

Fence XXIX

Cistern XLIII

Fence 17

hearth

LIV

edge of clay bank

XXXVIII

LV

Ditch

LVI

La

Bridge 1

preserved sill beam

SCALE
0   5   10   15 m

Conjectured lines of beams

Figure 5.1   The bailey buildings at Hen Domen in the late eleventh century

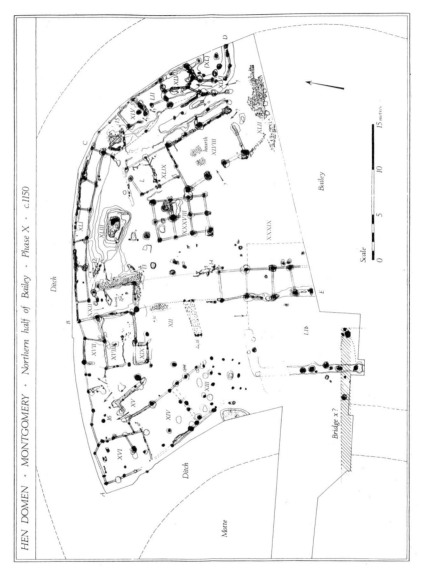

Figure 5.2   The bailey buildings at Hen Domen c. 1150

The discovery of what has been interpreted as another hall of the same date in the eastern half of the bailey has led to the suggestion that the castle was divided into households, the de Boulers family occupying the western part of the bailey, with its first floor hall. There seems to have been an equivalent building for the garrison or other occupants of the castle (building XLVIII), which succeeded a lodging or hall with a hearth dating to the first phase (LIV). Building XLVIII was a rectangular structure about 8m long and 5.5m wide on a clay platform, and it differed from the main hall in two respects. First, it was a ground floor hall, and second, its method of construction was radically different. Instead of timbers jointed into sillbeams, its main vertical timbers were posts set into the ground, and one wall may have been built of clay, strengthened with small uprights set in a trench. It is not known with what material the roof of this hall and the numerous other timber buildings at Hen Domen were covered, there being no evidence for tiles or shingles. The logical conclusion from this is that they were thatched. An internal feature of building XLVIII was a layer of red clay which marked the position of the hearth. The hall (XLVIII) was succeeded by another possible example (LII) (figure 5.3) in the late twelfth or early thirteenth century; its original length is uncertain, but it was a much narrower building, only *c*. 3.5m internally (Barker and Higham 1982; 1988).

The first hall at Goltho, built *c*. 1080, occupied half the area of the minute bailey of the castle, serving to emphasize that for much of the middle ages the planning of the domestic ranges within a bailey took second place to the defensive arrangements. It was a rectangular six-bayed ground floor hall 13.8m by 6m, with a single aisle down one side (figure 5.4). About 25 per cent of known aisled halls in England and Wales have only one aisle, but they do not relate to any chronological development, and were found throughout the middle ages (Sandall 1986). The main purpose of the aisle was to provide greater area within a building as the timber trusses of a roof could only span a certain width. The aisles then had their own roofs; they were either lean-to, pitched, or a continuation of the slope of the main roof of the hall.

The walls of the Goltho hall were probably constructed of timber and clay; some of the posts were set into trenches, whilst others simply rested on top of the ground surface. At each end of the hall there was evidence for a small room partitioned off from the main area, one of which may have been a solar or private chamber. Other features which were associated with the hall were a hearth, and an external garderobe pit against the south-east side of the building. The life of this first hall was short, for it was replaced about 1125 by another single-aisled hall which was built on the same site. This second hall (figure 5.4) was a larger building than its predecessor, 16.5 × 5.7m (at the gables); it was 6.9m wide in the centre, as one side of the hall was bowed. A large kitchen occupied the east end, and there was a small room housing an oven attached to the kitchen, with a garderobe just to the west of it. There was little evidence for the walls of the hall as they had been built sitting on the surface, but it was fortunate that an eaves-trench on two sides, together with the wear on the floor and rubbish deposits, marked the outline of the building. However, Beresford has suggested that the walls were of clay with timber-lacing, with only the aisleposts set into the ground (Beresford 1987: 106–10).

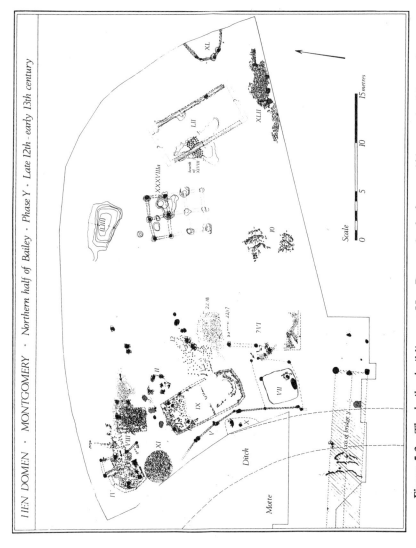

Figure 5.3 The bailey buildings at Hen Domen in the late twelfth to early thirteenth century

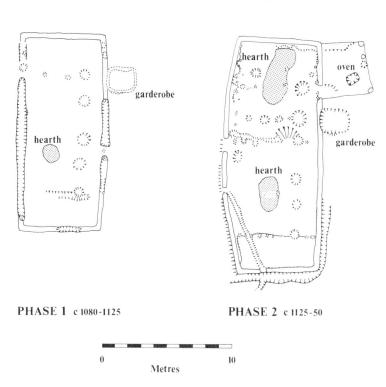

PHASE 1 c 1080-1125   PHASE 2 c 1125-50

0   10
            Metres

Figure 5.4   The early Norman halls at Goltho (after Beresford 1987)

The early Norman halls at Goltho could not have been particularly impressive buildings. Although the rebuilding did improve the facilities, the hall in its second phase was still not a substantial structure, especially when it is compared to the first floor hall at Hen Domen. However, the latter was associated with the castle of an earl, Goltho with a tenant of a Norman lord. More remarkable is the comparison with the hall of the Saxon manor which the castle replaced about 1080. The eleventh-century Saxon hall was 11.4m long and 7.2m wide, together with a bower at one end (6.9 × 4.5m); this may have been a separate building, not connected to the hall. The overall design produced a spectacular building with stave-built walls, and with the main structural timbers set in pits 0.9m deep (Beresford 1987: 74–81). The reasons behind the differences between the Saxon and the early Norman halls must have been a result of the status of the occupiers. Perhaps, as Beresford has suggested, the permanent resident of Norman Goltho in its first phase was the steward responsible for the running of the estates, with the Norman lord only occasionally visiting his property.

One further late eleventh-century timber hall has been uncovered, at Barnard Castle, Co. Durham. The building, like those at Goltho, was single-aisled, but at Barnard the hall was more substantial, with posts of the aisle set into large pits, and those forming the walls set in trenches; its dimensions were approximately 14 × 10.5m. The hall probably relates to the castle-ringwork founded c. 1095 (Austin 1982: 294).

It has been seen that the halls at Goltho and Barnard were single-aisled. At Sandal the hall associated with the earth-and-timber castle of the early twelfth century has been interpreted as having had two aisles, although one side of the building was partially destroyed when the timber building was replaced by a masonry hall. The Sandal example, about 13.5 × 7m, displayed yet another method of construction, for although the timber posts were set into the ground, the pits do not compare in size with those at Barnard nor those twelfth-century examples at Goltho and Cae Castell, Rumney, to be discussed below. The hall at Sandal consisted of three bays, with a chamber at each end, the southern room possibly having an upper storey. The usual pattern of an open hearth in the centre of the hall, seen at Goltho, was also a feature at Sandal. The entrance to the building was at the end away from the dais and private chamber which lay at the north (Mayes and Butler 1983: 32–4, 73–5). Although the evidence for kitchens will be discussed in another part of this book (pp.138–50), it is relevant to mention that the small timber kitchen at Sandal was adjacent to the northern end of the hall where the private chamber was situated. This was an unusual arrangement for if the hall and chamber were used by an officer of the household (the Warenne lord would have resided in a building on the motte) it would have been more pleasant for him to have used the room furthest away from the bustle and smells of the kitchen.

The evidence for a sophisticated double-aisled hall at Goltho in the middle of the twelfth century is irrefutable (Beresford 1987: 112–19). The rebuilding of the castle *c.* 1150, when the motte-and-bailey was levelled to become a low mound or motte, has been referred to above (figure 1.9, p.18). The one building which was definitely associated with this phase was a large timber hall (figure 5.5) in the centre of the mound whose dimensions (19.5 × 12.3m) made it similar in size to other twelfth-century halls such as those at Farnham Castle and the Bishop's Palace, Hereford. The main vertical timbers of the walls and aisles were set in pits of varying depths and widths, but not as large as those associated with the late Saxon hall, suggesting that the stability of the hall did not rest solely on the key vertical timbers.

Internal features of the Goltho hall included a central hearth and two small end-bays, which with the main aisles formed a continuous passage or arcade inside the building; the end bays were too small to be chambers or service rooms, a feature of several of the halls already mentioned. Beresford has suggested that the new Goltho hall may have had a clerestory, an upper level above the aisles. This theory is based on the layout of the timbers, and cannot be proved, although parallels are cited. A good example of a hall where there is evidence for a clerestory is the mid twelfth-century building at Leicester Castle (Alcock and Buckley 1987). The walls of the Goltho hall were probably of wattle-and-daub rather than staves.

The one external feature for which some evidence was found at Goltho was the roof. Earthenware roof-tiles, including a ridge-tile, were uncovered in the area of the hall and are the earliest known examples to have come from a medieval site (Keen 1987: 169–70). The implication is that the new hall not only would have looked very impressive from the outside (figure 5.5), especially if it did have a clerestory, but the carpentry required to support a heavy tiled roof must have been extremely sophisticated. Thus, we have a building of some status, and the second castle at Goltho must have been

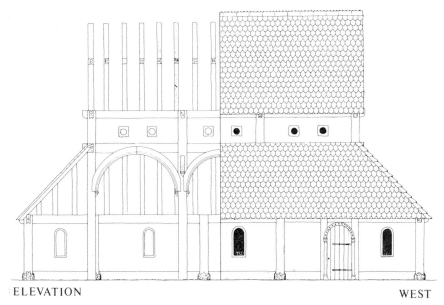

ELEVATION   WEST

Figure 5.5   Reconstruction of the hall at Goltho built *c.* 1150

designed to be the permanent residence of the lord of the manor. The new hall would have dominated the site, towering over the palisade which may have formed the only defences on the mound. It would, therefore, have been rather vulnerable to attack, but seemingly the new occupant made the defences of the site subordinate to the domestic requirements of his household.

The final building at Goltho is not the longest timber hall to have been discovered by excavation. The twelfth-century hall at Castle Bromwich, a motte-and-bailey in Warwickshire, was at least 21m long, but only 5m wide. Further information on the structure is sparse, but it did contain timber partitions, and there was a hearth at one end (Ford 1971).

The precise dating for the the ringwork of Cae Castell or Rumney Castle, near Cardiff, has yet to appear in print, although there is a useful interim report (Lightfoot 1983). It is assumed that the first phase was associated with the Norman occupation of Glamorgan in the early twelfth century, whilst the sixth and final period of occupation ended with the destruction of the site in the late thirteenth century, or possibly the early fourteenth century; a hoard of silver pennies of *c.* 1292–5 was found in the burnt remains of the later masonry hall (Boon 1986: 83–90). The hall of the second period, presumably twelfth century, was a single-aisled structure, with its timber posts set in wide pits dug into the rock, replacing an unaisled timber building. This makes the Rumney example one of the few known aisled halls to be found in western Britain (Sandall 1986: 23); Llantrithyd in Glamorgan is another (see below, p. 112). It was not possible to obtain the full plan of the Rumney hall, but it was a substantial building 10m wide and at least 13m in length. Its position in the castle, on the far side of the courtyard away from the main entrance, is a recurring feature in the domestic planning of castles, whether stone or timber, where the hall is an individual building in its own right, as opposed to forming part of a keep or gatehouse. In a later phase at Rumney the hall was replaced by another, also of timber, and with its main timbers set in postpits (figure 5.6).

Figure 5.6 Postholes representing successive halls at Rumney

At another Glamorgan ringwork, Penmaen, the hall of the twelfth-century phase is the smallest building (5 × 3.6m) to be considered in this section. If it were not for the fact that, on existing evidence, it was the main domestic building of the castle, one would hesitate to call it a hall at all. It was defined by a series of pits cut into the rock, and these holes would have taken the timber uprights of the hall. Apart from these features, nothing more can be said of the building, although it seems to have been kept clean, with the occupants discarding broken pottery and other rubbish outside the building (Alcock 1966: 190–2).

The hall at Cruggleton Castle, Wigtown, was not an aisled structure, but other aspects of its construction were similar to most other timber halls. It was built in the late twelfth century (figure 1.10, p.19), and lasted into the early years of the following century (Ewart 1985: 18–22). When the motte was built by extending a natural outcrop of rock, a hall which already stood on the site was left standing, although a major improvement was to double its length, making it 12.5 × 4m. At the end of the extension the hall was linked to the tower or chamber already discussed (p.20). The method of construction was the same as for the original hall, a building assigned to the excavator's phase 2 (mid–late twelfth century). The main timbers were set in pits, whilst the infilling (?wattle-and-daub) would have rested on the ground surface, leaving no trace.

There is some disagreement about the shape of another hall in Scotland, that built on the motte of Castlehill of Strachan when the castle was constructed about 1250. The excavator has interpreted the remains of this timber building as a hall 14 × 12m, with at least one end apsidal in shape, and it is possible that the other was also, so that the shape of the hall may have been akin to the possible fifteenth-century turf-walled oval hall at Macewen's Castle, Argyllshire (Marshall 1983). The external timbers at Castlehill were set in a soleplate laid in a continuous curving trench, whilst the main supports for the presumably thatched roof were placed in pits 1m deep on the inside of the walls (figure 5.7). The infilling between the timbers would have been of

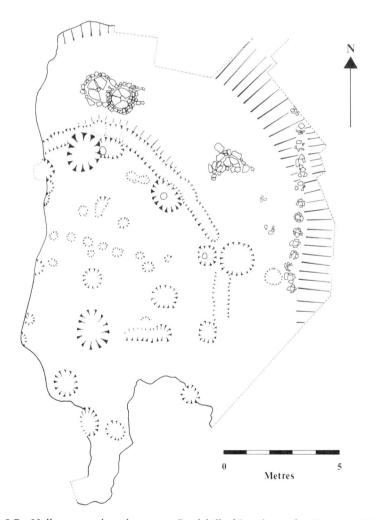

Figure 5.7 Hall excavated on the motte, Castlehill of Strachan (after Yeoman 1984)

wattle-and-daub, as much daub was found on the motte surface. At a later date, towards the end of the thirteenth century, three large posts were added either to support an upper floor or to reinforce the roof. Interior details included two possible hearths, one of which might have had a chimney, a theory based on a series of postholes in its vicinity. Originally a timber partition divided the hall into a small room at the north end, with the main chamber to the south, but the position was reversed in the final phase of occupation which lasted from the later thirteenth century until the destruction of the castle in the early fourteenth century (Yeoman 1984: 323–36, 344–5).

It was not possible to provide a complete picture of the features on the summit of the Strachan motte due to erosion of the site. Therefore, one cannot be certain of the precise plan of the hall. An alternative theory on the shape of the building was presented by Murray in an appendix to the excavation report (in Yeoman 1984: 346–7). It was proposed that the building should be seen as having a circular plan. This is not quite as remarkable as it may seem. The circular structure at Castle Hill, Peebles (Murray and Ewart 1978–80) has already been mentioned (p.20), and interpreted as a keep; that at Strachan clearly was not a keep. Murray also favours earthfast staves, planks or posts for the walling rather than wattle-and-daub; she suggests that the spacing of the posts is too close compared with known examples where wattle was employed in construction.

An argument in favour of a circular building on the motte at this site is the comparison of the dimensions of other excavated timber halls (Table 1). The widths of the halls given in the table are generally much narrower than the Strachan example, and those over 10m wide are aisled. The hall at Strachan was not of this design, and its dimensions and shape do provide a strong argument in favour of Murray's theory. The site is but one example of the problems of trying to reconstruct the original appearance of timber buildings from features such as postholes and slots.

The final two halls in this section, both late medieval, are examples of another type of timber construction. At both Sycharth and Bolingbroke the timber-framing was supported on low or dwarf walls to prevent premature rotting of the woodwork and to act as a stable foundation. It is unfortunate that the excavations on the motte of Sycharth (figure 1.3, p.9) in Denbighshire only uncovered about a quarter of the area (Hague and Warhurst 1966), for we have an elaborate poetic description of this manor or court (*llys*) of Owain Glyndŵr. The hall of Sycharth was described as this 'fine wooden house on the top of a green hill' (the motte) which was destroyed in 1403. Iolo Goch, bard to Glyndŵr, has left us a record, if somewhat exaggerated, of Sycharth and its environs about the year 1390. The verses (in Welsh) mention that it was cruck-built, 'each arch joined with the other', of French (i.e. foreign) workmanship, with various rooms or alcoves, a tiled roof, and 'a chimney that did not suffer smoke' (Hague and Warhurst 1966: 109–11).

The excavations at Sycharth revealed two buildings, the larger of which probably was the hall. It was not particularly wide, about 6m (5.3m internally), and no more than 13m long. The outline of the hall was preserved by the survival of dwarf walls designed to keep the timber-framing above the ground surface, although the evidence for the wall on one side was meagre.

Table 1. Timber halls: a comparison of dimensions

Site	Length × Width	Number of aisles	Date
Castle Bromwich	21 × 5m	–	12th cent.
Goltho 3	19.5 × 12.3m	2	c.1150
Goltho 2	16.5 × 5.7m	1	c.1125
Castlehill of Strachan	14 × 12m	–	c.1250
Barnard	14 × 10.5m	1	c.1095
Hen Domen (bldg LIa)	14 × 7m*	–	c.1080
Rumney	13 × 10m*	1	12th cent.
Goltho 1	13.8 × 6m	1	c.1080
Sandal	13.5 × 7m	2	12th cent.
Bolingbroke	12.5 × 8.1m	–	c.1400
Cruggleton	12.5 × 4m	–	c.1185
Sycharth	12? × 6m*	–	c.1390
Hen Domen (bldg LII)	9 × 3.5m	–	c.1200
Hen Domen (bldg XLVIII)	8 × 5m	–	c.1150
Penmaen	5 × 3.6m	–	12th cent.

(* = hall only partially excavated)

The best preserved section of the drystone foundation was 0.46m wide and 0.15m high, and it was set in a foundation trench 0.76m wide. A series of horizontal timbers or sillbeams would have run along the top of this walling, and small pieces of burnt oak were discovered on the footings. Little of the internal features could be deciphered, but large amounts of scattered charred oak and daub were an indication of the destruction of the building. It is quite feasible that the appearance of Glyndŵr's hall would have been similar to the timber-framed buildings that are still characteristic of the Welsh Marches today, with the panels formed by the vertical and horizontal timbers filled with wattle-and-daub (Smith, P. 1988).

The position of the original hall of Bolingbroke Castle is not known. It may have been on the site of the late medieval hall excavated in 1973 (Drewett 1976; Drewett and Freke 1974). However, a well in a corner adjacent to the later building may have been an earlier feature, associated with a service range. Such a range would have been further away from the thirteenth-century hall, suggesting that the hall lay elsewhere, not beneath the late medieval example. The interior of the castle was levelled-up either in the late fourteenth century or in the early years of the following century, and the new hall built (figure 5.8). The thirteenth-century hall itself probably occupied the southern rectangular area (12.5 × 8.1m), the suggestion being that an upper chamber such as a solar lay over the other end. The insubstantial stone foundations of the building seem to indicate that the hall was timber-framed, but the fragmentary remains do not help to provide much of a picture of the building. One wall collapsed in 1518–19 and was replaced by one with a brick foundation, and early in the seventeenth century the main body of the hall was demolished, leaving the wider section still standing and adapted for other purposes. That the building was roofed with tile was evident from the fragments of tile found during the excavations, but there were no other features to provide a clue as to the form of the roof.

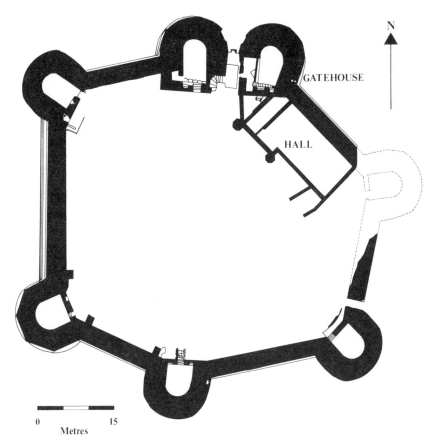

Figure 5.8   Plan of Bolingbroke Castle (after Drewett 1976)

Little can be said about the flooring of the halls discussed above, but some evidence did survive at Bolingbroke. The layers of mortar uncovered at the castle make it unlikely that timber was used, whereas a floor of stone flags or even tiles would have required such a mortar base. It was unfortunate that nothing remained in position after the destruction of the building. The one other remaining feature lay outside the south-west corner of the hall; this was a corridor which may have provided a link with the kitchens. It was not thought to be the original entrance.

Masonry halls

In contrast to the owners of castles with timber halls, the lords of the castles in this section were in most cases of a higher social rank. They were, therefore, either in a better position to build in stone from the beginning, or, like the Baliols at Barnard and the Warennes at Sandal, were able to convert earth-and-timber castles into major stone strongholds. However, two halls discussed in this section would have been noticeably inferior in quality when compared with, for example, the timber hall of Goltho 3; namely those at Llantrithyd and Penmaen. Not all stone halls were grand buildings; nor does a masonry hall automatically imply a larger structure than most timber examples, as a comparison between Tables 1 and 2 will show. The aisled hall of Goltho 3 compares very favourably in size with the stone hall built at Portchester later in the twelfth century, and which was left largely unaltered until the end of the fourteenth century.

Table 2. Masonry halls: a comparison of dimensions (some are approximate)

Site	Length × width	Number of aisles	Date
Degannwy	30 × 7.5m	–	1240s
Skenfrith	25.6 × 6.75m	–	early 13th cent.
Conisbrough	22 × 9m	?1	early 13th cent.
Launceston great hall	22 × 7m	–	mid 13th cent.
Corfe	21.95 × 5.18m	–	c.1080
Dover	21 × 9m	–	1239–40
Sandal	20.5 × 10.5m	–	mid 13th cent.
Dryslwyn	20.4 × 7.4m	–	c.1240
Aberystwyth	20 × 8	–	late 13th cent.
Portchester	19.8 × 7m	–	late 12th cent.
Threave	18.4 × 8.8m	–	c.1390
Huttons Ambo	18.3 × 7.6m	–	?late 12th cent.
Launceston admin. hall	18.3 × 5.5m	–	mid 13th cent.
Hadleigh 2	17 × 9m	–	c.1250
Stamford 3	15 × 12.6m	1	13th cent.
Barnard 3	14.8 × 11.7m	?	14th cent.
Llantrithyd	14.2 × 8.2m	2	early 12th cent.
Barnard 2	13.4 × 8.95m	–	13th cent.
Penmaen	12.5 × 5m	–	?early 13th cent.
Sulgrave	12.19 × 5.49m	–	c.1080
Stamford 1	12 × 11m	2	mid 12th cent.
Hadleigh 3	11.4 × 6.6m	–	c.1300
Deddington 2	10.5 × 5m	–	mid 12th cent.
Rumney	10 × 6.5m	–	late 13th cent.
Smailholm	10 × 6m	–	late 15th cent.
Deddington 1	10 × 3.75m	–	c.1100

The eleventh-century hall at Corfe Castle, Dorset, which dates to about 1080, is in complete contrast to the Goltho and other buildings discussed above, for at Corfe we have a royal castle begun by William I. The defences of his castle are represented by the curtain wall which surrounds what became the inner bailey, but on the western edge of the hill, outside the defences, there are the remains of a stone hall. The existence of this hall, which may be on the site of a pre-Conquest building, has long been known, for its southern wall is still upstanding. Its most notable feature is the high quality of its herringbone masonry. Excavations have revealed the extent of the hall, *c.* 21.95 × 5.18m, with a service room, possibly the kitchen, at the west end. The hall itself may have been at first floor level, but there is not enough evidence surviving to confirm this hypothesis. The reason why the Conqueror's hall at Corfe stood in the position it did, outside the main masonry defences, is not clear; no doubt this area of the hill was enclosed by a timber palisade, later replaced by the stone curtain of the west bailey built in 1202–4 (RCHM 1960).

When the Saxon manor at Sulgrave was replaced by a Norman castle ringwork soon after the Conquest the original wooden hall was taken down. It was replaced by one of masonry whose internal measurements were 12.19 × 5.49m, the walls being about 1m thick. The Norman hall at Sulgrave was, therefore, about the same size as its contemporary at Goltho, its small size being dictated by the fact that the ringwork defences at Sulgrave also enclosed a small area. The heightening of the defences shortly afterwards brought the edge of the rampart up against the hall, and the resulting pressure of the earth bank on the building led to its partial collapse. In spite of this, part of it was retained for some unknown use before the ringwork was abandoned at some time in the twelfth century. Unlike the halls at Goltho, there was no evidence for a hearth at Sulgrave, allowing for the possibility of the hall-chamber itself being at first floor level (Davison 1977: 112–13).

The ringwork at Llantrithyd, Glamorgan, is probably associated with the Norman settlement in south Wales in the early twelfth century. Building 3 (figure 5.9) was an aisled hall (14.2 × 8.2m) with rounded corners, possibly with a porch (Charlton *et al.* 1977: 18–20). It is debatable whether the hall really ranks as a masonry building, as its drystone walls were low. The reconstruction in the report simply shows the sides as having been less than a metre high, with the roof sloping down on to the upper course. In other words, there was no vertical timber-framing between the dwarf walls and the roof, unlike the halls at Sycharth and Bolingbroke. Such an arrangement would have left very little extra space in the aisles because of the angle of the roof, so that Llantrithyd cannot be considered to be in the same league as the hall of Goltho 3. Some specialists may not even consider it to be a true aisled building, although it does appear in Sandall's gazetteer (1986: 34). Its nearest comparison is the house on the motte at Lismahon, Co. Down, built about 1200 (Waterman 1959: 151, figure 56), and there are also similarities between Llantrithyd and the early thirteenth-century hall at Penmaen discussed below. An approximate date for the Llanthrithyd hall is given by a hoard of silver coins which had been deposited in the building in the 1120s.

At Deddington, Oxfordshire, a small L-shaped block was built close to the motte about the year 1100. This has been interpreted as a hall, with the main chamber 10 × 3.75m, the smallest of the halls reviewed in this section. At the end of the west wing there was a garderobe. Soon after the construction of the hall the area of the bailey closest to the motte was embanked to form a small inner bailey, and a few years later the area was enclosed by a curtain wall (figure 3.1, III and IV, p.59). Later in the century a range of buildings was built

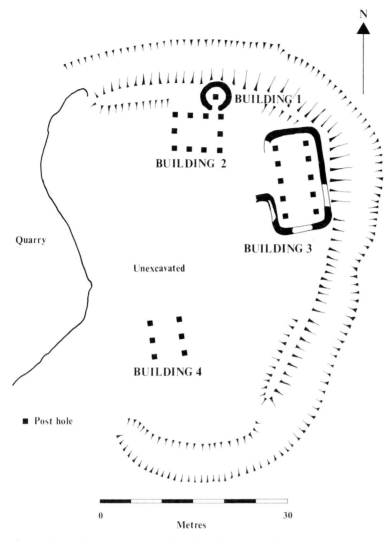

Figure 5.9 Llantrithyd castle-ringwork (after Charlton *et al.* 1977)

on the south side of the inner bailey (figure 3.1, V, p.59), including a new first floor hall (10.5 × 5m) which partially overlay its predecessor. Although the excavations only revealed the undercroft of this building, the hall had walls of mortared rubble *c.* 1.2m thick, reinforced with ashlar quoins. The refortification of Deddington in stone may have been the work of William de Chesney, one of King Stephen's loyal supporters in the civil war, who died some time in the 1170s. Whereas the stone curtain might date from the time of the civil unrest, the rebuilding of the domestic ranges is best assigned to the peace that followed at the end of Stephen's reign (Ivens 1984; Jope and Threlfall 1946–7).

Excavations undertaken at Stamford Castle, Lincolnshire, showed how the aisled hall, a fragment of which still stands, had developed from the middle of the twelfth century through to the fourteenth century (figure 5.10) (Mahany 1977; 1978). The original building was almost square (12 × 11m), and the foundations of the four stone columns or piers survived to a considerable depth. The plan (figure 5.10, II) shows just how much of the hall was taken up by the piers which provided a continuous aisle about the room. Whether these strong supports were required because of a point of weakness near the south wall, such as an old ditch, is not known, but the piers are regarded as supports for the roof of an aisled hall, not a vaulted undercroft for a first floor hall. As we shall see in more detail in the next chapter, the fine solar added to the west side of the hall later in the twelfth century was at ground level, the implication being that the hall must have been on the same level.

When the solar was added two extra piers were built in the hall, seemingly to buttress the north columns, but the first major alteration took place *c.* 1200 when the north and south walls of the hall were rebuilt inside the line of the original walling, thus narrowing the building slightly (figure 5.10, IV). In spite of this, the repositioning of the piers did provide greater space in the centre of the room. It remained as an aisled hall with a hearth centrally placed at the west end, although the solar in this phase was enlarged by the addition of an upper chamber. That the new hall was still not regarded as spacious enough is shown by the further improvements undertaken in the thirteenth century (figure 5.10, V). It was extended eastwards so that the interior of this, the third hall, measured 15 × 12.6m, and one aisle was removed. The east wall consisted of an arcade which may have led to a screens passage, and part of the arcade still stands. The only later alteration was the addition of a porch to the north-east side of the building (figure 5.10, VI).

The developments at Stamford, like those at Goltho, are a good example of the continuous sequence of improvements and patching that is a feature of many castles throughout the middle ages. Such alterations and additions are particularly obvious at Portchester where the palace range built by Richard II at the end of the fourteenth century dominates the inner bailey. Richard's new works did much to remove the evidence of earlier periods, but in the mid to late twelfth century, after the construction of the inner bailey curtain and the keep, various domestic buildings were added against the keep and curtain, including a hall (19.8 × 7m) on the south side. A fragment of an ornamental arcade or line of windows still survives. This survival is our only clue to the fact that the hall was a building of some quality, as was its successor. The hall may originally have been slightly shorter, by about 5m, because at the west end there was a door connecting the hall with the domestic range on the west side. It is likely, therefore, that the approach to this door from the hall would have been divided from the latter by a screen. There was also a twelfth-century first floor hall on the north side of the bailey, subsequently altered in the fourteenth century (Cunliffe 1985: 16–18, 37–8, 47).

There often are, however, reasons behind improvements at some sites other than a desire to modernize what the previous generation had built. This was the story at Hadleigh Castle. Here a new hall had to be built *c.* 1300 because its predecessor of around 1250 had either collapsed already or was in danger of doing so because of ground movement. Hadleigh at this time was in the hands of the king, but new works were kept to a minimum, apart from the hall, and largely consisted of routine maintenance and repair. Edward I rarely visited it,

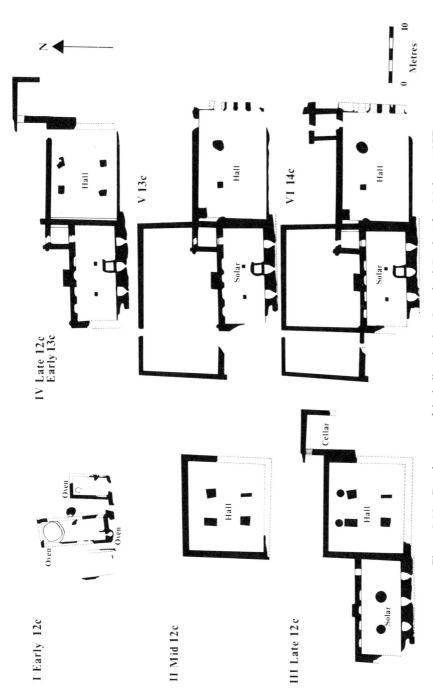

Figure 5.10 Development of the hall and solar, Stamford Castle (after Mahany 1977)

and it was not until the later fourteenth century that the defences and domestic accommodation were transformed by Edward III (Colvin 1963: 659–66). The mid thirteenth-century hall may have been built on the site of another earlier one, hence it appears as Hadleigh 2 in Table 2. Its position was close to the west curtain but independent of it. Although its remains were very fragmentary, it must have been a rectangular building 17 × 9m, with a series of external buttresses along its east wall; the destruction of the footings of the west wall meant that there was no evidence to show whether this side was also buttressed. The only internal features that survived were a line of eight pads for vertical timbers running down the centre of the hall and, on the inside of the east wall, buttresses which were added later to correspond with those on the outside. The purpose of both these features, the mortar pads and internal buttresses, must have been to prevent the collapse referred to above, but they were to no avail. The decision was taken to demolish the hall and build anew; the new hall (11.4 × 6.6m) lasted for about two centuries before it was systematically demolished. The west side of the new hall was built on the remains of the east wall of its predecessor, and whereas the walls of the old building were anything from four to seven metres high, those of its successor were probably much lower, judging by the foundations. The porch of the main entrance lay on the north-west, divided from the hall proper by a wooden screen, and adjoining the hall on the south was a first floor solar, a feature which it shared with the mid thirteenth-century building (Drewett 1975: 102–7).

Although both halls at Hadleigh have been systematically demolished, we have some idea of their appearance and plan. Both were roofed with tiles, and the internal walls were plastered and painted. The windows of the earlier building were glazed, the glass having red-painted decoration, including a floral design, but unfortunately the glass of the later period was preserved in an exceedingly poor condition.

It was mentioned above that when the mid thirteenth-century hall at Hadleigh had to be reinforced to prevent its imminent collapse, a series of vertical posts running up the middle of the building was added. A similar feature, dating to the late twelfth or early thirteenth century, was excavated at the fortified manor at Huttons Ambo, Yorkshire (Thompson 1957: 72–4, 89–91). But this hall, which was about 18.3 × 7.6m, was unusual in that its vertical timbers were part of the original design, a surprisingly primitive one for the period when compared to other contemporary buildings where the central area was generally kept free of obstacles. The line of posts meant that the hearth had to lie on the western side of the hall, rather than in the middle of the room.

The one certain domestic building associated with the second phase of Castle Tower, Penmaen, was a drystone-walled hall with curved ends, measuring internally 12.5 × 5m (Alcock 1966: 192–5). The walls as excavated stood only about 0.35m high, and were probably well under 1m originally. It was, therefore, similar in design to a hall in another Glamorgan ringwork mentioned above, Llantrithyd, although the latter had aisleposts. In the discussion on the stone gatetower at Penmaen (p.62) the problem was posed as to whether the Normans would have built a structure with unmortared walls. The Penmaen hall belongs to the same phase as the stone entrance tower, and it may be that the castle was in the hands of the Welsh at this time, the early thirteenth century. There is also firm evidence for the use of drystone walls at other native Welsh sites (Avent 1983: 7), although the examples cited are in north Wales where stone is abundant. An argument against the theory that the second phase at Penmaen (buildings with drystone walls) could be Welsh is that the Llantrithyd hall is Norman.

In the absence of aisle posts in the Penmaen hall, the whole weight of the roof must have been carried by the walls. There was no evidence for any central supports, but they could have rested on the stony floor, leaving no trace. The absence of evidence for the roofing material could be an indication that it was thatched, unless other material such as shingles had been totally removed for reuse elsewhere. As the hall was sited on sloping ground, part of the interior was levelled-up with stones and clay. The one other feature uncovered was the site of the doorway in the north wall; two postholes marked the site of the frame. Everything about the structure gives the impression of crudity and discomfort.

The construction of the keep and curtain wall at Conisbrough is assigned to Hamelin de Plantagenet, fifth Warenne Earl of Surrey, in the late twelfth century. However, the Norman internal buildings are regarded as the work of the Earl William, Hamelin's son and successor (1202–40), particularly as none of the domestic ranges is bonded into the curtain (Johnson 1984: 5-6, 18). Work began in 1967 on the bailey buildings prior to their display, and an early result was the identification of a single-aisled hall, a building against the northern section of the curtain wall (Thompson 1968). The hall was originally 22 × 9m, but in the early fourteenth century a wall was built to cut off the western end, creating an extra room with a new fireplace. Evidence was uncovered to show that an aisle ran along the southern side of the hall, supported on octagonal pier bases and creating a four-bay structure. The exact form of the roof is not known, one problem being that the west end of the hall in the thirteenth century was the curving corner of the bailey wall and, therefore, somewhat awkward to roof. The building contained a large central hearth, although its position against one of the piers is unusual, especially as the two features are regarded as contemporary. It is possible that this incongruity represents a change in plan when construction had already begun, an aisle being added to provide greater width than might otherwise have been possible. When the hall was shortened a mural fireplace replaced the hearth, its slightly raised position in the wall suggesting that the floor may have been heightened at the same time.

As the private lodgings of Conisbrough were situated against the western curtain wall, south of the hall, the dais would have been placed at the west end. A staircase would have linked the hall to the west range, whilst access to the pantry and kitchen was through a door at the east end, divided from the hall by a screens passage.

Another early hall is a feature of Skenfrith, one of the three castles of Gwent which were built in the twelfth century to control one of the routes between England and Wales, the other two being White Castle and Grosmont. The three came into the hands of Hubert de Burgh in 1201, but he lost them in 1205, whilst a prisoner in France. Hubert did not regain his properties in Gwent until December 1218, so most of the masonry at Skenfrith is likely to date to 1219 and later. The western range formed the main domestic accommodation at Skenfrith, with a long narrow hall (25.6 × 6.75m) to the north of a private room or solar, both at ground-floor level, although set lower than part of the courtyard when the latter was raised (see figure 6.3, p.134) (Craster 1967). The castle, however, is on a wet site, with a river flowing a little distance away from the eastern curtain, and flooding seems to have been a problem, certainly in the thirteenth century, when the level of the interior of the west range had to be raised. A cross-wall was inserted dividing the hall into two, the northern half being filled with gravel, the southern being left as a cellar below the new hall which was constructed above the original building.

The excavation of the first Skenfrith hall revealed several well-preserved features. The quality of the masonry of the doorway at the northern end of the hall is an indication that little weathering had occurred before it had been abandoned; this implies that the life of the first hall was short. A small window lighting the hall was uncovered with its iron bars still in position, whilst a finely carved fireplace was found to have been blocked when the ground floor went out of use due to flooding. A series of vertical slots in the eastern wall to hold timber uprights to support the roof were blocked when the new range was built. There was a second doorway at the southern end of the hall, reached by a flight of steps which postdate the original hall. The two doors into the building, coupled with its length, serve as a reminder that hall dimensions, such as those in Table 2, can be slightly misleading. There is no doubt that the northern two-thirds of the west range represents Hubert's hall, but the hall itself would have been a few metres shorter. The main entrance from the courtyard must have been at the southern end, especially as the solar was located beyond the hall at this point with its own connecting entrance. Presumably the door at the northern end was for service although no evidence for the timber screens survived. If there were screen passages at either end of the hall then the room would have been about 21m long.

The conversion of the Warenne castle of Sandal to masonry in the thirteenth century entailed the levelling-up of the bailey, a feature found on excavation at Conisbrough, another Yorkshire castle belonging to the family. The stone hall was built immediately to the east of its timber equivalent, and for a short period the latter was retained to house masons and other workmen involved in the construction of the stone castle (Mayes and Butler 1983: 194, 207). A similar feature was discovered during the course of excavations at Portchester (p.164).

As at Conisbrough, the various domestic buildings at Sandal were ranged against the curtain wall, but the hall differed from the example at Conisbrough in that it lay at first floor level, with an undercroft below; this contained the bases of two circular piers, the columns presumably forming the support for a vaulted ceiling. Although much of the eastern (outer) wall has vanished, enough is left elsewhere to indicate a series of windows in the wall fronting the bailey, at both floor levels. At least one of the undercroft windows had slots in its sill for shutters at the inner face (Mayes 1967: 7). The hall was reached by an external staircase running up the side of the building, supported by a column which was octagonal at its base. Another column beside the entrance to the undercroft once carried a projecting gallery or oriel at one end of the hall (Mayes 1967: 8: Mayes and Butler 1983: 55–6). The fragmentary remains of the hall contained virtually no evidence for any later improvements that may have been carried out, although stones from late medieval windows found in the barbican and bailey ditches may relate to a refenestration of the hall.

It has already been mentioned that a castle's hall might have administrative as well as social functions. At Launceston this dual role seems to have been divided between two buildings, both dating to the mid thirteenth century when Richard Earl of Cornwall, younger brother of King Henry III, transformed the castle. The probable administrative hall (*c.* 18.3 × 5.5m) lay just inside the southern entrance to the castle; its proximity to the gate would have afforded it little privacy, and this makes it unlikely to have been the main hall. It was a single-storey building (figure 5.11), its timber-framing consisting of six bays as indicated by the sockets still visible in the walls. The floor was made of clay, and there was a hearth at one end. Before the hall was refurbished in the later

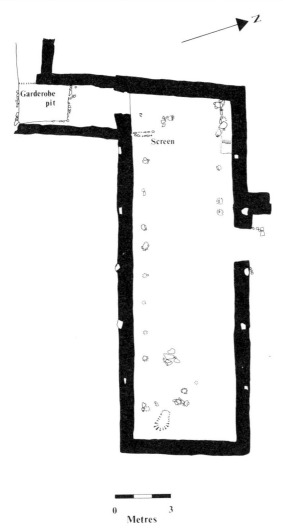

Figure 5.11 The administrative hall, Launceston Castle (after Saunders 1977b)

thirteenth century it underwent a change in function with part of it being used as a workshop, but the walls were then repaired and replastered, the floor renewed, and, judging by the the series of small postholes running parallel with the long sides, seating was provided against the walls. Although one cannot be certain that this building was an adminstrative hall when it was first built, the benching in its final phase is evidence enough for this role in the years immediately before its demolition about the year 1300 (Saunders 1977b: 134–5).

Richard of Cornwall's great hall at Launceston was built over earlier structures some 20m to the north-west of its administrative equivalent, and remained standing until the early seventeenth century. Originally it was a single-storey building, with a hearth at the dais end of the room, and benches, indicated by postholes, against one wall. Later the building's conversion to a first floor hall entailed the removal of the benching and the construction of what can be best described as an internal buttress. This buttress partially overlay the site of the original benching and probably supported a fireplace on the first floor, either in the hall or perhaps in a solar at one end of the block. Confirmation of the archaeological evidence for this alteration in the layout of the hall comes from a survey of the castle undertaken on behalf of Edward the Black Prince in 1337 where 'a certain hall with two cellars' is mentioned (Saunders 1984: 8). It is possible that the great hall acted as the local assize court from this time onwards, as Earl Richard's son, Edmund, transferred the machinery of government of the earldom of Cornwall from Launceston to the palace at Lostwithiel (Pounds 1979; Saunders 1981; 1982: 187).

Apart from the work undertaken at Hadleigh, discussed above, few royal halls have been the subject of excavation, although there has been limited research at two sites where Henry III was responsible for new works: Dover and Degannwy. Part of his hall in the inner bailey at Dover, later known as Arthur's Hall, has been identified by a small-scale excavation which revealed both the hall and a chamber beyond (Cook *et al.* 1969: 57–9, 73–4). The hall at Degannwy, Henry III's new and short-lived castle on the site of a Welsh stronghold (p.54), is the longest building (*c.* 30 × 7.5m) to feature in this chapter. Built on the western of two rocky hillocks which formed the inner bailey or 'donjon', it was so comprehensively damaged in the destruction of Degannwy by Llywelyn ap Gruffudd in 1263 that little can be said of its appearance, but well-dressed stone window embrasures were uncovered through excavation, and it was evident that the interior had been plastered (Alcock 1967: 195).

As there is some doubt as to whether a Norman or a Welshman was responsible for the construction of the stone hall at Penmaen, the hall at the hilltop castle of Dryslwyn is the only certain native Welsh masonry building to be discussed in this chapter. The castle was built in the first half of the thirteenth century, but considerable repair and rebuilding occurred when Dryslwyn was in English hands after 1287. The hall was on the first floor, so it is the walls of the basement rooms that have been excavated (figure 2.10, p. 55). The room was about 7.4m wide and 20.4m long, although the southern side was shorter, with an open courtyard to the south. The most noticeable feature of the basement is a large block of masonry, probably the support for a hearth and then a fireplace with chimney in the hall above. A similar hearth-support was mentioned above (Launceston), and a rectangular pillar may have served the same purpose in the hall of the Norman house at Bletchingley Castle, Surrey (Turner, D.J. 1987: 253–4). The hall block at Dryslwyn was enlarged later in the Welsh period by incorporating the area between the original hall and the curtain wall to the south. By 1338 part of the hall complex was in a state of collapse, the 'King's Hall' being mentioned in accounts which record its total reroofing, and the construction of a new door and window. A feature of the new roof was a series of stone corbels to support the timbering, and examples of these were indeed uncovered in the destruction debris of the hall. Roof slates and fragments of window moulding were also recovered by excavation (Webster 1987). The inner ward at Dryslwyn was a compact arrangement of buildings, the majority of Welsh build, situated on the highest part of the hill overlooking the river Tywi below; the only permanent open area or courtyard lay on the north side of the ward, between the round keep and the hall. Entry to the ward may have been dominated by the circular keep, but it was the hall, which traditionally played an important role in Celtic lordly society, that would have drawn the eye once one had set foot in the courtyard.

A good example of the evolution of a hall occurs at Barnard Castle in Co. Durham. The large single-aisled timber building (the first hall) has been mentioned above. It was succeeded by a stone building measuring 13.4 × 8.95m some time in the thirteenth century. The main surviving feature is the east wall, supported by four buttresses, but little is known of the internal arrangements because of later developments on the site. The entrance from the courtyard may have been up some steps in the south-east corner, somewhat removed from the lord's private doorway into the Great Chamber and keep to the north. The major surviving feature of the hall is the west wall of the building which was constructed in the fourteenth century. Excavation showed that this, the third and final hall, was larger than its predecessor (14.8 × 11.7m); its width suggests that it may have been an aisled building, but as with hall 2 very little evidence of its internal arrangements have been uncovered (Austin 1980: 79–82).

The ringwork at Rumney remained an earth-and-timber castle for much of its existence, from the early twelfth to the middle of the thirteenth century (Lightfoot 1983). It had a small stone keep in the twelfth century, with a new gatehouse of stone being added in the thirteenth century, although its domestic buildings remained built of wood. In the later thirteenth century the defences of the castle were levelled, with the spoil thrown into the interior. Thereafter Rumney became a shadow of its former self, as far as its defences were concerned. A new hall was built (10 × 6.5m) adjacent to the keep, and this time stone was used. It was roofed with sandstone slabs, with glazed earthenware ridge-tiles, and about half of its interior was raised to form a dais; there were also benches at one end. It was in the burnt-out remains of this hall that the hoard of late thirteenth-century silver pennies was found (p.105); when the hoard was concealed the building seems to have been transformed into a stable or barn, for horseshoe nails and grain were found amongst the charred remains.

At Threave, Kirkcudbright, a masonry hall was built in the late fourteenth century, presumably to augment the accommodation in the five-storey tower-house, and at the same time two rectangular buildings were constructed in the outer enclosure immediately to the east of the tower, one of which may have been a chapel. The other building has been interpreted as a first floor hall above an undercroft which was partitioned off into stalls. The excavators suggested that the stalls were either for storage or stabling, but the latter interpretation would surely be unlikely if there was a hall above. The hall floor was probably supported by timber joists set in sockets in the walls, but the interpretation of the building as a hall rests on a feature at the east end of the undercroft. This was the remains of a massive column which could only have been designed to support something on the first floor. However, as there was not a similar feature at the west end it seems very unlikely that the column was designed just to take the weight of the hall floor. The excavators considered that it must have been built to take the weight of a cross-wall forming a screens passage which divided the hall itself from the entrance (Good and Tabraham 1981: 99–101, 136–7). The life of both buildings was short as they were deliberately demolished in the middle of the fifteenth century when the defences of the castle were radically improved by the addition of the artillery wall around the tower-house (p.75).

One of the notable tower-houses of the Scottish border is Smailholm, Roxburghshire, built by the Pringles, a local family of modest means, probably in the second half of the fifteenth century. The tower was intended to be defensible, but only against small raids, and although it had five floors, the small rooms must have meant a generally cramped living style. Many tower-houses have been seen as providing the only accommodation available, a point that Tabraham has stressed (1987: 227), although some, such as Smailholm, lack a kitchen. It was not totally surprising, therefore, that excavations on the west side of the tower uncovered an enclosed yard containing a kitchen block to the south, and to the north, a small hall (10 × 6m) with a solar or private chamber at its east end. The hall had a central hearth, implying that it was a single-storeyed building, with smoke escaping through the roof. The function of the courtyard hall is uncertain; it may have been designed to be the main room for social entertainment when the Pringles had guests, with the rooms in the tower-house retained solely for family use. It has been suggested that whereas the preparation of food for the courtyard hall was undertaken in the kitchen opposite, that for the family, who ate in the hall in the tower, would have been carried out at a fireplace, possibly the one in the hall (Tabraham 1987).

The discovery of additional domestic buildings to overcome the accommodation problem in the smaller examples of late medieval Scottish tower-houses is one of the more interesting results from excavations. At Cramalt in Selkirkshire, however, there was a different story. The remains of the surviving tower-house, now under a reservoir, was found to have supplemented another, and hitherto unknown, tower (the South Tower) which stood some 25m to the south. It is not known what outbuildings there were at Cramalt, but a few years after the South Tower was built *c.* 1470, it was considered desirable to add a slightly larger tower to supplement, not replace, the original accommodation (Maxwell-Irving 1981).

The buildings discussed above are on the whole recognizable as halls, whether they were on the grand scale, as at Hadleigh and Barnard, or on a more primitive level, Penmaen for example. It is not always possible in an excavation to be certain about the function of every domestic building that is uncovered, and so at some sites identification has been tentative. This is the case at the castles of Bedford and Aberystwyth. Bedford Castle was destroyed after the well-documented siege in 1224 (Brown 1976: 191–4), but excavations in the early 1970s uncovered the remains of its defences as well as its domestic buildings. It was suggested in the report that one range may have been a first floor hall. A curved projection at its north-east corner could have been the foundation for a newel staircase, although there is the slim possibility that the remains represent a small mural tower. Another theory is that the domestic building was not so grand as a hall but simply a chamber. The problems of this particular site are well outlined in the excavation report (Baker and Baker 1979: 17–29).

Until the final report is published on the recent excavations at Edward I's castle at Aberystwyth we cannot be certain about the history of a rectangular building located to the south of the main gatehouse (figure 3.8, p.75). The approximate dimensions (20 × 8m) suggest that the room was indeed a hall, but which one is unknown, as there seem to have been at least three. Features of the room include a large mural fireplace, two loops or windows blocked in the seventeenth century, and in the south-west corner there are the fine remains of a moulded jamb of a door which led from a curious mural passage. It is possible that the hall was an afterthought, and not associated with the castle as begun in 1277 but rather with the work undertaken after 1282 following the destruction of the castle by the Welsh in March of that year (Thorburn 1983). The final report on this 'hall' and other areas of the castle which have been excavated is awaited with interest as the work has clearly emphasized that we should not take the Edwardian castles as necessarily the product of one master plan. Certainly at Aberystwyth the original plan underwent considerable alteration by the king's architects, possibly as a result of its capture by the Welsh in 1282 (see also p.74).

The arrangement and distribution of all the domestic buildings within the medieval castle, including the hall, is a subject that requires more detailed examination. The defences of a castle would often dictate the internal planning, but we have seen from the above that the halls could vary in their position. The majority of the timber buildings, particularly those in the earlier medieval period, were free-standing halls, although both at Rumney and Barnard they were close to the line of the ringwork defences. The situation differs with the masonry halls. In several of the major castles the builders made use of the masonry curtains to form one side of a hall, as at Conisbrough and Skenfrith. This was a sensible arrangement as it cut building costs and provided a wall of extra thickness which would have helped in the support of the hall roof. However, one particular disadvantage of employing this method is that light could only be admitted through windows on the bailey side; large windows in the curtain wall would have seriously weakened the defences. Some of the smaller masonry halls, including the unimpressive buildings at Penmaen and Llantrithyd, were independent of the defences, particularly where these defences were of earth and timber. This is also the case at castles such as Launceston where masonry defences ran along an earthen rampart. Nevertheless, even where the bailey was at the same level as the lowest courses of the curtain wall a hall might be built adjacent but separate from it, as at Hadleigh.

It is unfortunate that there are few really well-preserved castle halls surviving, although we are particularly fortunate to have buildings such as Oakham and Winchester. However, we do know from documentary evidence, particularly with regard to royal sites, that many of these medieval halls were elaborate in their carvings, furnishings and decoration (Brown 1976: 205–9). The archaeological record of some of the lesser castles has not provided us with an abundance of evidence to support the documents, due to the decay and destruction of the castles concerned. However, there is the decorated window glass from Hadleigh, already mentioned, and ornate glass was also recovered from Sandal. Unfortunately, it was not possible at Sandal to be certain where the glass was originally set; some of the fragments clearly relate to a chapel, whilst the secular glass may have come from the apartments rather than the hall. The walls of many halls were plastered and decorated, a common design being a series of vertical and horizontal red lines to give the effect of blocks of ashlar masonry. This pattern can still be seen in Marten's Tower, Chepstow, and was found on fragments of plaster from the hall at Okehampton (Higham *et al.* 1982: 109–10). The walls of one of the halls at Hadleigh had red geometric designs painted on the plaster. The finds from Sandal were particularly rich in architectural fragments, but, as with the glass, their exact position within the castle is not known with any great certainty, although some of the gargoyles may have come from the hall.

On a final note, the reader who is familiar with the archaeology of Southampton Castle may be surprised to find that there has been no mention of the recently excavated Castle Hall. The reason for this will be found on page 130.

6 Lodgings

The purpose of this chapter is to examine other residential buildings within various castles. In many cases the only evidence we have for such houses and chambers are the halls themselves which have solars or withdrawing rooms forming part of the hall unit. However, the main problem, particularly in regard to timber castles, is that it is exceedingly difficult to state with certainty to what use a certain building was put when it is only represented in excavations by a series of postholes or sillbeam trenches. An oven may well have formed part of a kitchen, but does a hearth in the centre of a house necessarily mean that it was a lodging for a family or retainers? It may, for instance, have been some form of workshop with all traces of its industrial use removed, however unlikely that may seem to an archaeologist, who might demand evidence in the form of metal fragments or the remains of furnaces for smelting. Nevertheless, for the purpose of this chapter the survival of a hearth as the only feature within a building has been taken as an indication that it was some form of lodging.

The study of the accommodation and social organization within a castle is not one that can be based solely on excavation, any more than can other aspects of military architecture. A particular drawback with the archaeology of halls and lodgings is that many were built on the first floor of a range, with the ground floor or basement area used for storage or less important accommodation. Excavations tend to reveal only the lower courses of the ground floor, and although some idea of a first floor chamber may be gained from these discoveries, as seen at Hadleigh and Sandal in particular, we can never hope to form a complete picture of such buildings.

In the previous chapter halls generally fitted neatly into two main types based on their building materials. This is not the case with lodgings, for there are several examples where a timber building did not consist solely of wooden walls with or without wattle-and-daub infilling. Archaeology has brought to light several examples where the main walls of a building, not necessarily residential, were partly or wholly constructed in other materials such as cob or clay, as in the early hall at Goltho, for example (p.101). A cob wall was made of unbaked clay which had been mixed with chopped straw, sand or gravel, and may well have been a common form of construction in areas where clay was freely available (Brunskill 1987: 50), and houses constructed of this material still stand today, particularly in the west country. Excavations at non-military sites have uncovered examples of houses which were originally built wholly or partly of cob.

The use of clay in castle building is not uncommon, and when available in the environs of a particular castle it was used in its defences. The ringworks at Bishopston, Glamorgan, Prudhoe in Northumberland and Chateau des Marais, Guernsey, all had banks of clay, whilst Mackenzie (1933–4) has published evidence for the use of clay or cob in various castles in Scotland. The problem with identifying buildings with walls totally of cob is that the structures often leave very little evidence behind once they have been abandoned and fallen into ruin. Archaeologists are rarely able to state with certainty whether remains represent all that is left of a complete cob wall or a dwarf wall. The virtually complete survival of the walls of a cob building, thought to be a kitchen, found at Wallingford Castle, Berkshire, is unique (see p.144). What is certain is that these lesser buildings of the medieval period employed a variety of methods of construction involving timber and cob: from walls totally of cob or cob walls reinforced with timber uprights, to timber-framed buildings with panels of wattle-and-daub.

Timber and cob buildings

The problems associated with the identification of the function of timber buildings found by excavation is most apparent at Hen Domen where over fifty different major structures have been uncovered in the northern half of the bailey. The first report (Barker and Higham 1982) does not discuss this matter at length, for the details of the reconstruction of the buildings will appear in a future volume, but some can be fairly certainly identified, and those which did not have a residential function will be discussed in the next two chapters. Most of the other Hen Domen bailey buildings of note appear in this chapter, although the reader should be aware that the term 'lodging' may be a misnomer in the light of future published work by the excavators. The domestic buildings from Hen Domen are examined in some detail below as a result of the amount of evidence that the excavations have produced.

The excavations have stressed just how cramped the bailey of Hen Domen must have been throughout most of its existence, a fact particularly apparent in the mid twelfth century (see frontispiece and figure 5.2, p.100). As Renn has stated 'The way that these structures were packed together has completely altered the traditional picture of a castle bailey as containing two or three widely-spaced buildings. A Norman castle was in its day a frontier town in miniature' (Renn 1988: 67). Apart from the possible hall with its massive timbers, mentioned in the last chapter, the other three main buildings (XXVI, XXVII and LIV) associated with Roger of Montgomery's castle were set close behind the rampart of the bailey (figure 5.1, p.99). It is assumed that houses XXVI and XXVII were built on sillbeams resting on the ground, as no postholes were found. XXVI was indicated by a clay floor, with a hearth against one side of the building; it overlay a wattle fence behind the bailey bank, so was not one of the first structures on the site. Building XXVII was represented by a large, basically rectangular area of charcoal with pits, and may not have been residential (Barker and Higham 1982: 31). The third building (LIV) was set on a clay platform, and the small postholes associated with it may have been for timbers set in clay walls (Barker and Higham 1988: 7).

From the late eleventh century until the middle of the twelfth century the structures in the bailey were post-built. To the east of the tower positioned at the extreme north-west corner of the rampart a series of rooms beneath the timber wall-walk were most probably sheds or storage areas; there is no evidence that such dark corners of the castle were ever used for human accommodation. South of the mural tower, and divided from it by a bakehouse, lay a jumble of postholes designated building XXV; in spite of its hall-like proportions (12 × 5m) the irregularity of the posts led the excavators to describe it as a 'somewhat incoherent building'. In the north-eastern area of the bailey a small building (LIII) stood on the site occupied later by the hall (XLVIII) discussed in the previous chapter (Barker and Higham 1983: 93–4).

Rooms beneath the wall-walk also occurred in the next phase of Hen Domen's history, about 1150, and again the majority of the buildings were post-built (figure 5.2, p.100). On the northern side of the hall (XLVIII) in the eastern half of bailey there were two post-built outbuildings (XLIX and L) partitioned from each other. It is possible that the one nearest the hall (XLIX) might have been directly associated with it as an extra room, although there does not seem to have been a connecting doorway; the other (L) certainly had an external door on the north side. Neither had a hearth.

Building XXII is the one structure where it is possible to be more certain of its function as a residence. The remains of the house revealed two different methods of construction: two walls had the usual arrangement of timbers set into the ground, whilst the east and south walls were of clay laid in a trench, and strengthened at the corners by stakes. The interior had a clay floor, and there was a hearth at one end of the room. It is not known whether the building was constructed in this manner originally, or whether two of the sides represent a rebuilding. The very fragmentary remains of another building (XII) lay close by, and this also had clay walls.

It is this mid twelfth-century phase that fits so aptly Renn's phrase of 'frontier town'. In the northern half of the bailey alone there was a complex of a great variety of buildings, surrounded by a rampart with a palisade and mural towers, with rooms beneath the fighting platform. In the north-western quarter of the bailey stood the large first floor hall with portico, a possible chapel, and an assortment of houses, whilst in the north-eastern area there was another hall with two attached outbuildings, a water cistern (XLIII), a possible granary (XXXVIII), and perhaps a guardroom (XLII) at the entrance to the bailey. An examination of the reconstruction and the plan (see frontispiece and figure 5.2, p.100) emphasizes just how little space there was, apart from an area to the south of the granary. There was no evidence for stables, the one building range that one would expect to find, so presumably these lay in the unexcavated southern half of the bailey, although there could only have been room for a few horses.

The evidence for buildings in the final two periods is more sparse when compared to the previous phase, particularly in the eastern area. However, enough remained to show that the majority of structures were built using sillbeams as opposed to posts set in holes. In the later twelfth and early thirteenth century various non-residential buildings such as the cistern and possibly part of the granary remained in use, and another hall-like building (LII) replaced the previous mess-room (XLVIII) (figure 5.3, p.102). In the area adjacent to the motte ditch the main structure was a possible chapel, but to its north, close to the mural tower at the north-west end of the palisade, was a small house with a porch (VIII), its clay floor surrounded by a series of large stones.

In the final period of occupation, *c.* 1223–1300, Hen Domen may have served as an outpost for the new masonry royal castle of Montgomery, for it was not abandoned when Henry III's new stronghold was begun. The observant visitor to Montgomery Castle soon realizes that it has superb views to the north and east, but that its view west into Wales is obscured by a hill. However, Hen Domen would have been visible just to the north of it, acting as its eyes into Wales. It is likely that Hen Domen was no longer the busy castle it must once have been, and perhaps it simply had a token garrison, only to be finally abandoned after the Edwardian conquest of north Wales. Features of this period include building I which lay near the motte ditch, and which had some form of extra chamber or outbuilding at its south-east corner, the wall being marked by lines of stones and sockets for the original posts. A path on the north side divided this house from a larger structure (II), and it is possible that the two buildings formed one unit, with the path forming a corridor between two rooms. The only other certain building (XXXVI) lay in the eastern sector.

The problem of reconstructing the original appearance of all the buildings at Hen Domen and those elsewhere is not one that can be completely overcome; the evidence is still insufficient. Barker and Higham stress that although the various postholes, sillbeam trenches and clay floors seem to indicate mainly primitive structures throughout the castle's history, the finished products may well have looked pleasing to the eye, with timber-framed houses having their wattle-and-daub panels painted white or some other colour. It is even possible that some of the woodwork may have been carved. One can be certain from the remains that all the Hen Domen buildings apart from the large hall at the foot of the motte were single storey.

The work at Hen Domen has been the subject of some criticism, namely that the research work is slowly resulting in the destruction of an unthreatened site (Olsen 1982). However, we will never come close to understanding how a castle was organized internally without such a meticulous excavation, and as Barker wrote in his reply to Olsen (Barker 1982: 222), the destruction of the archaeological deposits at Hen Domen is something few would grieve over in the light of the knowledge that has been gained. It should also be remembered that the southern half of the bailey has still to be dug.

Goltho is in marked contrast to Hen Domen; no 'frontier town' in the bailey here for there were no major buildings other than the hall, nor was there room for any, although the motte was big enough to support structures in addition to the timber keep. It is likely, therefore, that in castles such as Goltho where the hall forms the main domestic building such structures are best interpreted as hall-houses. In other words, they were lived in, and were not just used for social and administrative purposes. Many of these halls were divided by one or more partitions, some of the smaller rooms no doubt being service areas for the preparation of food, others being solars or withdrawing rooms for the lord and his family, the steward, or constable of the castle. We have seen that the first hall at Goltho, *c.* 1080–1125, had screens at each end partitioning off two small rooms. Neither had a hearth, but as the one at the east end may have had a garderobe, it is possible that this room was a small lodging. In the second phase of the hall, *c.* 1125–50, the hearth in the main area was supplemented by another in an adjoining room, this room possibly being a kitchen as it had a bakehouse next to it (Beresford 1987: 106–10).

Two other castles, both ringworks, have produced evidence for a series of timber buildings. The end of the promontory on which the village of Lydford stands is cut off by the bank of the small late eleventh- to early twelfth-century castle, about 130m south-west of the later stone tower and motte. Excavation there revealed the remains of five buildings (figure 6.1), with internal partitions, and walls of earth or clay between timber facings. They were set directly behind the rampart, against its massive internal revetment, and had been destroyed by fire. Their function is uncertain; one or more may have been granaries, for a vast amount of charred grain was found, but some must have been residences in this little Devon castle (Wilson and Hurst 1966: 196–7). Domesday Book records that forty houses were destroyed in the borough between 1066 and 1087, and it has been suggested that this was the result of the building of a castle here soon after 1066 (Colvin 1963: 733). A coin of Stephen was found in the upper levels of occupation, suggesting that the destruction of the ringwork probably occurred towards the end of the first half of the twelfth century (Wilson and Hurst 1965: 194).

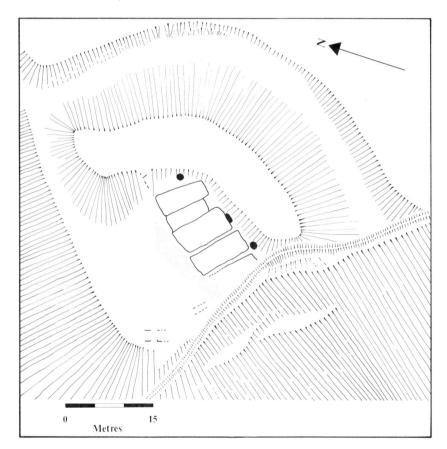

Figure 6.1 Lydford castle ringwork (after Wilson and Hurst 1966)

The other ringwork with remains of timber buildings is Llantrithyd in Glamorgan (figure 5.9, p.113). The first building on the site was a small timber-framed house with six main uprights set in pits. It lay in the southern half of the earthwork, not too distant from the entrance, but it is unlikely that it formed part of the entrance arrangements. It is more likely that it was simply a small dwelling during the initial phase of occupation of the site. The slightly later aisled hall (p.112) was succeeded by a smaller timber house with its main vertical timbers set in pits (Charlton *et al.* 1977: 16–18).

Excavations elsewhere have also uncovered clay or cob buildings, such as the twelfth-century example found at Okehampton Castle beneath one end of the still extant early fourteenth-century hall. Its hearth and finds of pottery and animal bones show that it was a domestic building; its foundations of stones bonded with clay supported the cob walls, of which slight traces remained. It could not be fully excavated, but it was at least 3.5m × 5m internally. The building underwent several rebuildings before it was abandoned or destroyed some time in the early thirteenth century (Higham *et al.* 1982: 36–7, 61–2, figure 14). At Totnes the remains of a cob house with a hearth, contemporary with the Okehampton building, was excavated on the motte (Rigold 1954: 238, 242).

Masonry buildings

One of the more interesting results of the excavations at the castle of Southampton was the discovery of a major rectangular building (18.4 × 6m) in the south-west corner of the bailey. This early twelfth-century structure is referred to as Castle Hall in the recent literature on the castle (Hodgson 1986; Oxley 1986). However, there are various indications that the building may have been purely residential, such as the elaborate garderobe possibly added in the thirteenth century. The south and west sides of Castle Hall were part of the bailey defences of the castle fronting the site of the medieval quay, although possibly with no access to it except through a passage on the north side. The building consisted of a ground floor or undercroft, with a floor above, and as there does not appear to have been an external access to the first floor, entrance must have been gained through the ground floor door in the east wall, and so on to the newel steps in the south-west corner. Originally the ceiling of the ground floor consisted of a series of timber joists set in sockets which ran across the width of the building. There are some traces of the windows of the first floor chamber, and these were the only features to survive from this room. At a later date, possibly in the thirteenth century, a major alteration was made to the building when the timber flooring was removed. It was replaced by a stone barrel vault, of which only a fragment remains, similar to the one that can still be seen in Castle Vault, a substantial rectangular building immediately to the north of Castle Hall. The new vault meant a raising of the level of the first floor, and a new door was inserted into the south wall to allow for this, as well as to provide access to the new garderobe (Oxley 1986: 16–29).

When Castle Hall was first built there was a stone-lined garderobe or latrine 5.6m deep situated against its south-east corner; the south and west walls of the chute were formed by parts of the bailey curtain and the lodging respectively. There is no surviving evidence to indicate how the garderobe was reached from the firstfloor chamber. At the same time as the vault was inserted a new latrine was built, and one on an impressive scale (figure 6.2). This lay on the south side of the building, outside the line of the curtain wall, leading down to the quay. All that remains today is the well-constructed channel, 7.38m in length and 1.16m wide, which slopes from east to west, designed so that the tidal waters of the sea could wash out the effluent. The floor of the channel was paved with limestone slabs, whilst the lower courses of the walls were built of good ashlar; the surviving upper courses of masonry were much rougher. At the west end of the channel an archway opens into an ashlar-built tunnel 2.36m long. This splendid garderobe, one of the finest to be seen in any castle, suggests that the building to which it was attached was one of some importance amongst the king's houses in the castle. Considerable documentation on works undertaken in the castle survives (Colvin 1963: 840–4), and there is mention of the king's cellar for his wines, and a new stone chamber built in 1186–7. It is possible that the second garderobe was associated with the queen's new 'wardrobe' that was ordered to be built in 1252. However, in medieval accounts, particularly those associated with the king's works, a wardrobe was usually a room where valuables and clothes were kept, but it could also be a room to which a 'privy chamber' (garderobe or latrine) was attached (Wood 1965: 377–88). Thus, the 'wardrobe' of 1252 does not necessarily refer to the thirteenth-century latrine.

At Launceston Castle two twelfth-century houses were located, their gables fronting the path which led from the southern gatehouse into the bailey. These were part of an array of buildings squeezed into the bailey, and may have provided lodgings for important guests visiting the castle. The first house was about 12m long and 5.3m wide, and had a central hearth; later, a partition divided the area into a smaller room and a hall. The second building was separated from the first by a lane down which ran a stone-lined drain, and it had a slightly larger hall than its neighbour. Traces of several other buildings belonging to the twelfth century were also found, some of which seem to have been dwellings (Saunders 1977b: 134, 136; 1982: 188). Together, the various houses and ancillary structures such as drains and yards create a pattern of occupation that comes close to the concentration of buildings that were a feature of Hen Domen in the mid twelfth century.

Another Cornish example is the manor of Penhallam, or Berry Court to give it its modern name. Most of the excavated buildings belong to the thirteenth-century manor house, but the site started as a castle ringwork, possibly in the late eleventh century, enclosing an area about 18m in diameter. The thirteenth-century occupation had removed virtually all evidence of the castle's defences and internal buildings, but one stone structure remained, incorporated into the later domestic range. This was a first floor private chamber (*camera*) standing adjacent to the Norman hall of the castle (Beresford 1974: 102–6, figure 27). It was built at the end of the twelfth century, partly cutting into the ringwork bank. An external stair provided access to the chamber itself which must have had a fireplace in one wall. There was a separate door into the undercroft below the chamber, and the excavations revealed that the first floor had been supported by three timber posts mounted on stone blocks.

A building similar in size and date to those at Launceston was a feature of the twelfth-century castle at Banbury; it was destroyed when the castle was drastically remodelled in the thirteenth century. The excavations were unable to reveal the full length of the house, which would have been over 10.7m, but it

Figure 6.2 Garderobe, Southampton Castle

was 4.6m in width, and there was an area of metalling around the outside. It had a central hearth, but apparently no internal subdivisions. It was originally a lodging of one long room with a timber screen shielding the door in the east wall. At some stage a new floor was laid, and a covering of gravel and sand was spread over the original surface. Further modifications were made following a fire inside the building: a new door replaced the first entrance, the house was subdivided by a partition, and the hearth sited against the east wall. The major addition, however, was the construction of a garderobe of drystone walling on the west side of the house, entered from a doorway of dressed stonework inserted in the original wall. In the third phase of the building's history the latrine chamber was abandoned and its door blocked, and at the same time a wall was built across the northern end of the building, thus creating a small sub-chamber. It was after these improvements had been carried out that the new ditch was dug for the castle. This resulted in the removal of the southern end of the building, with the rest of the structure then being buried under a dump of soil which formed the berm between the new outer curtain wall and ditch (Rodwell 1976: 103–9, 118).

The remains of the Norman domestic range on the western side of the inner bailey of Portchester are sparse, with some evidence for a Norman hall above ground level on the south-west side of the bailey. Excavations have produced only the fragmentary remains of lodgings along the west side of the courtyard, south of the keep, including a fireplace. The west range, which was about 15m long and 5m wide, was connected to the hall by a door, and presumably there was also a door leading out into the bailey (Cunliffe 1985: 16–18).

A fine ground floor lodging or solar was associated with the Norman hall uncovered at Stamford (figure 5.10, p.115), being added to the west side of the hall in the late twelfth century. It was a well-appointed building, with three windows in the south wall looking out from the castle, and a further three in the opposite wall overlooking the courtyard. The fireplace lay in the north, between two of the windows. The roof of the building was supported by two piers in the middle of the room, an unusual and inconvenient arrangement. The lodging underwent one major alteration in its history, and this took place soon after it was constructed, probably in the late twelfth or early thirteenth century. An upper storey was added, which must also have been a lodging, for the original chimney-breast was altered to take the flue from the first floor fireplace. The original chamber may then have gone out of use, for a garderobe was added against one of the windows in the south wall. The other addition to the solar at this time was a porch built in the northern corner where the solar met the hall (Mahany 1978: 25–6). The reason that lay behind the conversion of the ground floor solar to one at first floor level may have been that the two central piers were found to be an inconvenience; the desire for greater privacy may also have played a part. It is unfortunate that more of the internal features of the solar did not survive, for, judging by the carved corbel which came from it, the building was decorated with some handsome examples of medieval stonework.

The footings of a range of domestic buildings at Conisbrough, built against the west curtain wall, and lying between the hall and the gatehouse, have survived, together with other features, such as the first floor fireplace of the solar or great chamber at the north end of the range. The present fireplace was inserted in the fourteenth century, replacing the original one which dated to the period when the range was first built in the early thirteenth century. The 1300s saw several improvements to the domestic buildings of the castle, including a new staircase to the first floor at the southern end of the range. Whereas the first floor chambers south of the solar would have provided accommodation, there is no evidence for the function of the ground floor rooms which may have been storerooms, as at Sandal, another Yorkshire castle of the Warennes. The centre of the range was occupied by a garderobe. In the fourteenth century this was partly blocked by a substantial wall, and a bracing arch was added between the new masonry and one of the original walls of the latrine, presumably to prevent the collapse of the latrine down the shaft. The garderobe served the first floor lodgings, although there may also have been access from the ground floor. Garderobe pits required regular cleaning out, a job which commanded a high wage in the middle ages (Wood 1965: 385–6), and this particular latrine shaft was emptied freqently. Nevertheless, the lowest levels of this pit were never disturbed through cleaning, and excavation uncovered objects such as a chess piece, pins, ring and fragments of a glass urinal.

The domestic range of chamber and hall at Skenfrith was built against virtually the whole length of the western curtain wall, with the main lodging of the castle to the south (figure 6.3). The chamber also had a more private entrance situated at the extreme end of the range. Originally this lodging consisted of two rooms, the floor of one set lower than the other. Alterations were carried out in the late thirteenth century, creating a single room, and at about that time a fireplace with a stone kerb was inserted into the east wall of the chamber. It is not clear whether this fireplace replaced another in the same position, or a hearth in the centre of the room. The new work may have taken place when the castle was passed from Henry III to his second son, Edmund, in 1267 (Craster 1967).

Figure 6.3   Hall (foreground) and lodgings, Skenfrith Castle

The excavations of Sandal Castle have provided a detailed picture of the conversion of what had been a motte-and-bailey of earth and timber to a castle with masonry defences. This conversion by the Warenne earls of Surrey dates to the mid to late thirteenth century, and while the keep, barbican and curtain were under construction, work was also under way on the domestic buildings. On either side of the first floor hall various chambers were set above undercrofts, and the Tudor survey of 1564 provides an idea of the function of these rooms (Mayes and Butler 1983: 20). Adjoining the hall on its western side was a lodging chamber. This room was supported by a vault which sprung from a central circular column in the undercroft; the base of the column was revealed during the excavation. The main upstanding feature of the first floor lodging is a window in its west wall, overlooking the kitchen range, although at a later, but unknown, date this window was rebuilt as a door connecting the upper floor of the larder with the hall via the lodging. In one corner of the chamber a stair turret led up to the battlements, the turret being surmounted in the fifteenth century by a handsome carved stone finial. The stair was not accessible at ground level, so the lodging could only have been reached from the hall, presumably ensuring greater privacy. Such a stair, solid up to first floor level, is also a feature of the round keep at Skenfrith.

On the other side of the hall lay the great chamber. The square foundation of the central column which supported the springing of the vault was located in the centre of the basement chamber; the room also had a fireplace tucked into one corner, and garderobes in two other corners perhaps to serve both the undercroft and the great chamber. One of them was situated in the wall that divided the great chamber from the privy chamber to the north, and the excavations also revealed a further latrine in the privy chamber. It is distinctly possible that the privy chamber was literally that, a room containing the privies, as opposed to a private lodging. Privy chamber is a term used in medieval and later accounts to describe a room with garderobes. The position of the privy between the main domestic accommodation for guests (hall and great chamber) and the series of rooms to the north, nearer the gatehouse, known as the constable's lodgings, is entirely logical. It is a good example of the care and attention that went into the detailed planning of the domestic requirements of a medieval building (Mayes and Butler 1983: 54–7).

The series of small rooms referred to as the constable's lodgings in the 1564 survey represent the next tier down in the social organization of Sandal. The most important accommodation would be reserved for the Warenne earls in the keep, and then would come the lodgings for important guests, against the curtain wall of the bailey. In the absence of the lord, the control of a castle was invested in the constable, and there is evidence that in many cases the constable resided in the main gatehouse, or in a chamber close to the gate. The outer gate at Dover is known as the Constable's Gate, for example, and is still occupied by the castle's governor. A constable would, therefore, be in a position to control admissions to the castle. The remains of the constable's lodgings at Sandal, which include the porter's lodge, are fragmentary, and were much altered in the middle ages, but in the late fifteenth century the frontage overlooking the bailey was certainly timber-framed. When the survey was made in 1564 the constable of the castle, Sir John Tempest, still resided in these chambers near the gate.

It will be recalled that the mid thirteenth-century hall at Hadleigh had to be demolished and rebuilt on an adjacent plot by the end of that century. Both halls had a solar. The earlier chamber was L-shaped, with a door in the centre of its south wall leading out to a small courtyard which may have been for the private use of the residents of this range of buildings. It is uncertain whether the private chamber lay on the ground floor or at an upper level, but as the ground floor was at a lower level than the hall a first floor chamber would be the most likely. Another factor in favour of a first floor chamber is that the garderobe tower on the line of the curtain wall could only have been approached from an upper floor. Other excavated evidence showed that the walls of the solar were plastered, and that its glazed windows included red decorated glass (Drewett 1975: 102–3).

The new solar of *c.* 1300 at Hadleigh also lay on the south side of the hall to which it was attached. It was rectangular in plan, and its size (*c.* 11.5 × 5.5m) meant that the solar was only fractionally smaller than the hall itself. The discovery of the bases of two columns in the middle of the floor of the new building indicated that this later solar was certainly on the first floor. The columns would have supported either a vaulted ceiling or the timber joists of the floor. Further evidence for the position of the solar room itself came from the excavation of a rectangular foundation against the south wall. These footings were part of the support for a first floor fireplace, such as that in the *camera* at Penhallam. Immediately to the west, at the south-west corner of the chamber, there was a garderobe tower serving the solar. The excavated remains of this range did not show whether the solar could be reached from the hall through the undercroft or basement; certainly there was no evidence for a staircase. However, the angle formed by the meeting of the west wall of the hall with the north wall of the solar rectangular foundation may have supported an external timber staircase up to the chamber. Leading off from the south-east side of the solar were a series of rooms which may have been bedrooms and a chapel. One major difference between the hall and the solar is that whereas the hall was roofed with tiles, numerous examples of which were recovered from the demolition debris, the solar roof may have been covered with lead or shingles. The hall range lasted until the middle of the sixteenth century, for in 1552 the castle was sold by King Edward VI for £700, and demolition seems to have begun at that time. A series of hearths and pits was found in the floor of the hall in which the lead from the windows was melted down for reuse elsewhere (Drewett 1975: 104–6). Mid Tudor hearths were found in the hall at Okehampton, and probably served the same purpose (Higham *et al.* 1982: 54–6).

Examples of a different type of lodging, namely a dungeon or prison, have been uncovered at some castles, although it is not always possible to identify with any degree of certainty prisons or dungeons in castles. Examples of ill-lit basements can be seen in many great keeps and gatehouses, with perhaps just a ventilation shaft to provide air, and with access through a trap-door. Such chambers might have been used for storage, although it would have been inconvenient to keep goods in a room lacking easy access, and they were in most cases likely to have been dungeons. At Conisbrough a chamber stood on the west side of the gate passage, and in the fourteenth century this room appears to have become a guardroom or porter's lodge, and at the same time a basement was created beneath it, its construction undercutting the foundations of the curtain wall. In one corner of the basement stood a latrine seat of dressed stone, set on a stone base. Clearly the chamber was designed as a residence of some kind. However, the only method of entry to the room would seem to have been from the floor above, through the guardchamber, and this suggests that the basement was a prison (Johnson 1980). At Hen Domen there was a sunken room, with a possible latrine, which may have been a prison (Barker and Higham 1982: 44-5), and the prison tower at Lydford has already been discussed.

Archaeology has revealed evidence for domestic buildings in other castles, Loughor for example, but in many cases very little can be said about them. Also, the function of these buildings is far from clear; they might be lodgings, or they could form part of the service ranges. Most of the examples discussed above date to the twelfth and thirteenth centuries, and there is little excavated evidence for new buildings of the later medieval period. This is not totally surprising, as many thirteenth-century halls and lodgings, such as those at Hadleigh and Sandal, remained in use throughout the fourteenth and fifteenth centuries, although rebuilding and repair is known to have been undertaken in several instances. An example of a major building programme of the fourteenth century is to be found at Castle Rising, Norfolk, where a range of lodgings, including a chapel, was excavated in the area to the south of the great twelfth-century keep. These buildings are probably associated with the period when Isabella, the widow of Edward II, and known as the 'She-Wolf of France', came into possession of the castle in 1331; upon her death in 1358 the castle passed to her son Edward, the Black Prince (Brown 1983: 7, 16; Webster and Cherry 1975: 239; 1976: 185).

The duplication of apartments on the basis of social status is a recurring theme in the medieval castle; it can still be seen in some of the great castles, and also in some of the excavations undertaken over the last few years. A good example of two sets of lodgings can be seen at Edward I's great castle of Conwy, where accommodation for the king was provided in the inner ward, whilst the constable, garrison and servants resided in the outer ward (Taylor 1986a: 24–32). Excavations at Hen Domen indicated that in the mid twelfth century in particular the half of the bailey nearest the motte was reserved for the use of the lordly family, whilst in the eastern half lay the quarters of the garrison and the domestics. At Sandal the family apartments were probably located in the keep on the motte, with important guests lodged in the hall and chambers in the bailey. However, this dual arrangement was not necessarily a feature of all castles, particularly those which lacked the space. At Goltho the main domestic building was the hall which was situated in the very small bailey, or in the final phase of *c.* 1150 the large double-aisled hall on the mound that was created from the motte-and-bailey.

7 Kitchens and allied structures

It has already been mentioned that the survival rate of domestic buildings in castles has not been good. This applies in particular to kitchens, as well as allied buildings such as bakehouses. In many castles it is often impossible to identify the remains of such buildings, or there might be the remains of an oven tucked away in a corner to signify the previous existence of such a service range. In some cases the evidence has disappeared following the abandonment of a castle, but in other instances changes of ownership or improvements made by later generations of the same family have led to the loss or partial destruction of the original buildings. It is not surprising, therefore, to learn that some of the best examples are to be found in keeps or in towers which formed part of the defensive circuit, for it is these buildings that have tended to have survived better since the middle ages due to their size and their thick walls. One of the best Norman examples can be seen in the north-west corner of the first floor of the keep at Castle Rising, whilst in late thirteenth-century Caerphilly the kitchens were housed in two large towers, one square and the other D-shaped. Another fine example can be seen at Edward I's Caernarfon where not only has the seating for two cauldrons survived, with fireplaces beneath, but there is also evidence for the provision of piped water channelled from the adjacent Well Tower. In the late middle ages there is the fine Kitchen Tower built in the 1460s at Raglan.

Individual domestic buildings in castles often do not receive the treatment which they deserve. Recent excavations have made it possible to examine this subject in more detail, although we still cannot find an answer to all the questions posed. For example, why were the ovens added at a slightly later date to the original early fourteenth-century kitchen at Okehampton? Had there been a bakehouse elsewhere which served the castle's needs, but which was then brought within the walls? The bakehouse at Sandal would also seem to have been afterthought; although contemporary with the conversion of the castle from timber to stone, its walls were not bonded with either the kitchen or the curtain wall. Unfortunately, one cannot say whether there is any significance in such developments; in many cases where there is an oven still evident in the standing remains it is clear that it formed an original feature from the beginning. Hearths and ovens were obviously the most important features of a kitchen, but other ancillary features such as work surfaces that would be required in the preparation of food have either left virtually no trace in the archaeological record or have not been recognized for what they were. The type of feature that may throw light on such features was uncovered at Okehampton, in the eastern end of the kitchen. A narrow and unweathered surface against one wall was interpreted as possibly having been an area covered by a bench or a shelf.

Excavations have produced evidence for a number of kitchens, and as some of this work has been undertaken at monuments in State care, the remains have often been conserved and left open for display; for example, Montgomery and Okehampton. It is rare to find good evidence for timber kitchens, so the building uncovered at Weoley Castle, Warwickshire, was an important discovery, as was the cob-walled structure at Wallingford. For comparisons, the reader should also be aware of the report on the kitchen area of the moated site of Northolt in Middlesex (Hurst, J.G. 1961), as well as those at Penhallam, Cornwall (Beresford 1974) and Wintringham, Huntingdonshire (Beresford 1977a). Penhallam in particular produced valuable evidence for a series of rooms which made up the kitchen range.

In some cases where the remains are more fragmentary there is the problem of identification and interpretation. A building with a series of hearths may not necessarily have been a kitchen; it might originally have formed part of a range of lodgings, and, for instance, in the last chapter one of the buildings excavated at Okehampton could have been either a lodging or a kitchen. At some of the castles reviewed in this chapter, Penmaen for example, there are problems of identification which will become apparent, but where an excavator has suggested that a certain structure was a kitchen, this has been used as a basis for inclusion in this chapter.

It has been seen (p.97) that the accommodation within a castle may reflect two distinct units, the lord's family on the one hand and the household staff on the other. This is sometimes also indicated by the service ranges. The division is particularly noticeable in royal castles. The keep at Orford, Suffolk, built by Henry II in 1165–73, has a lower and an upper hall, both served by their own kitchens, and in 1244 two kitchens were built at Ludgershall, one of which was for Henry III during his visits to the castle (Addyman 1973: 10), whilst in the fifteenth century a 'privy kitchen for the king' (Henry VI) was required at Hertford (Colvin 1963: 680). Such arrangements can also be seen in castles of the nobility. At Bolton Castle, built in the late fourteenth century by Richard, Lord Scrope, the living quarters were divided up to accommodate eight main households, together with some lesser units. The main kitchen was located in one of the rectangular towers, and served the great hall, whilst the bakery and brewhouse were located in another wing. A smaller hall had its own kitchen (Faulkner 1963: 225–30).

The only evidence for kitchens at Goltho came to light with the excavation of the second hall, dated *c.* 1125–50, associated with the motte-and-bailey phase of the castle's history (figure 5.4, p.103). At the east end of the hall, and separated from it by a screen and passage, lay the kitchen which was 5.7m long. A large hearth dominated the room, whilst attached to the range on the south side was a small bakehouse with its oven (Beresford 1987: 110). The interesting aspect of this kitchen is its presence within the hall. Most medieval kitchens were separate buildings, but at Goltho there was very little space in the bailey for a separate kitchen. It was not until the end of the middle ages that a kitchen tended to be incorporated in the main building (Wood 1965: 247), for example at Wingfield Manor, Derbyshire, built by Ralph, Lord Cromwell in the middle of the fifteenth century (Emery 1985: 296–7).

Evidence for ovens and bakehouses comes from a number of castles. In the early twelfth century Stamford had three rectangular buildings equipped with ovens, adjacent to which were three corn-drying kilns (figure 5.10, p.115) (Mahany 1978). The kilns may have been used in the preparation of grain for malting. A similar, but later, arrangement can be seen at Montgomery Castle, where the ranges of domestic buildings date to the late thirteenth and fourteenth centuries. On the west and north sides of the inner bailey there is a kitchen with an oven and a brewhouse (figure 3.4, p.66). These buildings were timber-framed, and set on dwarf stone walls or sills to keep the timbers clear of the damp ground. The brewhouse contained a tank for soaking the barley which would then have been laid out on an adjacent area of paving to germinate. A small kiln for drying the grain following germination was also uncovered (Lloyd and Knight 1981: 22). In the fourteenth century a rectangular grain-drying kiln stood in the middle bailey; at this time most of the buildings in this area of the castle were apparently of an agricultural nature (Knight 1983: 173, 181). A malthouse with kiln was also found at Sandal, dating to the late twelfth or early thirteenth century (Mayes and Butler 1983: 41).

At the Glamorgan ringwork of Loughor (Llwchwr in Welsh), a circular structure set into the bank proved to be an oven; it was linked to the kitchen by a cobbled path. The position of the oven meant that the enclosing rampart would have helped to retain the heat. The kitchen itself was about 4m square, open on its east side but with a west wall of stone; the other two walls were presumably of timber (Lewis, J.M. 1975; 152). Dating to the first half of the twelfth century, its life was short, for it was destroyed by fire, possibly when the castle was sacked by the Welsh. The chronicles record that in 1151 the castle of Aberllwchwr was burnt as part of an assault on the Gower peninsular (Jones, T. 1973: 131). In the Gower itself, at the ringwork known as Castle Tower, Penmaen, there was a small building in close proximity to the small twelfth-century timber hall. This may have been a kitchen, although the evidence is sparse. A possible hearth was marked by a slab of rock, and there was a drain which might be seen as running down from the kitchen (Alcock 1966: 191).

The only firm evidence for cooking activities at the motte-and-bailey of Hen Domen comes from a structure dating to the first half of the twelfth century. This building (XXXIII) was situated in the north-west corner of the bailey, and seemingly rested against the back of the rampart tower. It has been described as a shed, and it contained a hearth as well as a substantial bread oven (Barker and Higham 1982: 32). It may seem surprising in the light of the detailed excavations of a bailey which had never been disturbed after it had been abandoned towards the end of the thirteenth century that there has not been more evidence for the cooking facilities in the castle, although there is still an area of the bailey to be explored.

The kitchen in the twelfth-century timber phase of the motte-and-bailey at Sandal was situated on the north side of the hall. A series of postholes and the remains of sill or dwarf walls marked the limits of the small wooden building. It had a central hearth, marked by a rectangular setting of stones, and there were deposits of charcoal and ash around it and over the kitchen floor which was made of clay and earth. It was later found necessary to extend the kitchen north-eastwards, and the additional area had a lean-to roof. A drain led from this extension to a sump. The bailey also contained two ovens, at least the larger one being for the baking of bread. The bread oven, however, was located well away from the kitchen, near the entrance to the bailey, whilst the smaller one lay to the south of the hall (Mayes and Butler 1983: 34–6).

The thirteenth century provides us with a greater number of excavated examples of kitchens and attendant facilities. At the motte-and-bailey at Great

Easton, Essex, the kitchen (which was burnt down possibly at the end of the thirteenth century) may not have been the first such building associated with the castle, for it seems most unlikely that the original kitchen would have lasted since the foundation of the motte in the middle of the twelfth century. The thirteenth-century building probably was a wooden structure set on clay sills: *c.* 5.8m square, with a hearth set in a depression in the middle of the floor. A later kitchen was built on almost the same site, and used the same area for a series of hearths, although the original hollow was filled in so that the hearths were at floor level; it also had an oven in one corner. A third building was also of timber set on clay sills, and there was evidence that it had had a tiled roof. Its relationship with the second kitchen is not certain, although the excavators have suggested that building 3 housed the main kitchen, and that the other simply provided additional facilities, such as for baking. It is worth noting that the finds included the remains of three mortars used in the preparation of food (Sellers and Sellers 1966; 1968).

The original buildings in the inner bailey at Conisbrough, including the hall, are likely to date to the very beginning of the thirteenth century (p.117). The kitchen uncovered in the late 1960s is also associated with this phase. It was in a separate building to the east of the hall; between the two lay other service rooms through which the cooked food would be brought prior to being served in the hall. In common with other medieval kitchens, particularly those of substantial build, the Conisbrough example remained on the same site throughout the occupation of the castle. However, the original kitchen at Conisbrough did undergo alterations during the fourteenth century when various improvements were made to the castle. The Norman kitchen had a central hearth, but later additions included an oven and fireplaces (Johnson 1984: 18), emphasizing that in many castles kitchens were improved throughout the middle ages. At Deddington, for example, the Norman kitchen floor and hearth were renewed six times in the twelfth century (Jope and Threlfall 1946–7: 168), and other examples will be discussed below.

One of the more remarkable discoveries of the 1970s was a building which was probably a kitchen at Wallingford Castle, Berkshire, remarkable owing to the nature and method of its survival. Cob-walled buildings have already been encountered in the last chapter, although the remains of the walls at castles such as Hen Domen and Okehampton were never substantial. However, when excavated the remnants of the late twelfth- or early thirteenth-century kitchen at Wallingford with its cob walls stood to a height of 1.8m (figure 7.1). The reason for its survival is that at some stage in the thirteenth century the ditch of the inner defensive work which surrounded the motte was deepened, and the spoil was spread across the inner bailey to a depth of 2m. Rather than go to the bother of demolishing the old kitchen, the spoil was placed in and around the cob building. The kitchen measured 12.5 × 8.5m externally, and was divided into three rooms, the central one being the largest. There was a hearth in each of the rooms, and the walls were plastered and lime-washed. The impressions on the cob left by the timber jambs of a door were also found, but there was no evidence for any windows, nor for the roof structure (Webster and Cherry 1973: 159-61). Documentary evidence for building works at Wallingford in the thirteenth century include a new kitchen, built in 1228–9 (Colvin 1963: 850). It is tempting to associate this event with the infilling and replacement of the cob building.

Figure 7.1   Cob building excavated at Wallingford Castle

It was mentioned above that in the majority of cases the main internal buildings of a castle tended to remain in the same place even when they were rebuilt, although sometimes a rebuilding did result in a slightly different alignment, as seen in the halls at Hadleigh (p.116). However, when a castle was being converted from timber to stone, it would be possible to relocate the domestic ranges within the walls. Such an opportunity presented itself to the Warenne earls of Surrey in the first half of the thirteenth century at Sandal. It has already been seen that the twelfth-century kitchen was situated to the north of the original hall, but although the stone hall was in a similar position to that of its predecessor, the service range was moved to the south, and consisted of a bakehouse, a kitchen and a larder, all built against the curtain wall (figure 7.2). The kitchen, which lay over the malthouse mentioned earlier in this chapter, had substantial walls on its other three sides, although their foundations, together with those of the larder, were not as substantial as those in the main domestic range. The building (*c.* 10.4 × 9.4m internally) had a floor of compacted earth mixed with sand and clay, and there were three hearths. The largest one had a posthole on each side, and it can be safely assumed that it was over this hearth that the roasting spit was placed; such evidence has rarely been located. The kitchen apparently had a drain which linked with a surface-water culvert to empty into the ditch which surrounded the barbican.

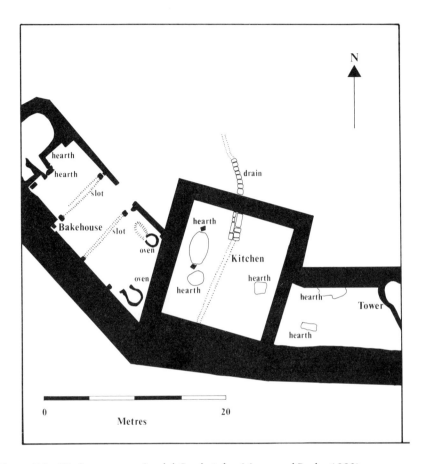

Figure 7.2   Kitchen range at Sandal Castle (after Mayes and Butler 1983)

On the east side of the kitchen at Sandal, and bonded with it, lay the larder, also a single-storey building, although by the time of the Civil War in the seventeenth century an extra floor had been added. The larder also had a floor of compacted earth, and the room surprisingly contained two small hearths, a feature not usually found in an area where meat and other foodstuffs would be stored. A doorway in the north-west corner led into the kitchen which had a bakehouse to the west. Although the excavators were unable to date the building precisely, its walls were not as substantial as the other buildings of the service range, and were clearly secondary to the kitchen. There was a cross-passage immediately inside the entrance, its walls marked by slots for sillbeams. There were two small ovens in the room which lay nearest to the kitchen, whilst on the other side of the passage were two much larger ovens, both sharing the same chimney. The smaller ovens still contained ash and charcoal, implying that they had been heated in preparation for a baking that had never been carried out. It is not known when the bakehouse went out of use, but in the seventeenth century the site was occupied by a stable which had a smithy at one end. Taken together, these three buildings provide a detailed picture of the services required to support the household of a castle owned by one of the great noble families of the thirteenth century. The surveys of Sandal undertaken in the sixteenth century show that the kitchen was still functioning, and that it had a roof of stone tiles at that time. The larder, however, was not in such a good condition (Mayes and Butler 1983: 20–1, 48–51).

When the kitchen at Launceston was excavated it was originally thought to have been built in the fourteenth century, but a review of the evidence has meant that it is now associated with thirteenth-century buildings such as the great and the administrative halls (p.120) (Saunders 1984: 14), and was still in use in the fifteenth century. The kitchen was about 8m square internally with walls almost 1m thick, and a door in one corner leading out into a yard which connected the kitchen to the great hall. The floor had been renewed on at least two occasions. A large hearth occupied the centre of the room, and a considerable area of the clay floor surrounding it had been scorched. There may also have been a fireplace against one wall where there was a further area of burning, and a capped and slate-lined drain ran out from the kitchen. Later in the middle ages various modifications may have resulted in the kitchen becoming a bakehouse; a similar alteration occurred with part of the kitchen range at Okehampton, as will be seen below. A setting near the oven may have been for a cauldron or vat used in brewing, although the similar features in the kitchens at Caernarfon Castle were used for cooking. The one other addition was a stone bench in one corner with a tank in front of it built of slate slabs; the purpose of the tank is unknown. At the same time a new drain was dug which cut through part of the burnt area surrounding the central hearth, and it contained a large quantity of fish remains, as well as Crustacea (Saunders 1970: 89–90).

Although the site at Weoley is known as Weoley Castle, it was really a fortified manor house rather than a castle; nevertheless, its inclusion in King (1983) means that it merits a mention here. There was a fortified site at Weoley, largely of earth-and-timber, before the stone building was built in the late 1260s and the 1270s, and associated with this original manor was a building which has been described as 'the first medieval timber building to be scientifically excavated in England of which anything more than post-holes remained' (Smith, J.T. 1965: 82).

The survival of many of the Weoley kitchen timbers to a height of about 1m was due to the same reason that led to the preservation of the Wallingford building. The spoil from the digging of the new moat associated with the late thirteenth-century stone-walled fortified manor was spread over the interior, resulting in the burying of some of the buildings, including the kitchen. The rectangular building (12.5 × 6.85m) lay against the earth and timber defences to the south of the stone hall, and the two were linked by a covered passage. Features in the interior included postholes which showed that the kitchen was divided into four bays, the remains of the hearth, whilst two further postholes marked the doorway (figure 7.3). There was evidence that the roof was thatched with reed, but it was not clear how the original roof was supported until the third phase alterations when the aisle posts were added.

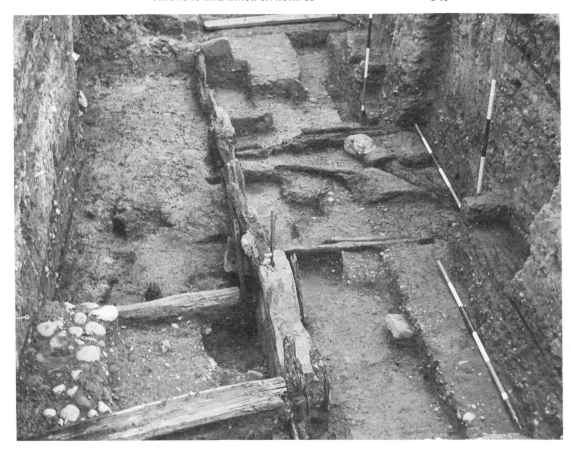

Figure 7.3 Timber kitchen at Weoley Castle, with entrance in the foreground

The kitchen at Weoley underwent various changes during its short life from *c.* 1200 until about the 1260s, possibly due to weakness in the construction of the building. Throughout the alterations the entrance remained on the north side because of the link with the hall. The kitchen as first built contained a small chamber at the west end, whilst the hearth lay on the opposite side of the buildings. In the next phase the chamber was made smaller, and partitions were added to the main area; at the same time the hearth was enlarged. A major alteration occurred in the third phase, for this was when the kitchen was divided into four bays by a series of aisleposts. Although the west room was retained, all other partitions were removed. Some of the original timbering, including sillbeams, was renewed at the same time. The kitchen remained an aisled structure to the end of its life, and the only major changes that were undertaken were the raising of the floor level and the reconstruction of the entrance, together with further renewal of some of the timber walling (Oswald 1962–3).

As the report on the Weoley excavation emphasizes, one of the remarkable aspects of this timber building is that the walls were clad with weatherboards (figure 7.4), as opposed to having timber panels filled with wattle-and-daub.

This type of construction does not seem to have been popular until the eighteenth century, and then mainly found in the south-east of England (Brunskill 1987: 64). However, it may be that many medieval buildings were constructed in this manner, but have simply not survived due to being weaker in design than the traditional timber-framed and panelled houses. There is a reference to 'viderbord' being used at Southwark in 1223, although this is apparently 'an exceptionally early, and isolated use of the term' (Salzman 1952: 244); documentary evidence for this type of construction is more common in the later middle ages. A more detailed analysis of the structure of the Weoley kitchen can be found in Smith, J.T (1965).

Figure 7.4   Weoley Castle kitchen, showing a section of the horizontal weatherboarding

A number of other castles have also provided limited evidence for castle kitchens in the twelfth and thirteenth centuries. In the twelfth century Eynsford had a masonry kitchen tucked into one corner of the courtyard, serving the hall which had been built a few years before. In the following century another kitchen was added on the opposite side of the courtyard against the south-east corner of the hall, but this was timber-framed on sill walls. The older building, however, remained in use until the castle was partially dismantled in the early fourteenth century, the large tiled hearth which is visible today marking the final period of occupation (Rigold 1971: 125, 135–7). A fire badly damaged the hall about the middle of the thirteenth century, and a certain amount of reconstruction took place as a result. The opportunity was then taken to improve the facilities by linking the timber-framed kitchen closely to the hall. At Barnard Castle there was a large twelfth-century masonry bakehouse containing two ovens partly constructed on the ringwork bank, as well as a timber kitchen dating to the same period (Austin 1980: 78; 1982: 296).

Other thirteenth-century examples of kitchens have been uncovered at Skenfrith (figure 7.5), Rumney, Hadleigh and Cruggleton. Although all that remained of a service range at Cruggleton was an oven, associated with the thirteenth-century rebuilding of the castle in masonry, the structure is of interest because of the evidence it contained for its firing. It was constructed of sandstone and shale, bonded together with clay, and the remains of its sloping sides indicated that it had had a domed roof. An analysis of the charcoal showed that the kindling had consisted of chaff, twigs and timber offcuts (Ewart 1985: 33–4).

Figure 7.5 Kitchen range at Skenfrith Castle

In the early fourteenth century Okehampton Castle underwent a dramatic rebuilding, with a chapel and lodgings on the southern side of the bailey and hall and kitchens on the northern (Higham 1984: 10–11; Higham *et al.* 1982: 63–5). Although we know virtually nothing about the earlier medieval service range, the walls of the later kitchen still stand, and it was separated from the hall by a passage, as well as a service room at one end of the hall-block. The kitchen consisted of two rooms, but in the eastern chamber the excavations went down no further than the late fourteenth and fifteenth century levels (see below). The western room, which was partitioned by a stone wall, also underwent later changes, but there was evidence for a mortar floor and a stone-lined pit which may have been used for cold storage. A major addition to this end of the kitchen range was made some years later; although the precise date is not known, the original mortar floor did not show any evidence of wear consistent with a long period of use. A new floor was laid 0.4m above the original mortar, and a masonry staircase was added which led to a new room created above the eastern half of this west range. The building itself was converted into a bakehouse, as two ovens were built at the west end of the room. Evidence for the use of the ovens was indicated by a layer of ash and charcoal which had been raked out before food had been placed in the heated interiors, and by the scorched floor in the area of the larger oven.

In the eastern room of the kitchen range at Okehampton the later medieval features included a large hearth set on granite, and with an ashpit. A quantity of rough plaster found in the room may have come from the fireplace hood. This end of the kitchen seems to have been partitioned, for the floor area nearest the hearth consisted of trampled ash, whilst the other half of the room had a stone floor sloping down to the north wall which had a drain cut through it. The suggestion is that food was prepared in the room with the stone floor, allowing debris to be washed out down the drain, especially as bones from fish and other animals were found between the stones. Another feature of this area of the eastern room was a circular recess which might have held a mortar (Higham *et al.* 1982).

The service range of the hall-house at Edlingham occupied the ground floor, with a kitchen at the west end. The first kitchen in the courtyard lay on the west side, and so it was in direct communication with the one in the hall-house. However, it was later demolished and its remains used in part of a rebuilding of the curtain wall as well as the courtyard paving; there are traces of a hearth as well as an oven. In the late fourteenth century there was a rearrangement of the domestic ranges. The new kitchen was moved against the northern curtain wall, although on the same side of the courtyard, and would appear to have been timber-framed with stone sill walls. The excavation revealed a series of hearths and ovens, and food was brought into the hall-house from the kitchen via a covered way in the manner seen above at Weoley. The existence of two kitchens at Edlingham may imply that the baking, roasting and the main preparation was done in the courtyard kitchen, whilst lighter work took place in the hall-house. Both continued in use in the sixteenth century, and were supplemented by a new range on the east side of the courtyard which included a brewhouse, the new building having replaced a late fourteenth-century lodging (Fairclough 1984: 53–4).

One other castle which saw considerable redevelopment of its domestic buildings, particularly in the fourteenth century, was Portchester. The east range of the inner bailey seems to have contained cooking facilities from the thirteenth century. An oven and a water-tank were features of the mid fourteenth-century kitchen; it is likely that the oven was used for baking, with the tank providing an immediate source of water, but it is feasible that both were used in the brewing process. However, in the early fourteenth century a small kitchen was added to the south-west range as part of the modifications made to the hall, and then rebuilt a few years later, in 1356. The existing kitchen, with its adjacent larder, at the east end of the hall dates to the time of Richard II's rebuilding in the 1390s, so little can be said about its predecessor. Richard II's kitchen, however, contained a drain which led out through the inner bailey wall, and the kitchen floor was paved with limestone. A staircase would have led from the kitchen to a service room on the first floor through which the hall was reached. No evidence was found for the fireplace or hearth, as most of the flooring had been removed; it may be that there had been a central hearth. However, if there had been a hearth associated with this kitchen it is surprising that no trace of ash or charcoal was found, even allowing for the loss of the original floor. It may be that as postulated for Edlingham the main cooking was undertaken elsewhere. This would have been in the east range of the inner bailey, with lighter preparations restricted to the kitchen by the hall. Another reason for thinking that the bulk of the food preparation would have been carried out in the east range is that the hall kitchen was small, only about 7m square internally. This surely could not have provided the necessary facilities for the palace of Richard II; the requirements of the royal household must have demanded a larger service range (Cunliffe 1985).

There is little archaeological evidence for major new kitchens being built in castles in the fifteenth century, but excavations have uncovered some small examples in Scotland. In chapter 5 mention was made of the hall at Smailholm, the small building that supplemented the accommodation in this Scottish tower-house. This was situated on the north side of a small courtyard or barmkin to the west of the tower. Although the preparation of food for the occupants of the tower-house was possibly carried out at a fireplace in the building itself, there was a kitchen in the barmkin opposite the hall. The range consisted of two rooms, each about 5 × 4m. There was a fireplace in both rooms, and the excavations revealed the remains of food scattered about the floors. In the seventeenth century, when a new house, with its own kitchen, was built on the site of the hall, the old kitchen was converted to a bake- and brewhouse (Tabraham 1987: 230).

A kitchen of a similar date to the one at Smailholm was excavated at Cruggleton, associated with the final phase of the castle's occupation, from the late fifteenth century to the middle of the seventeenth. However, most of the medieval deposits had been removed, and the large hearth is associated with the post-medieval phase (Ewart 1985: 38–40). A better example has come from Breachacha, Argyllshire. This castle consists of a tower and a courtyard, both built in the first half of the fifteenth century. Later that century a small kitchen was built outside the walls of the castle, although possibly enclosed by a rampart and palisade; certainly such a defence existed at the end of the sixteenth century. There is no obvious evidence to show how food was brought from the kitchen into the castle, but any doubt as to whether the extra-mural building was a kitchen is dispelled by the large fireplace, as well as the well and spring which lay close by. The building was about 8m long and 4.3m wide internally, and underwent various alterations in the post-medieval period (Turner and Dunbar 1969–70: 168–71).

The fifteenth-century kitchens at Smailholm and Breachacha were modest buildings to suit the requirements of lairds of limited means, and therefore a major contrast when compared to the kitchens of the great households associated with castles such as Sandal or Okehampton. The relationship of a kitchen with other domestic buildings is not always apparent from some of the above examples, particularly where it has by force of circumstance been excavated in isolation, for example Wallingford. It has sometimes been suggested that a kitchen would be built some distance away from the hall as a precaution against fire. However, it can be seen both from standing remains, as at Raglan, and from excavations at such castles as Sandal and Okehampton that in many cases there was a logical arrangement of the service range. The cooked food would be carried to an intermediate room where final preparations could be undertaken before the meal was carried into the hall.

There is obvious scope for further work on service ranges in castles, to extend our limited knowledge of these more ephemeral buildings; it is probably best done by incorporating all the known evidence from standing remains. However, some of the best evidence which provides a very detailed picture of service ranges in castles has come from excavation, notably Sandal. This Yorkshire castle produced one of the best sequences of rooms that made up a kitchen range, but few sites can equal the various structures which were associated with the moated site at Penhallam, with its larder, kitchen, pantry, bake- and brewhouse, buttery, and well-chamber (Beresford 1974).

8 Chapels, ancillary structures, and water supply

An examination of the building works which were carried out in the middle ages at various castles which were either permanently or temporarily in the possession of the English Crown (Colvin 1963) reveals that in many cases there was a variety of buildings serving functions other than those discussed in the previous three chapters. These included chapels, barns, stables, forges, dovecots, mills, sheds to house artillery, armouries, well-houses and cisterns. Some castles also had gardens, such as the one enclosed by the east barbican of Edward I's Conwy. Some of these structures might be housed in parts of the defences, such as keeps and mural towers, whilst others must have stood in the castle bailey. In many cases it is difficult to identify such structures from the existing remains even when a large percentage of a castle still stands. One exception to this is the chapel, for in many cases a fine east window, together with internal features such as a piscina, makes identification relatively simple. Another building type which does not constitute a problem is the dovecot with its nesting boxes.

Excavation has uncovered buildings which clearly cannot have been halls, lodgings or kitchen ranges, but whose function can be identified with a high degree of certainty. Various ephemeral structures which scarcely receive a mention in building accounts have also been uncovered; these include workshops built to house craftsmen employed on new projects. This chapter examines some of these other types of buildings associated with castles.

Chapels

Most castles would have had a chapel, although it is not always easy to see from physical remains, and documentary evidence is often a better guide. Chapels incorporated in more massive structures such as mural towers or keeps have often survived in a good condition, but free-standing buildings in the courtyard are more likely to have suffered from decay and stone robbing. Some ruined castles still have fine examples of chapels; one can be seen at Ludlow with its Norman circular nave (figure 8.1), whilst another is the early thirteenth-century building set below Dunstaffnage Castle, Argyllshire. Some of the castles which belonged to the Crown and the great magnates of England had at least two chapels, and medieval accounts for building and repair work show that there were sometimes more. At Edward I's magnificent castle of Caernarfon there is architectural evidence for at least four chapels, and it likely that there were another three, but this number is exceptional. Most of the Caernarfon examples were private chapels located in small chambers that led off from the main rooms in towers such as the Eagle Tower and the Queen's Tower, although there is a larger chapel on the first floor of the main entrance, the King's Gate.

When the great keep of Colchester, Essex, was built soon after the Norman Conquest a late Anglo-Saxon chapel, 14.9 × 6.8m in size, was left standing on

Figure 8.1   Norman chapel at Ludlow Castle

the site, its apsidal east end only about 2m from the south-east corner of the keep. In the early thirteenth century a certain amount of rebuilding took place, including the east end (Drury 1982: 323–33, 396). The keep itself contained a chapel, so presumably the Saxon building was retained in order to serve the spiritual needs of the garrison and household staff. The retention of a Saxon chapel within a Norman castle has been suggested at Hastings and Pevensey (Taylor 1969), and the same may be true of Pontefract (Youngs *et al.* 1985: 208).

Whereas the Colchester building was Anglo-Saxon in origin, the chapel excavated in the Castle Yard, Winchester, was early Norman in date (*c.* 1070), even though some aspects of its building show Saxon workmanship. It was situated at the north end of the platform occupied by the castle, and soon after it was built the motte was added at the extreme northern end (p.31), the mound's stone revetment wall lying close to the chapel wall. One of the interesting aspects of the chapel was that the quoins of the external north-west angle of the nave were laid in a style termed long-and-short work (figure 8.2), a feature known from many other Saxon buildings (Kerr and Kerr 1983: 37–8). It seems that Saxon masons were employed on this chapel, in the same way that they were used on the contemporary gatetower of Exeter Castle, where the upper windows are typically Saxon in design. The north wall of the apse is angled in a south-easterly direction; that is to say, it does not meet the wall of the main body of the chapel at 90°. This has led to two possible reconstructions (figure 8.3), of which the upper (a) seems the more likely as it represents a more symmetrical building. Once the main body of the chapel had been built, the interior was plastered, and a line was made in the wet plaster with a length of string to mark the setting for benches. The plaster was then painted in imitation of hanging drapery. The windows were glazed with coloured glass.

Figure 8.2   Early Norman chapel, Winchester Castle

The Winchester chapel had at least two doors, one in the north wall of the nave which was fully excavated, and another at the west end of the building, of which only the northern jamb was revealed. When the chapel was built *c.* 1070 both doors had frameworks of timber, but at a later date the west door was framed in rough masonry. The west door eventually went out of use, and a wall bench was later built across the inside of this doorway. The chapel probably only lasted about sixty years; the internal fittings were then removed, and the upper walls demolished. This was all part of a deliberate policy for the

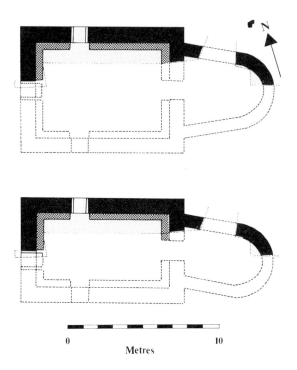

0   10
Metres

Figure 8.3 Two hypothetical reconstructions of the plan of the Norman chapel at Winchester (after Biddle 1975)

reorganization of the bailey which included the destruction of the motte and the construction of the keep (p.46) (Biddle 1970: 290; 1975: 104–9).

Building IX at Hen Domen (figure 5.3, p.102), from the late twelfth and early thirteenth century, is one of the few timber castle chapels to have been excavated, although its attribution is tentative (Barker 1987: 53). There may have been a chapel on the site as early as the middle of the twelfth century, for the remains of a holy water stoup were excavated from the fill of a posthole, clearly belonging to a phase earlier than building IX. The presence of a chapel on the site before the late twelfth century strengthens the argument for the apsidal-ended building IX being one, although its north–south orientation may suggest other interpretations (Barker and Higham 1982: 38, 45).

The twelfth-century chapel associated with the motte-and-bailey castle at Hen Blas, Flintshire, lay in the outer bailey (Leach 1960). It was a rectangular masonry building with a door in the north wall. The remains of one of the hinge-hooks for the wooden door was found nearby, and the stonework of a window which would have overlooked the altar was discovered in a state of near perfect preservation. Internal features included the remains of the altar set against the east wall and a bench. Its life seems to have been short, for some of the thirteenth and fourteenth century buildings in the inner bailey used stone from the chapel in their construction.

Pleshey is the only other castle with a major excavation of a chapel (Williams, F. 1977). There can be no doubt that the main building excavated there in 1959–63 was a chapel, and it was preceded by two structures which may have had the same function. It is known from documentary evidence that there was a chapel at Pleshey Castle in the middle of the thirteenth century, but on the evidence of the floor-tiles and carved stonework the stone chapel which was excavated is likely to have been built in the early fourteenth century. The building was rectangular (*c.* 18.8 × 7.6m), with side and angle buttresses, and an entrance towards the west end of both the north and the south walls. Its walls were built of flint with chalk and limestone dressings, although it is possible that they were timber-framed with wattle-and-daub on stone sills; however, there is no firm evidence for this, and a survey of 1558–9 describes the walls as 'pybble' or pebble. After the construction of the original building a small extension was added on both the north and south sides, possibly in the later fourteenth century, and perhaps to serve as side-chapels.

The excavation of the interior of the Pleshey chapel produced evidence for a series of tiled floors spanning the early fourteenth to the mid fifteenth century; in the later period the tiles were Flemish in origin. In spite of later disturbances in the chancel at Pleshey there was evidence for two burial vaults with flint and mortar walls, but both had been robbed in the post-medieval period; the chapel itself was in ruins by the middle of the sixteenth century. One other piece of evidence for the fittings inside the building was a pit at the extreme west end of the nave to house the base of a font. The ornateness of the chapel is not only indicated by the three different series of floor-tiles, but also by the large quantity of red, yellow, green and blue glass which came from the windows. Two fragments of painted wall-plaster may have formed part of the decoration of the chapel. The building of the chapel and its later history coincides with the ownership of the castle by the de Bohun family as earls of Hereford and Essex, and later the duchy of Lancaster when it formed part of the dowry of three fifteenth-century queens of England. Thus, on the basis of the owners' status, it is not altogether surprising that the interior of this externally plain chapel of flint was quite lavish (Williams, F. 1977).

Tudor surveys of Sandal Castle show it to have had at least one chapel, but there must have been two: one in the the keep on the motte and a second in the bailey. Excavations revealed no structure that might have been a chapel, but various finds, particularly from the barbican ditch at the foot of the motte, are likely to have come from an ecclesiastical building. These included fragments of carved stone, one possibly from the base of an altar. Firmer archaeological evidence for a chapel comes from the fragments of painted glass, the finest example portraying the Virgin and Child, and probably dating to the fourteenth century (Mayes and Butler 1983: 287, 289, 318–9).

Excavations of castles in Scotland have not produced definite evidence for chapels, but a building in the outer enclosure at the Douglas stronghold of Threave may have been one (Good and Tabraham 1981: 137).

Ancillary buildings

It is rare to find stables still standing in castles today. Some of the best extant examples date from sixteenth-century improvements, and include the Earl of Leicester's remarkable range at Kenilworth, Warwickshire, a small block added to Ludlow, and the range at Crichton, Midlothian. In many cases the stables were probably located away from the main domestic area of a castle, most conveniently beside the entrance. At both Kenilworth and Ludlow the stables stand near the main entrances against the earlier curtain wall of their respective outer wards.

Archaeological excavation in castles has tended to concentrate on areas other than the outer bailey, and this may account for the fact that the only certain evidence for stables has come from Hadleigh, Essex, and Farleigh Hungerford in Somerset. The range at Hadleigh is of uncertain date, but stands immediately inside the new entrance built in the fourteenth century, and against the north curtain wall. It was approximately 20m long and 3m in width, and its main feature was a stone-lined pit which could either have been used for storage or as a water trough (Drewett 1975: 108). The stable range at Farleigh Hungerford lay in the outer bailey; built in the late 1420s, this building also stood against the curtain wall. There was very little surviving evidence for its main walls, but the stable block was about 16m long and almost 5m wide internally. The interior contained a drainage gully emptying into the ditch through a drain which ran beneath the curtain wall. The floor itself was formed by smoothing the natural rock, with the addition of some stone slabs. Various postholes found in the interior probably supported the uprights for the stable partitions (Wilcox 1980: 95, 98–9). A different form of stabling has been found in the outer bailey at Portchester where two or three rows of posts suggest the presence of animal corrals (Cunliffe 1977: 36).

At Threave one of the buildings, interpreted as a first floor hall, might have had its ground floor used for storage or stabling (Good and Tabraham 1981: 99–101, 137). There was evidence for timber partitions which may indicate stalls, and if this were so the first floor above was probably not a hall but a room for the ostlers and stableboys. This was the arrangement at the sixteenth-century stables at Crichton and Kenilworth; the stables at Ludlow simply had a loft for storage above the stalls.

Dovecots are a common feature of medieval manor sites, and thirteenth-century examples are known from Ayton, Yorkshire (Rimington and Rutter 1967: 45–6), and Wintringham in Huntingdonshire (Beresford 1977a: 220–2), but few have been recorded at castles. At Richard's Castle there are three examples, ranging in date from the thirteenth (possibly) to the seventeenth century. The earliest lay on the bank of the town defences situated below the castle, whilst the latest is at a farmhouse not far from the castle. The third dovecot was inserted in one of the mural towers of the bailey of the castle itself, perhaps in the fifteenth century when the castle was in decline as a fortification but remained in use as a residence. The presence of the dovecot suggests that the tower was no longer militarily significant, and this in itself suggests a date in the late middle ages for its insertion (Curnow and Thompson 1969: 119).

Dovecots may also be directly associated with the main period of occupation of a castle, perhaps the best example being that on the top floor of the south-west tower of Bodiam Castle in Sussex, adjacent to the kitchen range. The basement of this tower contains the well, and sandwiched between the dovecot and the well are two floors which contained lodgings. The foundations of a dovecot can also be seen at Denbigh, and there is one at Carreg Cennen. In

Scotland dovecots are sometimes associated with the occupation of castles in the sixteenth and seventeenth centuries, and two very fine examples can be seen at the East Lothian castles of Dirleton and Tantallon. Others were inserted into the medieval fabric of castles such as Hailes, East Lothian, and Rothesay, Bute, but their date is unknown.

A granary is another type of building which may be found within a castle enclosure, but the remains of such buildings are rarely identifiable today. The 1322 survey of Sandal, for instance, showed that the castle had a granary containing wheat and oats, but the excavations found no traces of it. Its floor may have been raised above ground to keep rodents from raiding the supplies, and thus it would leave little archaeological evidence, but one of the buildings excavated at Hen Domen has been interpreted as a granary. Building XXXVIII at Hen Domen (see frontispiece and figure 5.2, p.100), originally thought to have been built in the mid twelfth century, is now known to date from the late eleventh century. Its plan was marked by twelve close-set postholes, some of which were almost a metre deep. They clearly contained posts supporting a heavy timber building, and certainly a granary would have needed to have been a robust structure. The setting of the posts would also have enabled them to support the essential raised floor (Barker and Higham 1982: 37–8, 47; 1988: 7–8).

Workshops in castles were generally ephemeral features associated with building campaigns, and they are discussed in the next chapter (p.164). Some may have been more permanent. Such a building was a shed associated with the mid twelfth-century phase of occupation at Hen Domen (figure 5.2, XV, p. 100). This was a post-built structure with a pebble floor, on which lay pieces of iron scrap, including bars, hasps and a damaged axe head (Barker and Higham 1982: 33). This building does not seem to have been a smithy for it had no forge, but it may have been the workshop for the castle's smith or armourer. A similar workshop, but dating to the fourteenth century, has been excavated at Bramber. The wooden building lay on the site of the ditch of the old motte, its main feature being a hearth. As with the Hen Domen workshop, the one at Bramber must have been used for metalworking, for the debris contained iron and copper-alloy waste, slag from a forge, and remnants of nails and horseshoes (Barton and Holden 1977: 38).

Water supply

The provision of water to a castle took two forms: a natural source of supply through the digging of a well, or water gathered in a tank or cistern. A cistern must have relied mainly on rainwater, but water supplies could have been brought in casks, either to be deposited in the cistern, or even to have remained stored in the casks. In many of the larger castles there was more than one source of supply, for although there might be a well in the courtyard there usually was another in the keep or a tower. This not only made for more convenient domestic arrangements, but it was also a wise military precaution, for if a besieging force took the bailey the garrison in the keep would have access to an all-important source of water.

A cistern in the form of a hollow, possibly lined with leather to minimize

seepage, was situated on the north side of the bailey at Hen Domen (figures 5.1
– 5.3, XLIII, LIII, pp.99–100, 102). It belonged to the late eleventh-century
period of occupation, although it was still in use in the later twelfth or early
thirteenth century. Rainwater from the roofs of surrounding buildings may
have been channelled to the cistern, and a line of postholes along the slope of
the bailey bank probably supported a gutter from adjacent roofs. A pit,
situated on the rampart at the north-east corner, was also used as a cistern
(Barker and Higham 1982: 36, 47).

In the twelfth and thirteenth centuries the castle at Okehampton also relied
on a cistern for its water supply. It was cut into the rock at the foot of the
motte, was 2.5m deep and enclosed on two sides by walls which probably
supported a covering or roof. It relied for its water on the natural seepage of
groundwater and also on rainwater collected in a drain which ran into the pit
(Higham *et al.* 1982: 31–5). The clearance and consolidation of various
features at Castell-y-Bere included a rock-cut cistern situated just within the
main gateway to the castle (figure 8.4). It was probably associated with the
castle as built in the 1220s by Llywelyn ab Iorwerth, and relied on the
accumulation of water in the same manner as the cistern at Okehampton.
When it was emptied in 1951 parts of the roof over the cistern and the winding
mechanism were retrieved, as were one virtually complete bucket (now
conserved and reconstructed: figure 8.5), and the remains of three others.
These fixtures and fittings are likely to belong to the period 1283–95 when the
castle was in the possession of the English Crown (Butler 1974: 80–1, 100–1).
Several other castles in Wales also relied on cisterns for a supply of water. At
the native Welsh castle of Criccieth in Caernarfonshire, the spring-fed cistern
was placed in in the gatehouse passage (Avent 1987: 3). Carreg Cennen had
two cisterns behind the gatehouse, whilst the main ditch was originally
clay-lined as if to hold water; the fact that no garderobe discharges into the
ditch suggests that it too was a cistern (Lewis, J.M. 1960: 9, 11).

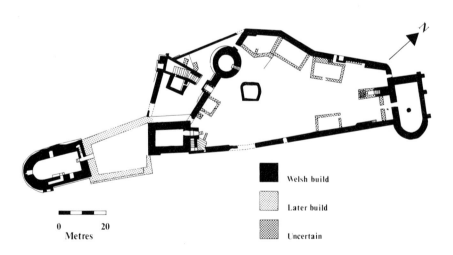

Welsh build

Later build

Uncertain

0   20
Metres

Figure 8.4   Plan of Castell-y-Bere (after Butler 1974)

Figure 8.5   Bucket found in the cistern, Castell-y-Bere

Other castles where there may have been a cistern include Baile Hill, York (figure 1.7, p.15) where one of the features on top of the motte may have been a well or cistern (Addyman and Priestley 1977: 131), and Goltho. One of the surprising results from the work at the latter castle was that there was no positive evidence for a well or other form of water source. Doubtless many earth-and-timber castles relied on cisterns, and at Goltho the only feature that comes close to this description is the brick-lined basement of the timber keep (p.17). If this were a cistern, the brick, together with some stone, which was bonded together with thick clay would have helped to prevent any loss of water (Beresford 1987: 103–4).

Most wells that have been excavated are associated with major buildings, such as keeps. This is not altogether surprising, as excavations have naturally tended to concentrate on the structures found within the defensive circuit rather than the open courtyard areas where wells would normally be located. In the tower at Lydford a well was cut through the rock to a depth of about 10m, and was associated with the first phase of the building (late twelfth century). The water for the well did not come from a spring, but from percolation of ground water. The objects retrieved from the well suggest that it went out of use in the thirteenth century and included various fittings associated with the well itself, such as the straps of the well cover and the remains of a bucket (Saunders 1980: 137–8, 165–6).

The late eleventh-century country house at Castle Acre contained two wells, located in the south-east and north-east corners (Coad and Streeten 1982: 151–2, 173). Both were retained when the walls of the house were thickened internally prior to the conversion of the building to a keep, but when the keep was built over the northern half of the site (p.49), access to the north-east well was restricted to the upper floors of the building. The south-east well remained in use until the upper ward of the castle was abandoned in the later twelfth century; the well was then filled with building rubble and debris which included pottery and animal bones. The area to the south of the keep may have been used as a kitchen with an open yard, for, besides the well, there were the remains of an oven situated on top of the south-west corner of the thickened walls of the country house.

Other good examples of wells within twelfth-century Norman keeps have been discovered at Aldingbourne and Farnham, the excavations at the former revealing evidence for the sinking of the well. At Farnham the shaft (4m square) was sunk through the centre of the foundations of the tower, whilst further down the well was just a circular shaft dug through the natural marl (Thompson 1960).

At Sandal the northern tower of the thirteenth-century keep housed a stone-lined well, and a second one was situated in the north-east corner of the bailey. The well in the keep could not be fully excavated, but it was at least 18.2m deep, with a flight of steps leading down from the ground floor to the well-chamber. It is possible that the presence of the well in the basement caused a weakening of the foundations of the tower, thus bringing about the need for the rebuilding of *c.* 1484 (Mayes and Butler 1983: 46).

A tower with a well on a larger scale than the one at Sandal was built on the west side of the inner bailey of Montgomery Castle (figure 3.4, p.66). Although the tower was originally built in the early thirteenth century, there were serious structural problems which resulted in its reconstruction some time in the fourteenth century. The well-shaft is cut through the rock, and is mainly square in shape, but the upper section is circular and stone-lined. The well was reached via a ground floor doorway in the tower, and as in similar structures, there would have been some form of accommodation in the upper levels. The first floor of the Montgomery well-tower contained a dining room (Knight 1983: 171; Lloyd and Knight 1981: 23–4).

During the large-scale thirteenth-century improvements undertaken at Launceston a new ditch was dug around the motte on the bailey side. Between the new ditch and the foot of the motte a wall, which ran from a small tower that protected the bridge and stairs to the motte, enclosed a terrace in which a well was dug, set into the inner face of the original ditch surrounding the motte. The position of the well, set within its own enclosed yard and overlooked by the defences both on and running up the motte, was obviously designed to serve those who might be accommodated in Earl Richard's circular keep on the summit of the motte; the water supply for the bailey with its halls and kitchens has yet to be located. The terrace was raised several times in the medieval and early modern period, and the well-head followed suit until it went out use in the late eighteenth century (Saunders 1970: 84–6).

Piped water supply is a feature of two of the great keeps of Henry II: Newcastle, built in the 1170s, and Dover, dating to the following decade. It is an aspect of domestic life in a castle for which very little evidence has survived, although another good example can be traced at Caernarfon, where water was channelled from the Well Tower to the kitchen. Also at Caernarfon there is a rainwater tank at the top of the Cistern Tower from which water could be piped to the Queen's Gate. The excavations of two castles in Devon have uncovered similar evidence. At Lydford a small carved water spout projects from the south-west wall of the basement of the prison, about 1.5m above the floor (Saunders 1980: 156). A channel in the spout leads to a small circular hole which could have been sealed by a bung. It probably was part of a water system leading from a cistern on the roof forming the prime source of water before the well was dug. When the bailey at Okehampton was refurbished in the early fourteenth century a lead pipe 40mm in diameter was laid across the courtyard from the earlier cistern to the domestic buildings on the south (Higham *et al.* 1982: 38, 40).

Archaeology has shed some light on castles and water supply, a subject which in the past has not attracted much attention. The problem has often been that whereas some castles seemed to have been provided with a supply of fresh water, at others there is no obvious sign of a well or cistern. At Ashby de la Zouch Castle, Leicestershire, there are four wells: one in the fourteenth-century kitchen, another in the fifteenth-century Hastings Tower, with a further two of unknown date immediately outside the entrance to the Hastings Tower. This does not mean that all four were in use in the fifteenth century; of the two outside the main tower, one might have been sunk after a collapse in the other. In contrast to this, there do not appear to have been any wells at two Pembrokeshire castles, Carew and Pembroke. In the sixteenth and seventeenth centuries Carew relied on water piped in from a well a considerable distance away (King and Perks 1962: 274), and this may have been the system in operation in the middle ages. At Pembroke even the great round keep of *c.* 1200 had no well. The town of Pembroke depended on piped water, and the castle may also have done so; alternatively, the water was stored in cisterns and barrels (King 1978: 104). Although today we might think that a lack of water sources, or dependence upon a supply which could easily be cut off, was a major weakness in a castle, the builders of Carew and Pembroke did not view the matter in this light, for these castles developed into two of the most powerful castles of the middle ages.

The popular image of life in the medieval castle tends to be one of hardship and great discomfort, but some of the less obvious domestic arrangements show that considerable planning went into the layout of various buildings, whether keep or kitchen. The examples of piped water supply at Caernarfon and Okehampton, mentioned above, are a case in point, as is the system at Orford that enabled the garderobes to be flushed by the drains from the kitchen.

Our knowledge of the lesser buildings found within the defences of medieval castles is largely based on documentary sources, and almost all these relate to major castles. Nevertheless, the results from several excavations have confirmed that there was a great variety of buildings within medieval castles, although little has been gleaned as to the decors and furnishings of these structures. Archaeology has also emphasized the ephemeral nature of many of these buildings, indicating that the layout and organization of a castle courtyard was often changing.

9 *Archaeology and castle life*

This chapter is concerned with excavated finds which give some indication of daily life within castles. The finds by no means present a complete picture; organic materials, for example, need waterlogged conditions for their survival and much must have decayed. Nevertheless, several of the categories discussed below help to emphasize that a castle was not just a fortress, but that it was also a home. Excavation reports of castles deal exhaustively with some categories of artefacts such as pottery and coins, and catalogues such as those in the Castle Acre report provide an insight into these categories. This chapter, however, will concentrate on those aspects which provide an altogether more informative picture of life within castle walls than can be given by coins and pottery. An invaluable introduction to the various types of medieval small finds, although originally published many years ago, is the old London Museum's catalogue (reprinted 1967); the finds reports in published accounts of excavations have in many cases updated the museum catalogue entries, as have the first two volumes in a new series published for the Museum of London (Cowgill *et al.* 1987: Grew and de Neergaard 1988).

It should not be thought that items included in this chapter are unique to castles; they are also found on other types of medieval upper-status habitations, for example moated manors. There are also problems regarding finds in connection with castles in towns, such as Newcastle upon Tyne and Oxford, for not all the material found on these sites can be associated with those who resided on a permanent or semi-permanent basis within the walls. The wealth of artefacts found in ditches of these castles are clearly the result of dumping by the urban inhabitants. At Newcastle few finds from the medieval period seem to have been thrown down into the ditch from the castle walls, but with the decline of the castle the ditches were used by the townspeople for the disposal of rubbish, and the bulk of the finds date from the sixteenth century and later (Harbottle and Ellison 1981). At Oxford the situation was slightly different; although some of the remains of shoes and other items of clothing belonged to the post-medieval period, many more fragments had been deposited by the citizens of Oxford in the thirteenth to fifteenth century, particularly in the ditch of the barbican (Hassall 1976).

Evidence for different aspects of life in a castle will be covered in six sections here: castle building, militaria, household objects, costume, pastimes, and food and diet. The examples cited are not exhaustive, and more detailed information can be found in the reports themselves.

Castle building

The richest source of evidence for the construction of castles is building accounts. These survive in considerable quantity for the castles which were built by the English Crown, or which the king had taken into custody. The accounts for building programmes and repairs were maintained by the Exchequer, and so with other documents of government are housed in the

Public Record Office, London. The history of these royal building works has been treated in great detail in Colvin (1963). Documentary evidence for the works of the kings of Scotland have not survived in such quantity.

Most of the records of the works undertaken by the nobility and others have been lost, but there are some interesting survivals. For example, the financial records of the late thirteenth-century works carried out by Roger Bigod III, Earl of Norfolk, at Chepstow still exist, as do the building accounts for Lord Cromwell's Tattershall, Lincolnshire, for the period 1434–72.

Evidence for the construction of castles has been found in a few excavated examples where traces of temporary workshops have been uncovered. These workshops were sometimes set up in pre-existing buildings which were then either demolished or rebuilt. When the early Norman chapel at Winchester was being dismantled the remains became a masons' lodge; while it served as this the motte was removed and a keep built in its stead. The timber hall at Sandal was also used by masons, and perhaps carpenters, whilst the castle was undergoing reconstruction in stone, and at Portchester the hall range was used by workmen employed on the late fourteenth-century rebuilding. Two lead-melting hearths were set into the floor of the hall, and a temporary smithy erected in the courtyard, backing on to the old kitchen, where the necessary iron fittings required for the new hall were probably made. Lead- and ironworking hearths were also used at Sandal when the castle was being converted from timber to masonry, and the tracks of a horse- and ox-drawn cart used in the building works have also been traced by excavation.

One of the more obvious pieces of above-ground evidence relating to the construction of a castle is the rows of horizontal and vertical putlog or scaffold holes which can often be seen running through a curtain wall or tower, left as a result of the removal of the original horizontal timber scaffolding. The holes were blocked by rubble and mortar after the scaffolding was removed, but over the years the filling may have weathered out. Another form of scaffolding can be seen in some of the Edwardian castles in north Wales, where the putlogs run up a tower in spiral fashion (helicoidal scaffolding). Excavations at the east gate into the lower ward at Castle Acre uncovered a series of ledges or benchings, associated with traces of mortar, which had been dug into the inner slope of the ditch. The benchings could have been cut to provide firm bases for the scaffolding used in the construction of the gate, but more usually postholes for vertical scaffolding set into the ground are found, as at Portchester, associated with the reconstruction of the hall block in the 1390s.

Kilns used in the construction of masonry castles are commonly found. Most were used for the burning of limestone or chalk to produce the quicklime which, mixed with sand and water, makes mortar (Davey 1961: 97–101), although the kiln from Sandal produced ridge-tiles for the new stone buildings which were under construction from about 1240. A fine series of thirteenth- and fourteenth-century limekilns remain at several castles in Wales, mainly discovered during the twentieth-century clearance and consolidation of monuments in State care. They can be seen at Carreg Cennen, Carmarthen-shire, Denbigh, Denbighshire, Ogmore and Weobley, Glamorgan, and Cilgerran in Pembrokeshire. More recently, limekilns have been excavated at Bedford, Bramber, Castle Acre, Portchester and Southampton.

It is impossible to say whether the two different types of kilns, the basic pit variety and the more elaborate stone-built structure, reflect the needs for which they were required. It may be that the more primitive unlined examples from Castle Acre, Portchester and Bramber were designed to provide enough lime for routine maintenance, and were short-lived. The more solidly built kilns, on the other hand, were constructed for a major programme of works, and had to stand up to repeated firings. The need for the continual firing of limekilns is shown, for example, by the fact that just two fuelled by timber cut from 26 acres of woodland were used in 1229 for the work in progress on the town defences and castle of Oxford. The quantity of timber required may well have been influential in the use of coal as the main fuel in kilns (Salzman 1952: 150).

The earliest example of a limekiln comes from the eleventh-century country house phase at Castle Acre. It was built into the upper part of the ditch of the upper ward, and although only a small part of the kiln itself was examined, one flue was fully excavated. The kiln had been dug through the original top soil and into the rock below, and then lined with mortar. As would be expected, the area around the flue contained pieces of charcoal, for timber was the fuel used in the limekiln. It was not until the later thirteenth century that coal was used as an alternative fuel, and this is borne out by archaeology as well as contemporary documents. When the Castle Acre kiln had served its purpose it was backfilled with rubble. Traces of what may have been a second kiln were discovered near the south-west corner of the upper ward. Other pit limekilns have been found in the outer bailey at Portchester, Bramber and Southampton, dating to the thirteenth century and later. The Portchester example may have been associated with repairs to the castle which were undertaken in 1296.

The most impressive limekiln from a castle is the example at Bedford which was scheduled as an Ancient Monument following its excavation (figure 9.1), although temporarily backfilled and no longer visible. It may have been built for the refortification of the castle between 1216 and its siege and destruction in 1224–5. The bottom of the kiln was divided into four sections with channels running between them; when they were originally excavated the channels were found to be full of pure lime, but their prime purpose was to allow the heat from the firing of the fuel to spread evenly throughout the chamber. In both the east and west walls of the kiln there was an arch, leading to the flue or stoke-hole. The other major feature associated with the Bedford kiln was a cobbled path which ran from the surviving top of the chamber, probably for carts bringing in their loads of limestone directly to the mouth of the kiln chamber.

The pit limekiln at Southampton was followed by a more sophisticated structure which consisted of a lined central chamber or shaft with three stoke-holes. When first built the chamber seems to have had gravel sides, as these had been scorched by the heat, but later a stone lining was added to give greater strength to the kiln. This lining consisted of small blocks of limestone, some of which had been fused together as a result of the heat from several firings. Pieces of burnt clay recovered from the site probably came from one of the cappings applied to the kiln prior to a firing (Oxley 1986: 54–63). A similar kiln was found at Portchester (figure 9.2).

Figure 9.1   Limekiln, Bedford Castle

The chamber of the late thirteenth- or early fourteenth-century limekiln at Ogmore is similar in diameter to the flued example from Portchester (2.03m), but with two flues on opposite side. Quantities of both lime and coal were found in the kiln, whilst a deposit of both materials lay nearby. On one side of the kiln, butting against it, is a buttress which may have been the base for steps so that blocks of limestone could be carried up to the mouth of the kiln chamber. In contrast to the majority of the above limekilns, the Cilgerran example, which dates to the fourteenth century, has a very small chamber, less than a metre in diameter. The flue arrangement also differs, for as the kiln was built in a corner of the castle the two flues could not be positioned opposite one another, so they were constructed at right angles. It is not possible to associate the Cilgerran kiln with any particular work at the castle, although in the fourteenth century major works were undertaken in two areas. It is, therefore, somewhat surprising that the kiln chamber was built so small, for this would have meant that its production rate would have been slow (Craster 1950–1; 1983).

Figure 9.2 Limekiln, Portchester Castle

Tools associated with a number of trades or crafts have been found at several castles. No doubt they were used in connection with works and routine maintenance undertaken on the castle buildings. Three types of woodworking tools were discovered at Goltho; there were two claw hammers, two auger bits and an adze. One of the Goltho bits was big enough to make mortises for the construction of the timber buildings at the castle. Other early auger bits have come from Bramber and Castle Neroche, both dating to the late eleventh or twelfth century. A particularly fine example, with the remains of another, comes from Threave Castle, associated with the Douglas period of the late fourteenth and first half of the fifteenth century (Good and Tabraham 1981: 112, 115).

The artefactual evidence for the work of masons is by no means prolific; this may be explained by the fact that after the construction of a castle a mason would have departed, taking his tools with him. A trowel and a wedge of the late fifteenth century come from Sandal, as does a mason's compass, and at Okehampton a fourteenth-century lead plumb-bob was recovered. The daily work of masons, however, can also be seen from the masons' marks carved in ashlar blocks so that the work of each mason could be checked and the number of blocks counted to enable a mason to be paid his due. Fine examples are preserved at Flint and Raglan, and at Skenfrith twelve different marks were revealed when the west range of the castle was investigated; several identical marks also appear at Llanthony Priory, Monmouthshire, where there was also a major programme of building in the early thirteenth century. A total of thirty-seven different marks have been identified at Sandal, and a table of comparisons made giving details of other buildings where the same marks appear, emphasizing the mobility of the medieval mason as he moved from one contract to another.

Although destruction and stone-robbing have often led to only a bare outline plan of a building being left for the archaeologist, some sites have yielded up the remains of fixtures and fittings, such as roofing materials, glass, and architectural fragments. This has enabled us to obtain a more complete picture of these buildings than otherwise might have been possible. The vulnerability of chimneys to damage, particularly by stormy weather, has meant that few survive to be seen in castles today, although Christchurch in Hampshire has a fine example of the twelfth century, and there is a tall chimney dating to the fourteenth century at Grosmont, Monmouthshire. The fact that the majority of the remains of chimney pots found on excavations date to the fourteenth century or later may be interpreted as confirmation of just how prone these objects were to damage. It is most unlikely, for example, that the newly-built thirteenth-century domestic buildings at Sandal did not have chimneys, although the fragments recovered have been dated to a later period.

However, parts of chimney-pots of twelfth- and thirteenth-century date are known. The examples from Pleshey are of baked clay, closely paralleling examples from the Continent. The earliest are attributed to the period post-1140 to the early 1200s, whilst the later type is dated to somewhere between 1180 and the late thirteenth or early fourteenth century. At least one of the chimneys at Pleshey was polygonal and made of brick. Evidence for seven baked clay chimney-pots has come from the outer bailey at Portchester, and although mainly attributed to the thirteenth and fourteenth centuries, one example was Norman. The inner bailey at Portchester also had clay chimney-pots, the majority associated with the refurbishment and rebuilding that were a feature of the fourteenth century. The tall stone chimney at Grosmont suggests that this aspect of roof furniture was becoming more elaborate from the late thirteenth/early fourteenth century, and this is borne out by the remains of other stone examples found at castles, Criccieth for example (O'Neil 1944–5: 43–4; see also Wood 1965: 281–91). The Conisbrough ashlar chimney, originally part of a fireplace in the gatehouse, was octagonal with a circular flue and a surround of ball-flower carving. Another octagonal chimney came from the domestic ranges rebuilt at Okehampton in the early fourteenth century, and various fragments of late medieval circular and octagonal ashlar chimneys were found at Sandal.

Other forms of roof furniture for which there is considerable evidence, notably from Sandal, include tiles and slates, ridge-tiles, and finials; flattish roofs would have been covered with lead, the metal long since robbed for reuse. Earthenware tiles roofed the hall at Goltho (dated about 1150), and also many of the domestic buildings at Sandal in the thirteenth century. Stone tiles were also used at Sandal in the thirteenth century, although some date to the fifteenth century and may be associated with the works ordered by Richard III, whereas west country slate was found in fourteenth-century contexts at Portchester. Documentary evidence shows that slate from the west of England was being used at Portchester from 1180. Sandal has produced a large quantity of ridge-tiles, all made in the kiln in the bailey (p.164). The shape of these tiles varies, and no doubt they reflect the pitch of the roofs for which they were intended. Roofs clad with tiles must be more steeply pitched than roofs with thatch or shingles, hence the difference in the design of ridge-tiles. Ridge-tiles were also found in the outer bailey at Portchester; ceramic roof-tiles were rare here, and as with the buildings in the inner bailey west of England slate seems to have been the main material used. It is interesting to note that the fourteenth-century hall in the west country castle of Okehampton was roofed with ceramic tiles rather than slate, even though stone tiles or slates were brought for the castle in 1422.

Architectural fragments other than chimneys have been found at a number of sites, and provide an indication that although the glories of the medieval carver in stone are best seen in our ecclesiastical monuments, the castle was not always the bare and stark building it is sometimes made out to be. At Castle Acre the main stone used was the local chalk and flint, with architectural details made of stone from Barnack in Northamptonshire. Barnack had one of the great limestone quarries of the middle ages, and was a source of good quality stone much used in East Anglia. The Castle Acre fragments include the base of a shaft which may have been part of arcading on the outside of the keep, and the remains of corbels, one being a human head with a hairstyle in keeping with a late eleventh-century date.

A carved head and another piece of Romanesque carving from Okehampton have been compared with late twelfth-century carved stonework in some churches in Devon and Cornwall, and it may be that the sculptors responsible for the work in these churches were brought to Okehampton in the 1170s or 1180s to assist in the work on a new building, perhaps even a chapel.

Thirteenth-century examples of corbels include the head associated with the Welsh phase (early thirteenth century) of Degannwy (figure 9.3). The Degannwy head may represent the likeness of Llywelyn ab Iorwerth, the lord of the first castle. Another handsome corbel depicts a woman's head wearing a wimple, this example coming from the solar of the castle at Stamford. Sandal has also produced a range of carved stonework, including pieces of animal and human sculpture, mostly of fourteenth-century date. Some were external features, such as gargoyles and fragments of string-courses, and others came from inside buildings. Two fifteenth-century items of note are a rainwater spout in the form of a falcon and a knight's head with chain-mail surmounted by a chaplet or garland of suns and roses; the knight figure may have been part of a string-course, or mounted free-standing on the battlements in the manner of such castles as Alnwick and Chepstow.

The fragments from the chapel at Pleshey suggest that there was a major refurbishment of the building in the late fourteenth century, possibly when the castle was in the hands of Thomas of Woodstock, and when the floor of the

Figure 9.3   Corbel from Degannwy Castle

chapel was retiled. A lead ventilator with a floral design which was probably positioned to one side of a window is a further indication of the decoration of the chapel.

Some window glass has been mentioned in earlier chapters (p.124), but one of the earliest castles in which it has been found is Ascot Doilly with its plain glass from a window in the early twelfth-century keep. Despite this example, glass does not seem to have been common in non-royal castles until later in the thirteenth century. Fragments found at Dover may be as early as the time of King John (1199–1216) (Cook *et al.* 1969: 85, 101), and later in the same century when the hall at Eynsford was rebuilt (*c.* 1240) decorated glass was set in the windows. Fragments dating to the thirteenth and fourteenth centuries have been found at Bramber, Bedford, which produced painted and coloured fragments, and Sandal, with several examples of plain and decorated pieces.

Two fragments from Okehampton are likely to be associated with the great rebuilding of the domestic ranges from about 1300.

There is documentary evidence for plain and decorated window glass at Portchester in the late fourteenth century, although none was found from the excavations of the inner bailey, whose buildings would have contained much of the glass. This lack can be explained from the excavations which had been undertaken in the outer bailey, for it was discovered that some time in the early sixteenth century the glass, together with plaster, tiles and slates, was used to fill in an old gully, presumably following the clearance of and repairs to the inner bailey ranges.

Although most British castles have been roofless and ruined for centuries, the remains of plaster adhering to the internal walls of halls, chambers and other rooms may still be found. Traces of decoration on the plaster occasionally survives, often as vertical and horizontal red lines painted on a white background in order to give the impression of blocks of ashlar. This pattern can be seen in Marten's Tower, Chepstow, and the chapel at Okehampton, whilst further evidence for 'false ashlar' at Okehampton came from wall-plaster fragments found in the hall. At Castle Acre the late twelfth-century fill of one of the buildings of the upper ward contained pieces of chalk which were painted red and yellow, whilst the hall at Hadleigh in about 1300 had geometric patterns painted in red on its walls.

Militaria

Spurs and arrowheads have been found at a number of sites, but other categories of equipment, such as hand weapons and armour, are much rarer.

The two types of spur (prick and rowel) are well represented in castle excavations. The prick-spur is the earlier form, dating to the eleventh, twelfth and thirteenth centuries, but in the thirteenth century the point behind the heel was gradually replaced by a rowel with six or more points. Late eleventh- and twelfth-century prick-spurs are known from Castle Acre, Goltho and Portchester, and thirteenth- and fourteenth-century spurs with rowels have been found at Bramber, Castle Acre, Hadleigh and Lochmaben. The Castle Acre spur is a particularly early example of a rowel-spur, dating to the first half of the thirteenth century. Most spurs (of both types) are of iron, usually with a coating of tin, but Sandal has produced copper-alloy examples from a late fifteenth-century context.

Arrowheads are notoriously difficult to date, although some excavations have been able to provide good dated contexts. Most were for military use, and some of these were designed specifically to pierce armour, but others may well have been for hunting. Several castles have produced one or more arrowheads, but the best collections of eleventh- and twelfth-century examples have come from Castle Acre and Goltho. Thirteenth-century and later examples are known from Bramber, Brandon and Baile Hill, York. Some of the arrowheads from Bramber, and the majority from Brandon, are remarkable for their size, one at Brandon being about 190mm in length. Such heavy arrows must have been intended for use against armoured men in order to shatter the plate armour. The more than thirty arrowheads found at Baile Hill probably result from the motte having been used as an archery butt in the late medieval and post-medieval periods, but the finds included one with a forked terminal which must have been used in hunting. Another example of this type came from Hadleigh, whilst a barbed and socketed arrow with a large head from Sandal has also been interpreted as for use in the hunt.

Some of the Baile Hill arrowheads were bolts or quarrels for crossbows. Dover Castle has produced a thirteenth-century example of a crossbow bolt, and in this connection it is interesting to note that the castle has the earliest example of a tower (the late twelfth-century Avranches Tower) built with slits specifically designed for use by crossbowmen (Renn 1969). Cruggleton has produced an example of a bolt of uncertain date, and at least one from Portchester is likely to be thirteenth century. Another form of evidence for the use of crossbows in castles comes from finds of bone or antler 'nuts' (Credland 1980). The nut formed part of the release mechanism, holding back the bowstring when the crossbow was cocked (Wilson 1976: 2–4). A twelfth-century example has come from the keep at Wareham, Dorset (Renn 1960: 61–2), and another, probably from the late fifteenth century, was discovered at Sandal. Crossbow nuts found at other castles at various dates include Castell-y-Bere, and an example of uncertain date was found at Urquhart, Inverness-shire (MacGregor 1975–6: 318). The crossbow nut found at Goltho has been attributed to the late Saxon phase, prior to the construction of the castle, but as the crossbow was not a weapon used by the Saxons it is more likely that the nut belongs to the Norman period of occupation.

Discoveries of other forms of militaria are rarer. A fragment of fourteenth-century armour came from Bramber, and links from chain-mail were found at Threave in late fourteenth- or fifteenth-century contexts. Buckles and buckle-plates from armour were discovered at Sandal, and other forms of weaponry such as spears and javelins have come from Goltho dating to the late eleventh or early twelfth century, and from Dover in a late twelfth- or thirteenth-century context, as well as late medieval examples from Sandal. This Yorkshire castle also produced a silver chape from the end of a scabbard.

Artillery shot was found at Bedford, associated with the siege of 1224–5, and at Dolforwyn and Dryslwyn, besieged by the English in 1277 and 1287 respectively, presumably fired into the castles from the siege lines. Although gunpowder artillery and handguns begin to be mentioned more frequently in historical records from the second half of the fourteenth century, little evidence for this weaponry has come from excavations. At Threave thirty-four examples of stone cannonshot were retrieved from the harbour and ditch. They are difficult to date, and may have been used for small wrought-iron cannon in the seventeenth century, but it is equally possible that they formed part of the armament associated with the artillery defences built about 1450; in 1512 a quarrier is recorded as having supplied a gun at Threave with shot. Some unfinished stone cannonballs were also found at the castle, which showed that they were roughly shaped at the quarry before being delivered to the castle where the cube-shaped shot would have been chiselled and polished into shape.

Household objects

Pottery vessels of various types are the most common items under this category, and little more will be said here other than to give some idea of the range of objects which might be found. Other examples of household objects are much rarer, but some of the finds have helped to provide a better idea of life in a castle.

Artificial light would have been provided by cresset-lamps, candlesticks and lanterns, and some examples of the first two types have been found. An early example has come from Launceston, carved from local stone, associated with a Henry I penny dating to about 1120–5; the main distinguishing feature is its pierced handle which has few parallels (Saunders 1978). A stone cresset of uncertain date was found in a pit at Portchester, and a late thirteenth- or early fourteenth-century example came from Bramber. Pottery lamps of the late eleventh or early twelfth century were amongst the finds from Castle Acre. Finds of candlesticks or holders include an iron fragment from Lochmaben and one of bronze from Conisbrough, with a fine bronze example dating to the fifteenth century coming from Laugharne (Avent 1977: 20–1). A notable find from Knaresborough was a lamp made of glass, probably imported from the Mediterranean in the thirteenth or fourteenth century (Le Patourel 1966: 607).

Other objects of glass have been found, but the remains are usually fragmentary. Several examples of urinals have come from castles, including Conisbrough, Hadleigh, Laugharne, Pleshey (Rahtz 1960: 25) and Richard's Castle and, whilst medieval pottery urinals were found at Sandal, glass examples dating to the 1500s were found in the garderobes. Sandal produced a quantity of other glass vessels, and most of these appear to have been used for an industrial process such as distillation, as did one vessel from Bramber. Another basic household glass object besides the urinal was the linen-smoother, the one from Therfield probably dating to the eleventh or twelfth century, and another of uncertain date comes from Conisbrough. Finer glass is even rarer on castle sites, although parts of various vessels have come from Hadleigh, including a bowl which may have been French in origin, and flasks. An exceptional discovery was the remains of a yellow and blue stemmed 'chalice' from Knaresborough, possibly Venetian and dating to about 1400; it may be associated with a period when the castle was in the control of the king, as indeed the lamp mentioned above may have been.

Mortars for pounding and grinding were items that would have been found in most kitchens, and some castles have produced several examples. One of the Portchester examples, dating to the thirteenth or fourteenth century, was made of Purbeck marble, and had pierced handles; a second mortar of uncertain date was made of a much coarser stone. The date range of the nine mortars from Sandal is from the thirteenth to the fifteenth or sixteenth century, and Hadleigh is another castle where several mortars have been found, dating to about 1300 and later. Not all mortars were stone; one from Castell-y-Bere was a pottery import from north-west France, and decorated with face-masks. Other imports are represented by the remains of Caen stone mortars, examples of which have come from Dover and Sandal.

The range of pottery vessels that one would expect to find in a medieval household is best seen in the evidence from major excavations. However, sites occupied for a long period of time present problems as far as pottery analysis is concerned, for such castles would have been kept relatively clean, and even if considerable amounts of material were dumped in ditches, such as the barbican ditch at Sandal, recutting and scouring of ditches in the medieval period must have destroyed crucial evidence. Both Castle Acre and Sandal provide a good variety of medieval pottery, the various forms including cooking pots, jugs, bottles, costrels, curfews, pitchers, cups, bowls, skillets and plates. Sandal also provided a range of imports from the Continent, including stoneware. Wooden vessels may have been more common than one might think from the general lack of evidence for this type of artefact, but only one castle, Threave, has produced a range of bowls and plates. These date to the Douglas period (late fourteenth and first half of the fifteenth century) and some of the items are stamped with a heart, the Douglas family badge.

Costume

Buckles, shoes, jewellery, lace-ends, pins and combs are the usual evidence for dress found in excavations. Clothing has rarely survived, although a considerable amount was dumped by the inhabitants of Oxford in the barbican ditch. Although illuminated manuscripts and paintings are a rich source for medieval costume, the finds from excavations do throw further light on the minutiae of this subject. Copper-alloy buckles and belt fastenings have come from Bramber and Sandal. The majority of the lace-ends at Sandal date to the later fifteenth century, a time when these objects appear to have become more common in the fastening of costume. Their form is usually of rolled sheet metal, with one end closed up, and sometimes secured by a pin. Hadleigh has also produced a range of these ends.

Items of personal jewellery include rings, brooches and pendants. The decorated penannular brooches and finger-rings from Castle Acre are copper-alloy, as was a third ring which was white in appearance and had a setting for a stone. Silver wire rings (perhaps ear-rings) are known from Sandal, whilst a fine gold ring with a garnet, dating to about 1200, came from the garderobe of the solar at Stamford. A circular and a hexagonal brooch came from Bramber, the hexagonal having grooved bosses for decoration at each corner. Although a silver locket at Threave was found in an unstratified context (in the backfill of earlier excavations), it has been assigned to the fifteenth century for stylistic reasons. One side was removable so that some form of memento could be kept inside it.

Although pins have been found on a number of medieval excavations there has been little study of these objects, particularly those made of metal; carved bone pins by their ornateness have tended to attract greater attention. Two castles in particular have produced a large quantity of these objects, Sandal and Castle Acre. The pins would seem to have been mainly used with clothing, although one cannot be totally certain of this; there have been suggestions that bone examples may have been used as gaming pieces or even pointers to enable someone to follow text in a manuscript. Over 100 metal pins and wires came from Sandal, the majority dating to the middle ages. The twenty-four carved bone pins from Castle Acre date from the late eleventh to the twelfth century, and include several with decorated heads. It has been suggested that the decorated pins were designed to be seen, and that as most of them have short shafts they were more likely to have been used with head-dress as opposed to holding clothing together. The small silver pin from Castlehill of Strachan may have had a similar purpose, but the longer bronze example could have been used for securing clothing such as a cloak.

Pastimes

Evidence for gaming has come from a number of recent excavations, both gaming counters and 'boards' on which various games were played. Other pastimes for which evidence has been discovered include sewing and the playing of music.

The remains associated with board games are found more often in twelfth- and thirteenth-century contexts rather than later. Bone dice from Castle Acre have been dated to the twelfth century, and the one from Threave belongs to the late fourteenth or first half of the fifteenth century. A series of bone counters with ring-and-dot decoration from Castle Acre dates to the same period as the dice. A crude counter also came from the castle, made from a sherd of pottery. Ring-and-dot bone counters were associated with the final Saxon phase of occupation at Goltho (1000–80), and have been discovered in late twelfth-century contexts at Loughor, as was possibly the box in which they were kept, whereas the Portchester gaming piece has been dated to the twelfth or thirteenth century. A particularly fine ivory counter came from the garderobe of the keep of Brandon Castle; the circular piece has at its centre a collared griffin, an animal with the head of an eagle and the body of a lion. Later medieval gaming-pieces include the shale counters from Threave. The most exciting find, however, as far as games are concerned was the discovery in a late eleventh-century pit at Gloucester of 150 pieces of carved bone (figure 9.4) (Stewart 1988; Stewart and Watkins 1984). They represented the remains of a board for the game known as tables (*tabula*), a form of backgammon, and together with these finely decorated pieces was the full set of thirty counters (figure 9.5). The central carving of the counters or tablemen varies, but include a centaur with a bow and a harpist sitting on a stool. It is not possible to say why the tables set was thrown away; although it seems that the board had been broken before it was discarded, that would not have been a reason for throwing out the thirty counters.

Chess pieces were also found associated with the counters at Loughor, and it was possible to identify one as a knight and another as a pawn. The pawn is thimble-shaped and hexagonal, and is closely paralleled by a find from the castle at Totnes. Various small pieces of carved chalk from Castle Acre may well be twelfth-century gaming pieces, although it cannot be said for what game. However, one with a crenellated top might have been a castle in a chess set.

Castle Acre has also produced several examples of twelfth-century graffiti gaming boards, designs crudely scratched on pieces of stone, and possibly soon discarded. Three of these, with fragments of others, were for merels, otherwise known as nine men's morris, whilst a fourth was a tables board. All four

Figure 9.4   View of the Gloucester *tabula* set during excavation

boards are rather rough and ready in appearance, and it would seem unlikely that they were devised for permanent parlour games. Pieces of merels boards dating to the fifteenth century were excavated at Okehampton, incised into slates, another west country example was found at Launceston, and a medieval board has also come from Peel Castle, Isle of Man (White 1986: 30, 60).

The main evidence for sewing and spinning comes in the form of thimbles and whorls. Thimbles do not tend to appear in contexts much earlier than the

Figure 9.5 Four tablemen from the Gloucester *tabula* set: the Virgin (top left); musician with rebec (top right); archer (bottom left); two birds (bottom right)

mid fourteenth century (Holmes 1988). An example from Sandal has been broadly dated to *c*. 1270–*c*. 1400, but the majority belong to the late medieval or post-medieval occupation levels. A thimble lighter than the Sandal examples was found at Bramber, and was probably in use in the fourteenth century, as was another solitary find, this time from Burton-in-Lonsdale (Moorhouse 1971: 94, 96). Other late medieval thimbles were found at Threave. Spindle whorls are known from a number of sites, but not in great numbers. They are either made of metal, pottery or stone, each whorl having acted as the fly wheel at the base of a spindle. Lead examples are known from Hen Blas, Llantrithyd and Threave, the last also producing stone examples. Further stone whorls come from Castle Acre and Totnes. Clearance at Castell-y-Bere produced a single pottery example.

A number of bone pipes or flutes were recovered from castles in the nineteenth and early twentieth centuries, one of which, discovered at White Castle in the 1920s, has been published in detail (Megaw 1961); it probably dates to the late thirteenth century. Two pipes have since come from Castle Acre, the largest carved from a sheep bone, the smallest from the bone of a goose; they are both mid twelfth century in date. The castle has also produced the remains of a jew's harp which may be medieval, but could be later. Other bone pipes come from Rayleigh, *c.* 1300 (Helliwell and Macleod 1981: 68), and Okehampton, where an unfinished bone piece was discovered in the fill of a fourteenth-century pit. One other type of musical instrument represented in castle excavations is the harp; at Dolforwyn a carved bone harp peg was discovered in the courtyard of this native Welsh fortress.

One very important pastime that was both practical as well giving pleasure has already been touched upon above. It was noted that amongst the collections of arrowheads there occur some types which would have been used for hunting as opposed to warfare. Further evidence for hunting comes from the remains of birds of prey retrieved from environmental deposts. Although bird remains are discussed in the following section (as food), it is more relevant to mention hunting birds here. At Llantrithyd, an early Norman ringwork in the Vale of Glamorgan, the bones of goshawks and a young sparrow hawk were found, as well as the remains of several rooks. The falconers may well have released their birds against rooks as part of their training, a custom not unknown today. The bones of hunting birds were found at Portchester in the twelfth-century deposits, but none in the later middle ages, so it may have been that other methods such as netting were used in order to provide food for the table. At Hadleigh a male merlin was part of the household in the late middle ages. Although no remains of hunting birds were identified at Sandal, a small bell is likely to have been part of an attachment to a leg of a hawk, as in fact depicted in fragments of painted glass from the castle.

Food and diet

A particular aspect of medieval archaeology in recent years, and mainly associated with large-scale excavations, is the development of the detailed specialist report on faunal and floral remains. It has, therefore, been possible to learn more about the medieval diet, the corpus of material supplementing the information that exists in household accounts, at least for the upper echelons of society. The analysis of plant remains has also made it possible to provide an idea of the environment in the vicinity of a castle in the middle ages, such as Hen Domen and Sandal. A useful survey of the historical and archaeological sources for diet towards the end of the middle ages is provided by Platt (1978: 184–91), whilst Alcock has discussed some of the problems that can be associated with the archaeological evidence (Alcock 1987: 16–19).

Assuming that most of the animal and plant remains were discarded as kitchen refuse, it is not always possible to state whether the remains represent food prepared for the lord of a castle or the servants and garrison. Nevertheless, some types of meat such as venison were presumably for the lord's table, and no doubt both lord and servant ate beef, mutton and other meats, the only difference being that the better cuts went to the high table. It is also impossible to know just how representative the collection of bones is, and whether, therefore, it is possible to gain an accurate picture of the diet at a particular castle at any given time. As Alcock mentions, sieving has not always been used to collect biological remains on castle excavations, so that small bones, of both animals and fish, and plant remains will be missing from the evidence. Another factor is that not all bones will be preserved, especially if the soil in which they have been concealed is acidic or if the material thrown out had come from young animals, with the bones not yet completely ossified. Another factor, mentioned in the report on the Portchester fish material, is that some bones may well represent species which reached the castle in the guts of larger fish. Nevertheless, allowing for such shortcomings, botanical and zoological specialist reports, even with a small amount of material, do help to illustrate the dietary aspect of castle life, and tend to confirm that much of what is eaten today was being eaten in the middle ages.

Household accounts will naturally throw light on aspects of food and diet that cannot be obtained from the archaeological record. For example, an examination of the 1420–1 accounts of Elizabeth Berkeley, Countess of Warwick, informs us that 18,950 gallons of ale were consumed in that period. The document also lists the quantities of foodstuffs purchased, as well as the range of spices used in the preparation of food (Ross 1951).

Castle reports with useful biological reports include the earth-and-timber castles of Hen Domen, Llantrithyd and Baile Hill, York, whilst the excavations of larger castles such as Portchester, Sandal, Barnard, Hadleigh and Threave have provided a large quantity of evidence for diet and environment. Most excavations have produced quantities of bones from the larger animals such as cattle, sheep/goat (it is almost impossible to separate the two due to bone similarity), as well as deer, whether red, roe or fallow (or all three). Pork was another meat that was served at the table. At Hadleigh the amount of rib-bones and vertebrae that was found amongst the kitchen refuse suggests that, at least in the thirteenth century, the preferred cuts of meat were steaks or chops. The remains of deer at some castles, for example Castle Acre and Portchester, were few in number, implying that venison was not a major feature of the diet at these castles. At Llantrithyd deer bones accounted for a large percentage of the bones, although cattle, sheep and pigs were still in greater quantity.

The evidence for particular birds and fish is of considerably more interest when it comes to the study of the medieval diet, although not all the bird remains represent animals eaten. The more common bird remains tend to be goose and fowl, as well as pigeon which were no doubt reared in dovecots close to or within castles. At Okehampton, however, very little pigeon was found, just three fragments from the medieval deposits, and domestic fowl dominated everything else, over 60 per cent of the main species of bird from medieval rubbish being fowl. Other remains included goose, duck, woodcock, with partridge being more common than goose in the fourteenth and the fifteenth century, although the bones came mainly from two particular deposits. Species of other game served up for banquets at Portchester included swan, curlew and woodcock.

Bones of marine fish are found particularly in castles close to the coast or by navigable rivers, and shellfish also formed part of the medieval diet. None of the fish remains from Okehampton, representing at least twenty-seven species, were from a freshwater environment; presumably they were all caught in the fishing grounds around the west country. Sturgeon, herring, eel, bass, mackerel and mullet were just some of the seafood prepared at the castle. Oysters were also consumed, and the analysis of the remains suggests that they were deliberately cultivated, the majority being harvested when three to four years old. Portchester also produced a large range of sea fish, as might be expected from this coastal site, whilst at other sites such as Sandal and Baile Hill in York only a few varieties were represented; these included cod and haddock. In contrast, there were only a few fragments of fish found in the kitchen waste at Threave, in spite of its position on the river Dee.

The examination of the late medieval contents of the kitchen drain at Barnard Castle has revealed details of a late fifteenth-century feast, or perhaps feasts, the remains providing one of the best environmental deposits from a northern site (Austin 1980: 86–96). Plant remains included grain, which may have been intended for a pottage, and peas and sloes. Both freshwater and marine fish formed part of the diet, and included herring, trout, pike, eel and haddock. Oysters, cockles and mussels were also eaten. Goose and fowl dominated the bird remains, with other bones coming from grouse and partridge. Amongst the mammal bones, the larger animals (cattle, pig, sheep/goat) naturally dominated, but there was also deer, hare and rabbit.

It is by no means unknown for reports on artefacts to be generally overlooked by the student of the castle. The more peaceful aspect of castle life has been touched upon by Brown (1976: 200–13), although the information used tends to be documentary and thus relate to royal buildings, but these sources are but one form of evidence. In their useful discussion on the results from Castle Acre, Coad and Streeten, when referring to the information provided by the finds, state that 'Interpretations such as these push the archaeological evidence to the limits of inference but can only be speculative' (Coad and Streeten 1982: 196). Nevertheless, the discoveries have thrown light on the way buildings were built, decorated and furnished, given examples of the food which was eaten, particularly meat, and the way in which people entertained themselves in the middle ages.

It is too much to expect that archaeology, or even historical sources, will provide a complete picture of this aspect of life in a castle throughout its period of occupation, whether it was for a few decades or five hundred years, and of course speculation should not be taken to extremes. What is important is that the two sources, archaeological and historical, should be used in conjunction. This is particularly the case with foodstuffs, for documents such as household accounts provide so much extra information than that obtainable from the archaeological record. However, although we have learnt much about the social aspects of castle life from a number of examples, this is counterbalanced by some sites which, although occupied for a long period and excavated extensively, have produced little in the way of artefacts. The picture gained from the excavations at Hen Domen, for example, suggests that life was austere and simple. In a review of the evidence Barker has commented that at Hen Domen there has been 'nothing, apart from the defences themselves, to suggest that the site was occupied by a succession of wealthy and powerful families' (Barker 1987: 51). The evidence from this fortress on the Welsh border is in marked contrast to the material from Castle Acre.

Part 3

10 *Town defences*

Medieval town defences have tended to be the poor relation as far as studies of medieval military architecture are concerned, and only Harvey's book (1911) has taken both castles and walled towns as its theme. Good examples of upstanding remains are few in number, and they lack the appeal of castles, except for some exceptionally fine walls such as those which are to be seen at York and Conwy. H.M. Turner (1970) provides a useful introduction to the subject with a gazetteer, and more recent general surveys of the subject will be found in Barley (1976) and Bond (1987). T.P. Smith (1985) has emphasized most cogently that the primary function of these walls was defensive, in contrast to some recent statements which he cites suggesting that other factors played a greater role, status for example. As far as descriptions of individual circuits are concerned, one should cite in particular the publications on Canterbury (Frere *et al.* 1982), Exeter (Burrow 1977), Pembroke (King and Cheshire 1982) and York (RCHM 1972b).

Anyone using this author's bibliographies (1978; 1983) will be made immediately aware that there has been a considerable amount of work undertaken on town defences. However, much of it is piecemeal, not really producing results that merit a mention in this chapter. Worcester is a case in point. The medieval city has been the subject of an issue of the *Trans. Worcestershire Archaeol. Soc.* (3rd series 7, 1980), and there are several sections on the defences, including a valuable documentary history. However, as much of the archaeological work was undertaken by machine in advance of the construction of a bypass, it was mainly a case of uncovering the medieval wall and recording it, although some areas received a more exhaustive examination.

The precise number of defended towns in Britain in the middle ages is not known, but Bond has stressed that the figure for post-Roman sites has risen considerably since Turner's publication which listed over 130 examples, and one school of thought has suggested that the final number may be as high as 200 (Bond 1987: 92). The origin and development of medieval town defences are varied. In several instances towns in the post-Conquest period were able to make use of earlier defences, such as the Roman walls at Lincoln and Gloucester, and the Saxon ramparts at Hereford and Wareham, although a certain amount of work would have been required on them by the twelfth and thirteenth centuries, as at Winchester for example (Cunliffe 1962: 60). New circuits built in the twelfth and the early thirteenth century tended to be earth ramparts, presumably surmounted by a timber palisade, and archaeology is increasingly providing us with a greater insight into urban defences of this period. However, it was from the thirteenth century in particular that new stone walls with mural towers and gatehouses were built to enclose the larger towns.

The burden of paying for these works was often alleviated by the granting of a murage tax by the king, a system which had appeared by 1220. This enabled citizens to levy taxes on certain goods brought in from outside their town, the money raised then being used towards the cost of the walls. It was from the mid thirteenth and through the fourteenth century that the great masonry town walls, such as Southampton, Canterbury and Newcastle, were erected. Their construction often took a considerable time, although few towns can rival the time taken at Coventry (almost two centuries), but at Conwy Edward I's defences, begun in 1283, were almost complete by 1287. In contrast to these examples, other towns were only furnished with gates, and cannot be regarded as true defended towns. In other instances the defences enclose such small areas that the term 'town' is a misnomer, and perhaps are best regarded as village fortifications, although the defences at some of these are still impressive as, for example, Castle Acre with its massive rampart and twin-towered gatehouse.

The growth of many towns from the later eighteenth century, particularly in England, has resulted in the destruction of several originally great circuits of walls with gateways and towers, for some centres considered them too restrictive and an obstruction to growth as well as communication, particularly with the development of coach travel. Some towers and stretches of walling survived by being incorporated into later buildings, or were made use of for other activities. For example, the Gunner Tower at Newcastle-upon-Tyne was leased to the Company of Slaters and Tylers in 1821. This particular tower serves as an object lesson in not always to accept what appears to be an old building as necessarily being one, for an excavation inside the D-shaped tower revealed that the structure was a complete refacing of the late nineteenth century, although traces of the original wall were found within (Harbottle 1967).

The different aspects of town walls are examined in four sections, namely ramparts and walls, gateways, mural towers, and ditches, although references are made to some or all of these features in any one section.

Ramparts and walls

The increasing amount of rescue excavation undertaken in towns since the 1970s has led to the investigation of a number of town defences. Although several excavations have simply confirmed the line of a wall and ditch, others have shed light on the development of defences through the middle ages. The majority of the excavations examined in this chapter are either concerned with defences in England or those built by the English in Wales. Very few examples are to be found in Scotland (Bond 1987: 94), and there has been correspondingly less work in that country.

Urban expansion has resulted in the total loss of defences in a large number of cases, Leicester being but one example. The evidence from this town is that the walls were being destroyed in the sixteenth century, if not before, although the ditch was evidently still visible two centuries later and the gates were left standing until 1774. However, work in the 1950s and later has confirmed the line of the Roman and medieval walls in a number of places (Buckley and Lucas 1987). The encroachment on and demolition of a town's defences by its citizens, as at Leicester, is a common enough feature in the post-medieval period, but at Barnstaple in Devon it occurred haphazardly as early as the fourteenth or fifteenth century (Markuson 1980: 78). A similar occurrence took place at Shrewsbury *c.* 1400, when a section of the town walls was levelled almost down to the plinth; the remains of the defences were then used as foundations for new houses (Carver 1977–8).

Excavations other than those at Leicester have also proved invaluable to the understanding of the plan of the defences, but for some instances there has been a different story. The Welsh border town of Oswestry, Shropshire, has provided another aspect to recent work in this field. As in the case with Leicester, Oswestry's walls have long since been razed to the ground, but the line is known in some areas, whilst subject to conjecture in others. Excavations in 1979–80, however, found no traces of the wall, a result which is almost as valuable as discovering the defences themselves, allowing corrections to be made to the conjectural plan (Border Counties Archaeological Group n.d.: 34–40).

Later in the middle ages many twelfth-century earth-and-timber defences were improved by the addition of a stone wall, usually with mural towers, whilst others never progressed from the earth-and-timber stage. The early twelfth-century ramparts which surrounded the Norman town and castle of Devizes, Wiltshire, possibly built by *c.* 1121, fall into this last category (Haslam 1977–8). Unfortunately, very little remained of the bank at Devizes, for medieval and post-medieval expansion has removed all evidence of the nature of the original ramparts. In other towns a similar occurrence has been the result of the addition of a wall to the original bank. Taunton in Somerset also had a bank and ditch, first recorded in 1158, and there excavations have also indicated that the town never had a stone wall, even when the fortifications were improved in 1215–16 (Leach 1984: 59–74). The defences at Richard's Castle, which may date to *c.* 1200, also simply consisted of a bank and ditch; no trace was found of a palisade (Curnow and Thompson 1969: 117–19). A similar story occurred at Wareham, where the Saxon defences, including a stone wall, were remodelled. This probably took place in the twelfth or early thirteenth century, and it led to the rescarping of the rampart and the redigging of the ditch; it is likely that the bank had a timber palisade, for there is no evidence for a post-Conquest stone wall around the town (RCHM 1959: 128–30).

Not all town defences which were built of earth-and-timber, and which remained so, were Norman in date. Those at Tonbridge, Kent, were probably built about 1260 following a licence to enclose granted in 1259; the town also received a murage grant in 1318 for three years, presumably to repair and improve the existing fortifications. Excavations, although on a small scale, have indicated that there was never a stone wall about the town (Streeten 1976).

The town fortifications associated with the foundation of the Edwardian castle of Rhuddlan, Flintshire, in 1277 were constructed with a rampart fronted by a wide flat-bottomed ditch, a counterscarp bank on the far side, and a palisade. Rhuddlan, like Flint but unlike Conwy and Caernarfon, never had a stone wall surrounding the Edwardian borough (Miles 1971–2: 7–8). In other instances, whereas the main circuit consisted of an earth bank with palisade, the gateways may have been built of masonry. An example of this comes from Ipswich, Suffolk, a town where an early thirteenth-century earth rampart was built along the line of the old Saxon defences (West 1963) but with the West

Gate being of masonry (Owles 1971). A further example is the standing Bargate at Southampton, the main entrance through the medieval walls; the building incorporates a twelfth-century gate which may have been associated with the earth-and-timber defences of the town, although the rampart may not have been built until *c*. 1202.

Another town which had extensive Saxon fortifications is Hereford, and the post-Conquest defences followed the same line on the south-west and south-east, but with a new circuit in the northern sector to enclose a greater area, and possibly a short stretch of wall to the south of the river Wye (Shoesmith 1982). This refortification and extension was undertaken in the late twelfth century, for there is reference to the construction of four gates (perhaps of timber) in 1190; the defences themselves consisted of a gravel rampart. The bank at its base was probably *c*. 15m wide and 3m high, but no evidence was found for a palisade. However, there may have been a fence of some description which has left little trace archaeologically, and fences may also account for the absence of palisades at other towns. The only real evidence for a structure on the bank was traces of what may have been a wooden internal tower. Hereford is one of several towns which had their twelfth-century earth-and-timber defences rebuilt with a stone curtain and mural towers in the thirteenth century. In some areas the new wall fronted the Norman rampart, and in other areas it was cut into the pre-existing defences; altogether there were six gates and a minimum of seventeen mural towers flanking the walls.

The gravel and sand rampart at Newark, Nottinghamshire, was formed by dump construction, a method employed at other sites; there was no evidence for timber-lacing to hold the bank together, although at least one side of the circuit was revetted with masonry. In the early fourteenth century a stone wall was added along the top of the rampart (Todd 1974; 1977). Although one excavation at Nottingham produced some doubt as to whether the thirteenth-century town wall did in fact replace a Norman rampart (Ponsford 1971), later work has shown that this was the case (Carter 1971). The stone defences were cut into the earlier bank, and the circuit was surrounded by a ditch; evidence for the ditch associated with the Norman defences was not forthcoming. At Norwich the defences were built from the early thirteenth century, destroying several small houses or huts in the process (Hurst, J.G. 1963: 139). The stone walls were built mainly in the first half of the fourteenth century, although the work began in the 1290s. In the St Benedict's Gates area of the town excavations revealed that when the walls were constructed a large section of the bank was removed, creating a U-shaped trench. This was then filled with material to form a firm foundation for the wall (Hurst and Golson 1955: 24–30).

The carefully laid foundations at Norwich were not matched at Southampton where the defences also consisted originally of a bank and ditch, an outer ditch being added later. Excavations on the north-east section showed that the foundations consisted only of about three courses of masonry, on top of which was built a thin wall which had to be supported by a bank. Southampton's walls originally ran along the north and east sides of the town, the sea and merchants' wharves lying on the other undefended sides. As mentioned above, the original earth-and-timber defences were probably begun in the early 1200s, whilst the masonry wall began to be added to the earthworks later in the thirteenth century. However, at the north-east corner the poor quality wall is likely to have been built in the late fourteenth century, an indication that at several towns the process of walling in stone took many years. The wall was certainly built after the late thirteenth-century circular Polymond Tower which lies at the extreme north-east corner of the town, as the two were not bonded together. When a comparison is made between the width of this wall (0.76m) with other town defences (Bath 1.9m, Bristol 1.5–2.5m, Newcastle 2.1m) it can be seen just how poor a construction the late medieval work at Southampton was. The weakness of the fourteenth-century curtain was recognized in the following century, for a trench was dug into the rampart immediately behind the wall and filled with masonry in order to strengthen the defences at this point (Wacher 1975: 142–7, 149). A similar thickening occurred at Swansea, but here the original width was a more substantial 1.4m (Lightfoot 1979), and another example, Dryslwyn, will be discussed below.

Other excavations have taken place in towns where early earth-and-timber defences were later supplanted by a stone circuit. These include Warwick, where the new defences may have been very early, possibly the late eleventh century (Klingelhofer 1976–7), as was the Norman work at York (Radley 1972: 49–50). However, as intimated above, the peak period for the building, or rebuilding, of town defences in stone was the thirteenth and fourteenth centuries. Examples of some of these have been mentioned above where they formed the refortification of an existing circuit, such as Norwich and Southampton, but other useful research on town walls has been undertaken at Shrewsbury, Oxford, Hull and several other sites.

The wall at Shrewsbury was built in the first half of the thirteenth century, and the excavations at Roushill, not far from the old Welsh Bridge entrance into the town, provided an insight into the building of the defences. Before construction began the area was cleared down to the natural clay which was then partly scarped. The waste clay was then used to form a low bank and it was fronted by a stone wall, the foundations of which were set deep in a trench. The exterior of the wall was formed of sandstone ashlar (figure 10.1), with coursed rubble against the clay bank. A core of rubble lay between the two faces, and the whole wall was 1.37m wide. A large pit (*c.* 1.8m wide and at least 2.5m deep) dug into the bank behind the wall revealed traces of lime, and must have been used for slaking lime for the mortar used in the building operations. The wall was built with a stepped plinth at its base, following the line of the slope of the ground. A cobbled path ran behind the defences, and there may have been wooden steps leading up to the wall-walk; a similar path lay in front of the defences, with a low bank running parallel with it. When the wall was constructed the marshy ground in front of it made a ditch unnecessary, although by the fourteenth century much of the marshland had dried up (Barker 1961).

At Oxford in the late 1200s an attempt was made to build a concentric defence on the north-east side of the city, with two lines of curtain running parallel with each other (figure 10.2). Although a document of 1484 mentions two walls as being in existence as early as 1311, the first archaeological evidence for this system, unique in Britain, came with excavations in 1974–5. Much of the inner wall with its mural towers still stands in the grounds of New College, and dates to about the middle of the thirteenth century. The later outer wall,

LIME PIT

Figure 10.1   The town wall, Roushill, Shrewsbury (after Barker 1961)

which also had towers, was built into the outer scarp of the city ditch, and the main feature revealed in the initial excavations was a stairwell which led down to a postern (Palmer 1976). Further excavation in 1980 to the west of the original archaeological site confirmed that the outer wall had been built in the city ditch, with about 10m separating the two lines of fortifications, the ditch then being infilled. This outer defensive line was only about 1m thick, implying that it was lower than the inner wall, as would be expected with a concentric fortification (Durham *et al.* 1983: 27–8, 37–8).

Figure 10.2   Reconstruction of the concentric town defences of Oxford (after Durham *et al.* 1983)

Some towns were associated with the outer bailey of a castle, for not only were they founded in close proximity to a castle but the areas which the boroughs occupied were minute when compared to other urban centres. Barnard Castle is one such example, and another is Dryslwyn (figure 10.3) which was surrounded by a wall and ditch, and although most of its documentation dates to the period when the castle was in English hands (post-1287) it may have been founded before that period. The town expanded in the late thirteenth and early fourteenth century so that by 1324 it was granted a weekly market. The excavations at Dryslwyn have concentrated on the inner bailey of the castle (p.35), but some work has been undertaken in the town. The section of town wall uncovered was in reality a double wall. The outer line was the earlier, for when the wall was strengthened with a second line, the later wall was built over a timber building which lay against the original defences. A gap in the later wall probably accommodated a flight of wooden steps leading to the wall-walk, but this feature was obscured later by another house. Not enough work has been done to give a dated sequence to these features, but the strengthening of the town wall may have been carried out by the English after the capture of Dryslwyn in 1287 (Webster 1987: 97–8).

Town walls dating to the fourteenth century include Hull, Yorkshire, and Hartlepool, Co. Durham. The interesting feature about the Hull defences, begun in the 1320s, is that they were built of brick, and they had rectangular mural towers; as will be seen below, semi-circular or D-shaped mural towers were the usual design. There was some indication that the brick wall had been added to a clay bank, suggesting that the rampart came first, although brick and stone are listed in accounts for 1321–3 (Bartlett 1970). Although the walls of Hull are depicted in a seventeenth-century view of the town, the little we know about their actual design has come from the limited excavations.

More survives at Hartlepool, largely in the form of the Sandwell Gate. The defences at this port date from about the same time as those at Hull, the first murage grant dating to 1315, the year in which the Scots are said to have burnt the town. Further grants followed during the fourteenth century, and continued into the following century, the grants coming from the Bishop of Durham as well as the Crown. Unlike Hull, the Hartlepool wall was built of stone. The building sequence entailed the digging of a shallow ditch backed by a low bank about 1.5 m high designed to define the defensive line. The ditch was then deepened and

Figure 10.3 Aerial view of Dryslwyn. The castle lies at the top, with the town at the edge of the hill below

made wider, and the rampart was raised to 2m. If this work dates to the years 1315–18, then the wall was probably added soon afterwards, perhaps associated with the murage grants of 1326 onwards (Daniels 1986).

It was mentioned in the introduction to this chapter that very little work has been done on the few medieval walled towns of Scotland. Nevertheless, the work at Perth and Edinburgh has been a useful start. At Perth a large ditch, 20m wide and 5m deep, was a feature of the defences, certainly in the fourteenth century (Holdsworth 1987: 56–8), and at Edinburgh a short section of the King's Wall of *c.* 1425–50 was uncovered, together with a house built against it (Schofield 1975–6: 160, 181). It was not unknown for houses to be built against, or even partially on, town walls, as we have seen at Dryslwyn. At Edinburgh a decree was issued in 1473 ordering the destruction of houses built along the wall; it may even be that the building mentioned above was incorporated into the defences. This occurred at Southampton in the late fourteenth century with the houses of the merchants which fronted the quay; this measure, although unpopular with some of the citizens, enabled the town to become completely walled.

Gateways

The destruction of medieval town gateways was a feature of urban expansion, particularly in the eighteenth and nineteenth centuries, and the loss of all four at Leicester has already been mentioned. Fortunately some remarkable examples still stand, such as the Southampton Bargate and Canterbury's West Gate. Most of the gates that have been lost are known from documentary and pictorial evidence, and a few have also come to light as a result of rescue excavations over the last two decades or so. Most town gates belong to the period which saw the construction of some of the finest castles in the land, so it is not surprising that they were sophisticated buildings in terms of defence. They also had an economic role to play, enabling the burgesses to control merchandise coming into the towns, and were a point where tolls could be paid.

Denbigh's late thirteenth-century Burgess Gate is a very fine example of an extant gatehouse, lacking only its floors and roof. The small defended town at the foot of the Edwardian Castle also had a second entrance, close to the castle, known as the Exchequer Gate. Very little of this remained by the last century, but excavations have shown that it was even larger than the Burgess Gate. Examination of its remains has helped to shed further light on the development of the town defences. Originally, in the 1280s, the short stretch of town wall designed to connect the castle with the Exchequer Gate was intended to run almost due south. The foundations were laid, but the work did not proceed any further as the north front of the castle had yet to be constructed. When this part of the castle, including its main gatehouse, was eventually begun in 1295, there had clearly been a slight change in its plan. If the town wall had been built on the original line it would have met the castle curtain only to leave an angle awkward to defend. So the line was moved slightly to the west to run into one side of the polygonal Red Tower, to the west of the castle's gatehouse. A mural passage in the town wall connected the Red Tower with the

Exchequer gate at first floor level.

The Exchequer Gate itself consisted of twin towers, rectangular within, but with rounded external fronts and buttressed. There is no evidence for a ground floor entrance from the gate passage, but this can best be explained by the fact that most of the passage and the northern gatetower lie under the modern street which cuts across the remains. It is likely, however, by analogy with the Burgess Gate's west tower, that the north tower was entered from the entrance passage, whereas both the east tower of the Burgess Gate and the south tower of the Exchequer Gate had entrances at the back where the gatehouses met the town walls (Smith, C. 1988).

The Roman East Gate at Gloucester may have formed part of the Saxon defences, but it was largely demolished in the early Norman period to make way for another gate. This was replaced in its turn by a twin-towered gatehouse, in keeping with the thirteenth-century work on the town walls. One of the rounded towers of the gate was uncovered in 1974, built against the earlier gate walls (figure 10.4). It had a small postern door which would have led out to the berm between the town wall and ditch, but this was later blocked and converted into a garderobe (Heighway 1983: 53–7). The passage between the towers was defended by at least one portcullis, and probably had double-leaf gates at each end. The addition of the towers to the East Gate serves as a reminder that the citizens of Gloucester were not slow to update their defences according to the fashions of the day, but they do not seem to have undertaken similar work at the North Gate (Heighway 1983: 33).

Another example of a twin-towered gateway is the East Gate at Rochester in Kent, it too being an addition to defences that were originally Roman, and possibly replacing an earlier medieval gate. Here the similarity to Gloucester ends, for at Rochester the building, with the adjacent curtain, dates to the fourteenth century, and probably towards the end of that period. The gate consisted of parallel lengths of wall, at the end and to the side of which were D-shaped towers; the unusual feature of the plan is that the towers project out along the line of the town wall rather than out towards the main approach (Harrison 1972: 125–6, figure 5). The constant threat of French raids on southern England in the second half of the fourteenth century, particularly in the reign of Richard II, led to a considerable amount of work being undertaken on defences on or near the coast, or by navigable rivers, such as the West Gate and several mural towers at Canterbury; the Rochester East Gate may have also been built as a result of those troubled times.

Part of the main gateway through the fourteenth-century defences at Hull, the Beverley Gate, came to light in 1986 (Youngs *et al.* 1987: 147). Like the town walls described above, it was built of brick, and the remains stood to a height of 2.45m. The examination of the gate and a short stretch of the town walls showed that the two had been constructed independently of each other, and that the gate was built with a higher quality of workmanship than the adjacent wall. A guardroom, a socket containing part of the post for the setting of the wooden door, and a length of projecting wall, which was probably part of a barbican in the manner of the gates at York, were revealed. It has been suggested that as the lower courses of the town wall do not bond with the Beverley Gate at least two gangs of bricklayers may have been employed on the defences. Although some bricks in the gate were left to project as toothings so

Figure 10.4   The East Gate, Gloucester

that the town wall could be bonded with the gate the differences in the construction techniques may result from the Beverley Gate having been built a few years before the walls.

The majority of town gates are associated with the main period of the construction of urban defences, the thirteenth and fourteenth centuries. There are later examples, such as the South Gate at King's Lynn, Norfolk, dating from 1437, and the Sandown Gate of 1455 at Sandwich, Kent. This gate was part of a programme of improvements made to Sandwich's defences in the fifteenth century, largely necessary because of the threat of French raids. However, its construction, along with other works, was unable to deter a disastrous French raid in 1457. The gate with its two rounded towers was constructed in brick, which was rendered, although the gate arch was ashlar; the window jambs and the vaulting of the entrance passage may also have been of stone (Tatton–Brown 1978). The advantage of using brick was that it was a cheaper building material than stone, and also easier to stack and bond together due to its regular shape. There is evidence for its use at Hull and several other sites, including the South Gate at King's Lynn where the brick building is ashlar-fronted, and also at Norwich.

Not all gateways were twin-towered structures, however. Work on a section of the walls at Norwich suggested that the St Benedict's Gate, one of several entrances into the city, was simply a square gatetower. Such a basic structure is not unknown in the context of Norman defences where earth-and-timber ramparts had stone gates, as at Southampton, and possibly with Ber Street Gate at Norwich itself. However, the evidence suggests that this gate at Norwich was built in the late thirteenth century or early fourteenth (Hurst and Golson 1955). Although St Benedict's Gate was a small structure, even smaller gateways are found in some defensive circuits, some of them are best interpreted as posterns such as at Oxford. The purpose of the small Ham Gate at Bath was not in any way defensive, and as such could be considered a positive weakness. It was built in the late thirteenth century to provide access from the priory to its agricultural land lying just outside the walls, between the town and the river Avon. It was eventually blocked in 1643, but not for any defensive reason; its closing was due to the insistence that all tolls had to be paid at the four main gates of the city (Wedlake 1965–6).

One of the few posterns in the London city wall had a similar function as the Bath example. It was inserted in the stone defences some time after the middle of the thirteenth century, and blocked probably towards the end of the medieval period when the city wall was strengthened by a series of brick arches, a refortification that had already come to light with the post-war work on the walls (Grimes 1968: 82–4). As with the Ham Gate at Bath it had an ecclesiastical function, linking as it did the Priory of Holy Trinity, Aldgate, with its property just outside the walls (Maloney and Harding 1979: 348–50). Another ecclesiastical postern was built by Franciscan friars in the 1370s at Southampton, connecting the friary to its gardens, and this also was blocked at a later date (Youngs *et al.* 1987: 134, 136). It may seem strange that an extra gateway was provided at Southampton at a time when the town was making strenuous efforts to improve its defensive capabilities, but the postern was part of the 'garret' that the friary had built for the defence of the town. A town would naturally have kept strict control over its gateways for both economic and defensive reasons, but clearly the citizens in some places felt that the provision of additional small gates for religious houses would not be detrimental to their security.

In contrast to the functions of the above gates, the Oxford postern in the outer circuit of the town defences which led down to the ditch between the two walls may have been provided to give access to a stretch of the ditch that was used as fishponds (Palmer 1976: 159). A second and more important postern through the London city wall also had a secular function. This was the Tower Hill Postern which was probably built by 1308, and the remains of which were discovered in 1978. It stood immediately to the north of the Tower of London, and consisted of a three-storeyed tower which overlooked a narrow gate passage with a portcullis. Anyone passing through the postern would have needed to negotiate two right-angle bends before reaching the other side, an unusual security arrangement (Brown and Curnow 1984: 88–90).

Mural towers

Just as the mural tower became a common feature of castles from the early thirteenth century onwards, so it was with town walls. The building of such towers naturally added to the cost of urban defences, and whereas larger towns such as Norwich were able to provide a large number, other towns such as Oswestry depended just on gates and walls. The shape of mural towers could vary, and at Norwich circular, D-shaped and polygonal designs were all used, and a similar variety may still be seen at York, including square examples. However, the most common form overall was semicircular or D-shaped.

There is virtually no evidence for timber towers on town ramparts apart from the possible example at Hereford, dating to the early thirteenth century (Shoesmith 1982: 56). The only chance of finding examples will be where the defences were never rebuilt in stone, and where the ramparts have survived any post-medieval disturbances. Masonry towers, in contrast, have been uncovered at a number of towns. One late thirteenth-century tower at Bristol formed part of the defences built to enclose the area into which the town had expanded that century (Barton 1964). Excavations revealed that the tower still stood to a height of 2.5m, and that it was D-shaped or semicircular in plan; two of its three arrow embrasures survived, both with a wide alcove or standin where archers could be positioned (figure 10.5). This is one of the best examples of a tower with its embrasures for archers, and it would have been a formidable obstacle to an attacker trying to escalade the wall at this point, for there would have been at least one more floor above the existing remains, no doubt similarly furnished with arrowslits, and with battlements and wall-walk above. Another example of a semicircular tower, this time dating to the early fifteenth century and not in such good condition, comes from Coventry (Gooder *et al.* 1963–4: 105–6).

Mural towers were added to the Roman walls of Gloucester in the thirteenth century. The one example which has been uncovered is not a particularly impressive structure, for it is small, and does not project boldly from the curtain. Conditions inside would have been cramped for an archer, and its main defensive capabilities may have rested with archers positioned on the

Figure 10.5   Mural tower at St Nicholas's Almshouses, Bristol

battlements (Hurst, H.R. 1986: 27–9). The Roman defences were also used at Lincoln in the middle ages, but at some stage in the thirteenth century the western line was extended by about 100m to the south, until it reached the north bank of the Brayford Pool. The new section culminated in a small circular tower, the Lucy Tower, not to be confused with the tower in the castle which is similarly named; another similar extension was built on the eastern side. The purpose of the Lucy Tower may have been to protect commercial quays centred on the Brayford Pool. The wall and tower projecting out in this way is closely paralleled by the spur wall of Edward I's town defences at Conwy, built in the 1280s. The Conwy spur not only ended in a round tower, now vanished, but it also closed one end of a quay. The excavation of the Lucy Tower revealed that the medieval builders were fully aware of the problems of building in a marshy area. Initially the area was covered by fibrous vegetable 'matting' which included sticks and reeds; this may have been laid down to provide a reasonably dry surface on which to work. The tower itself was supported on foundations which consisted of both horizontal and vertical timbers, as well as large stone slabs, and the town wall was built in a similar manner (Colyer 1975: 259–66).

The Half Round Tower at Southampton was formed from a pre-existing dovecote. The west wall of the dovecote was demolished and the tower built on the eastern half; the date of this conversion is uncertain. The town wall was found to butt against the dovecote, but no evidence has been given to suggest whether the dovecote predated the earth-and-timber defences of the town or not (Youngs *et al.* 1987: 136).

Rectangular mural towers are rare, and where they are found they tend to date to the fourteenth century. The brick town walls at Hull, which have already been mentioned, had towers of this form (Bartlett 1970: 3–5, 15).

The late fourteenth- and fifteenth-century refortification of Canterbury employed both semicircular and square towers. Tower 18 on the northern side of the city was one of two square towers built to protect the lock controlling a branch of the river Stour which flows through the middle of Canterbury. The tower was fundamentally altered in the nineteenth century, but a short excavation undertaken recently confirmed that the tower was built at the same time as the town wall, probably some time in the last two decades of the fourteenth century. An interesting aspect of both tower 18 and its fellow guardian of the lock (tower 17) is that it was faced with blocks of Kentish ragstone, as was the town wall in this area. This finish to the tower was in marked contrast to the flintwork of many of the other towers; the reason for this may have been that the ditch on the north side of Canterbury was filled with water, so ragstone was used to provide a more watertight finish to the defences (Frere *et al.* 1982: 105–7).

Ditches

An examination of the 'Medieval Britain' section in the journal *Medieval Archaeology* reveals that many excavations have discovered the line of walls and ditches, but the width and depth of a ditch will often mean that archaeologists are unable to excavate the remains fully, and it is then impossible to obtain an accurate picture of how the defences developed and declined. Therefore, only a certain number of excavations have been particularly significant.

One excavation which was able to reveal the full width of the ditch (15.8m) took place in Bristol in 1965; it lay outside the walls in the southern sector of the defences, possibly built in the 1230s. Unfortunately, the trench across the ditch only went down just over 4m so that the full history of the defences was not revealed. Nevertheless, the excavation showed just how substantial such defences could be, although by the seventeenth century it could no longer be regarded as a defensive feature, for it was recut to make it a more effective obstacle, perhaps in the 1640s (Hebditch 1968).

Although the Bristol ditch in at least one sector was obviously a considerable obstacle when first dug, not all town defences, such as those at Coventry, were so effective. It is difficult to consider the defences at Coventry in a general way for they took virtually two centuries to build, and the work would, therefore, not have been consistent. However, in one area the ditch was only *c.* 2m deep, although about 10.5m wide. It was also flat-bottomed, making it easier for attacking forces to occupy it comfortably before assaulting the walls. This apparent weakness was partially compensated for by the steep sides of the ditch (Gooder *et al.* 1963–4: 102). Elsewhere in Coventry a novel method was used to create a ditch, possibly some time in the fourteenth century. The area to be defended was close to the river, and the excavation of a ditch at this point would have been extremely difficult, if not impossible, due to flooding. The solution was to build parallel ramparts of dumped earth, the space between them forming the ditch. The main or inner bank must have carried a palisade, for it was not until *c.* 1530 that the town wall was constructed on this side of the town (Bateman and Redknap 1986: 50–8). There are other examples where insubstantial defences were built around towns; for instance those at Northampton which were only about 4m wide and 2m deep (Williams, J.H. 1982: 63, 65).

A considerable amount of walling with mural towers still survives at Great Yarmouth, Norfolk, but until the excavation in 1955 the only evidence for a ditch was contained in a documentary reference to the digging of a moat around the town at the beginning of the Civil War. However, an excavation revealed that there had been a ditch in the middle ages, probably first dug in the late thirteenth century. Considerable care was taken with the ditch, for not only was the inner, and perhaps the outer, scarp revetted with a wall of flint, but at least part of the base of the ditch was lined with flagstones. The reason for this is unknown, although the town wall set in the ditch was able to use the flags as a firm foundation. It is possible that the flags extended across the full width of the flat-bottomed ditch (Green 1970).

Investigations at Dukes Place and Houndsditch in London have revealed more than just the priory postern mentioned above. It has been shown that London's medieval defences in at least one area originally had a ditch in the early thirteenth century; this later went out of use, being cut through by a second ditch some time between the early fourteenth and late fifteenth century. The distance between the city wall and the earlier ditch varied from 12m (Houndsditch) to 18.45 (Dukes Place), and it was at least 22m wide, whereas the later example was no more than 5.8m from the wall in one area, and it was considerably narrower, somewhere between 12–18m. It has been suggested that the new ditch was the work of Ralph Joceline, Mayor of London, who began to improve the defences between Aldgate and Aldersgate in 1477. However, its effectiveness had declined by the early sixteenth century when much of it had been filled by silting and rubbish, even though the survey of London by the Elizabethan John Stow shows that the citizens regularly cleaned the city ditch, no doubt for both social and defensive reasons (Maloney and Harding 1979: 350–4).

Future work on town defences needs to involve both archaeological excavation and studies of standing remains, either of individual sites or perhaps on a regional basis. We are fortunate in having valuable descriptions of such walled towns as Exeter and York, but, as Bond has emphasized (1987: 108), attention should now turn to the smaller walled towns. Some, like Oswestry, have already benefited from archaeological work on their walls, but in many cases the excavation has been small in scale, and, as was the case of Oswestry, may create more problems than answers. There are also several towns which are known to have had defences of some kind, but where nothing now remains, and where there is no clue as to the original line of the ramparts and walls; it is only recently that the line of the town defences at Farnham has been discovered, and they may date back to the twelfth century (Youngs *et al.* 1986: 164–5). The major fortifications of the thirteenth and fourteenth century have naturally dominated recent work, although there has been a considerable advance in our knowledge of the Norman defences of towns. Problems remain to be resolved even where major excavations have been undertaken, Rochester being a case in point, for here the two excavators have different theories as to the disposition of the southern defences in the early thirteenth century (Flight and Harrison 1986: 19–26). So much has been discovered since 1945 on this subject, through study and excavation, that a volume on urban defences, equivalent to Brown's work on castles (1976), is now greatly needed.

Part 4

11 *Aftermath and future*

The present book has examined aspects of both castles and town defences from the time of the Norman Conquest until the end of the fifteenth century. However, the history of these fortifications extends beyond 1500, and this chapter looks at some aspects of the later history of some of the sites which have been excavated, as well as suggesting where future work should best be concentrated.

The decline of the castle and castle building is a complicated subject, and one that is inappropriate to discuss in depth in a book of this nature. The reader is advised to consult the relevant chapter in Brown (1976: 128–53), and more particularly Thompson's recent analysis (1987). Platt's survey of castles in England and Wales (1982) is also useful for its coverage of the later medieval castles, and the documentary history of royal castles up to 1660 has been published (Colvin 1975).

Although the decline in the building of castles can be charted from the fourteenth century, castles were still built, notably the numerous tower-houses in northern Britain which date from the later middle ages through to the seventeenth century (Cruden 1963; Rowland 1987). The uncertainties of border politics in the late middle ages is a major reason for the tower-houses of the north, whilst in the south several new castles and town defences included primitive artillery defences because of the threat of French attacks. Only one English royal castle was built after 1300, Edward III's Queenborough in Kent, although existing royal buildings were not totally neglected, as witness the massive improvements undertaken at Windsor by Edward III. We have also seen from the excavations at Barnard and Bolingbroke, for example, that major improvements were undertaken at other castles in the later middle ages. In Scotland, although James II began the castle of Ravenscraig, Fife, in 1460, the kings also concentrated on the improvement of existing defences and domestic buildings, particularly in the first half of the sixteenth century, notable works being the forework and hall at Stirling built by James IV.

Besides the northern tower-houses, a few new castles were built by the nobility in fourteenth- and fifteenth-century England and Wales, including Nunney in Somerset, Bodiam in Sussex, and Raglan, Monmouthshire, all of them grand status symbols. The design of both Nunney and Raglan shows the influence of contemporary castles in France on the builders of these two castles in England and Wales. Impressive new defences were built at other castles, such as the magnificent Caesar's and Guy's towers at Warwick. Some scholars have suggested that many of these late medieval buildings scarcely justify the term 'castle'; Bodiam has even been dismissed as 'just an old soldier's dream house' (quoted in Turner, D.J. 1986: 267). Although Turner has reminded us of this scathing comment on Bodiam, he disagrees with it, and has emphasized, quite correctly, that this fortification is fully justified in taking its place amongst the last of the true castles of England (Turner 1986).

The decline of the castle is not indicated only by a drop in the number of new edifices under construction after 1300, but also by the fact that many once important buildings began to deteriorate in the later middle ages. Leaking roofs were often the initial cause of the decay, particularly where the lead had been stripped for reuse elsewhere, or melted down and sold. The pattern of distribution of occupied castles was of course constantly changing, even from the early days. The majority of the ubiquitous earth-and-timber motte-and-baileys and ringworks which were never converted to stone would have been abandoned by the first half of the thirteenth century. There are exceptions, and as we have seen, Hen Domen remained in use as an outpost until about 1300, Sycharth was still occupied in the early fifteenth century, whilst Castlehill of Strachan was not built until about 1250.

However, by the end of the middle ages descriptions of some of the large castles show that the burden of upkeep was having its effect on their condition. Bristol is a good example, for in 1480 not only was the great hall in ruins, but the chambers in the inner ward and the constable's lodging were in a very poor condition (Colvin 1963: 581). In the first two appendices to his book, Thompson (1987: 170–8) lists those castles which were derelict or had been abandoned in the fifteenth century (Appendix 1), and the condition of a large number in the 1530s as recorded by John Leland in his *Itinerary* (Appendix 2). Of the 258 listed by Thompson, 137 were ruinous, and several had been in this state for some time before Leland recorded their condition. Others, such as Caerphilly in Glamorgan and Trematon, Cornwall, were derelict, yet still used as prisons.

All was not a picture of gloom at the beginning of the Tudor period, however, for several castles received a new lease of life, admittedly as residences and centres of adminstration rather than for their defensive capabilities. One of the best examples of a castle that took on an important role in the Tudor and Stuart period was Ludlow, the centre of the Council in the Marches of Wales. Nevertheless, it must also be remembered that some castles, such as Manorbier in Pembrokeshire, referred to as ruinous by Leland, also played a role in the Civil War in the 1640s. The same applies to town defences, for many of the great towns, such as Bristol and Gloucester, endured major sieges; here the defenders relied primarily on the medieval fortifications, although these were sometimes augmented by new earthworks, as at Newark and Oxford. Several castles were refortified in the Civil War, some only on a small scale; for example, the pit dug into the roadway at the Black Gate, Newcastle (Ellison *et al.* 1979).

The four sites mentioned below illustrate what happened to some castles in the post-medieval period.

The effective life of Okehampton ended in the sixteenth century, for the castle was forfeited to the Crown about 1540. Although the clearance and partial restoration of the castle in 1911–13 removed much of the later archaeological deposits, enough survived for recent excavations to show that Okehampton was systematically stripped of its fittings at the time of its forfeit. Lead was removed from the roofs, and the metal was melted down into ingots in four lead-melting hearths in the floor of the hall. Some of the iron fittings seem also to have been removed from Okehampton, with a few pieces left lying about the castle, together with fragments of the carved stonework. The result of this robbing was that the castle was no longer in a fit state to be a domestic residence, a centre of administration, or a military stronghold, but this did not prevent part of the site from being utilized as a bakery in the late seventeenth century. A small lodging which had been added about 1400 was converted into a bakehouse with a fireplace and two ovens, and at the same time the remains of the barbican gate was used as a residence, whilst a new entrance to the castle was built on the north side of the bailey (Higham *et al.* 1982: 54-60, 78–9).

In 1584 Elizabeth I granted the castle of Laugharne in Carmarthenshire to Sir John Perrot, who died whilst confined in the Tower of London in 1592. Although his main seat was at Carew in the neighbouring county of Pembroke, where excavations have recently begun, Sir John began to transform the ruinous thirteenth- and early fourteenth-century castle at Laugharne into a Tudor mansion. He did the same at Carew, and his impressive north range still dominates the Carew River at its upper tidal limit. Perrot retained much of the medieval fabric at Laugharne, while restoring and modifying the castle to meet the requirements of a Tudor gentleman. The battlements, together with the inner and outer gatehouses, were repaired, and the outer ward became a formal garden.

Very little of Perrot's sixteenth-century work within the inner ward has survived above ground, presumably as a result of demolition following the garrisoning, siege and final capture of Laugharne in 1644. The inner ward has been excavated down to the Tudor and the medieval occupation levels (figure 11.1). Small areas of cobbling from the Tudor courtyard have been found, but there was no evidence of the 'proper fountaine' that was described in a survey of 1592 as standing in the centre of the ward. The foundations of the 'stately round stairs' which led up from the courtyard into the 'faire hall' have been exposed, along with the entire extent of the basements under the hall. The most recent excavations have revealed the plan of the medieval and Tudor buildings which originally occupied the eastern side of the inner ward (Avent 1981; personal communication).

Montgomery shows a similar story. In the sixteenth century the castle passed into the hands of the Herbert family to whom the site still belongs. It was habitable in the 1530s, for a certain amount of work was undertaken by Bishop Lee, President of the Council in the Marches of Wales (1534–43), but by the end of the sixteenth century the castle was in a poor state, containing few household goods and fittings. At that date the main family residence of the Herberts was a house in the town of Montgomery, but this changed *c.* 1622–5 when Sir Edward Herbert built a new brick house for himself in the middle ward of the castle. Herbert's 'new building' must have been an impressive structure, for in 1649, the year of its total demolition on the orders of the Council of State, it was valued as £4,731.

Sufficient foundations of the 'new building' remained upon excavation to show that the seventeenth-century brick house occupied the southern end of the middle ward, and was built over the demolished medieval walls and gatehouse. Its kitchen occupied the area of one of the medieval gatetowers with the principal accommodation on the first floor. A lodging ran along the west side of the ward, whilst the remainder of the area was a courtyard, a brick path connecting Herbert's house with the inner ward with its ancillary service buildings. A writer in the late seventeenth century recalled that Herbert's house was 'an elegant and noble pile, beautiful without and richly furnished within', and an indication of this was the large amount of decorated plaster from the

Figure 11.1   Excavations on the site of the Tudor hall at Laugharne Castle in 1978

ceilings of the main rooms which was discovered during the excavations
(Lewis, J.M. 1968). One does not have to look far for the reason behind the
placing of Herbert's 'new building' in the castle of Montgomery; not only
would it have provided the owner with one of the most picturesque views in
the Welsh March, but it would have stood out at the southern end of the

promontory for all to see and admire, particularly when viewed from the east.

Montgomery sustained two sieges in the Civil War. The first, in early September 1644, was a short-lived affair, for Herbert surrendered to a Parliamentarian force the day after it arrived. The second siege, two weeks later, was also short, for a Royalist army failed to recapture the castle. In spite of Herbert's mansion in the middle ward, the castle was evidently still capable of being a defensible stronghold.

There was nothing new in the partial demolition of a castle, and rebuilding within the original circuit as Herbert did in the 1620s. It had been done about two hundred years previously at Tattershall, Lincolnshire, where, in the second quarter of the fifteenth century, Ralph, Lord Cromwell demolished parts of the thirteenth-century castle in order to build the great brick tower which now dominates the site. This tower has to be seen as a symbol of 'dignity and authority' rather than as a keep in the tradition of the twelfth century (Thompson 1987: 74). However, by the beginning of the seventeenth century quasi-fortified buildings, or 'show-castles' as Thompson has described late medieval castles, were not only unnecessary but things of the past in England and Wales until the mock castles and follies of the eighteenth and nineteenth centuries.

Despite late fifteenth-century improvements Sandal had lost its importance by the middle of the sixteenth century. As with so many other castles, the English Civil War in the 1640s saw the last moment of glory for this medieval stronghold. Sandal declared for the king, and its garrison built some earthwork batteries to supplement the medieval defences. However, it was not until early in 1645 that the Parliamentarians were in a position to set about besieging the castle. Success was not achieved until September in that year, when the garrison surrendered as preparations were being made to storm the various breaches made by the artillery. The garrison then marched away from the castle on the morning of October 1st. The effective life of Sandal was then at an end, for Parliament ordered the destruction of the castle, and it was dismantled (Mayes and Butler 1983: 5–7).

The excavations at Sandal have shown that various modifications and building works were undertaken by the Royalist garrison, and that by the end of the siege little of the medieval keep remained. The garrison had dug a communication trench between the gateway of the keep to the tower rebuilt by Richard III, containing the well; the only purpose of the trench would have been to provide a measure of protection for the garrison, protection which was no longer afforded by the walls of the keep. It may even be that the top of the keep had been demolished to make it less vulnerable to gunfire, and also to permit the defenders to mount their own ordnance on its walls. Further evidence for the use of the castle in the 1640s comes from the graves of some of the defenders, as well as from various buildings. In the area of the medieval kitchen range, on the site of the medieval bakehouse, there was a stable, with a smith's forge at one end, built against the curtain wall. A rectangular workshop lay close by, and both this and the stable had very thin walls, suggesting that the buildings were timber-framed structures set on low walls; all-masonry structures would have required thicker walls for stability. Such buildings would have been necessary for the maintenance of the garrison, and presumably had to be built because the medieval buildings of the castle had either disappeared or were in a state of advanced decay (Mayes and Butler 1983: 50–1, 80).

It has sometimes been said that castle studies tend to concentrate on the period up to the late thirteenth-century Edwardian castles of north Wales, generally accepted as representing the peak in castle building in Britain, and that this has been to the detriment of the castles of the later middle ages. That this should be the case is not totally surprising, as what attracts the student to the study of castles are the fortifications, and the finest period for these is the twelfth and thirteenth centuries. Nevertheless, the post-medieval history of castles is a subject that tends to be considered only when individual castles are studied, so the importance of the excavations of the above four castles has been to show that the archaeologist can reveal much of interest about the castle in decline.

What of the future? What can we hope to learn from future excavation and publication? Certainly one would welcome the full report of some of the more important excavations of castles that have taken place over the last twenty years or so. We know enough now to suggest that the overall picture of the development of the castle is unlikely to alter fundamentally in the light of future work, although research will no doubt throw fresh light on aspects of the history of individual castles. Most of the major British castles are in State care, and in many cases have been cleared and consolidated, with a certain amount of excavation also undertaken. In Wales excavations are continuing (1988) at two castles taken into guardianship in the 1970s, Laugharne and Dryslwyn, and will contribute further to our knowledge of the Anglo-Norman and native Welsh castle.

Other castles which were of considerable importance in the middle ages, and where much masonry still stands, today lie overgrown and slowly crumbling. Only when such sites are brought into State care will there be an integrated programme of excavation, consolidation and research; this is the only approach that will increase our understanding of castles throughout the middle ages. There are various castles which can be categorized as being of both great importance as well as very ruinous. One thinks of Wigmore in Herefordshire, for example; it fully warrants being placed in the care of the State, and no doubt there are others throughout Britain.

The excavation of earth-and-timber castles has been the most important archaeological contribution to castle studies, with the amount of information gained from Hen Domen and Goltho emphasizing the importance of large-scale excavations for the archaeological study of earthwork castles. Nevertheless, we still need to know more about them. The evolution of the defences, the types of buildings in the baileys, and methods of construction, for example, still need to be elucidated. Of course, the work of Barker and Higham at Hen Domen is of paramount importance, and although it will take many years to accomplish, it is fervently to be hoped that the excavations at this motte-and-bailey will continue until both the bailey and motte have been totally investigated. Unless there is another rescue opportunity similar to that at Goltho, it is unlikely that funds will be found in the immediate future for the large-scale excavation of another earthwork castle comparable to Hen Domen.

Some recent archaeological reports have included detailed examinations of the above-ground fabric of castles, notably Colchester (Drury 1982) and

Portchester (Munby and Renn 1985), and this is another important aspect of castle studies. Surveys on these levels need to be undertaken at other British castles, for undoubtedly they will shed further light on the history and architectural development of the buildings. The disposition of arrowslits in castles is also a subject which will repay investigation for the information it will provide about the defensive capabilities of a building. The only recent example of this type of study is the work carried out at White Castle, Monmouthshire (Jones and Renn 1982), and a much greater sample is needed before general conclusions can be drawn from an exercise such as this.

The recent work at Farnham (p.199) has shown the value of being able to examine those towns where documentary evidence for defences exists, but for which there is little or no indication on the ground. Also, thorough above-ground surveys, such as those undertaken at Exeter (Burrow 1977) and York (RCHM 1972b), ought to be applied to other town defences, as the analysis will result in a better understanding of the constructional history of these monuments.

We know from documents that the walls around some towns took many years to build, depending on the funds available, and that murage grants often continued over several decades, and in some cases centuries, whilst at other towns defences were built comparatively quickly. Archaeological projects should throw more light on the constructional history of these defences, such as whether a wall was built by separate gangs of workmen, as has been suggested at the Beverley Gate in Hull, or whether the differences relate to more than one period of construction, building having taken place only when money was available.

Research and rescue excavations since 1945 have transformed our knowledge of medieval fortifications. It is unlikely that many new excavations of castles will be on the scale of those undertaken at such sites as Launceston and Portchester, for this type of work is becoming increasingly expensive. Besides future major excavations which may be confined to sites where a castle is taken into State care, some local archaeological groups and societies may find themselves in a position to undertake smaller excavations at sites not in the care of the State which are threatened by building development or farming; even if this work is on a small scale useful information will be forthcoming. Local societies, as well as individuals, are also in a position to initiate studies of above-ground remains, and it is through all these contributions that castle studies will undoubtedly continue to flourish. The formation of the Castle Studies Group in 1986 can only act as a further stimulus to the study of these monuments, for amongst its aims is the promotion of research into castles through such means as excavation, architectural history and fieldwork.

Glossary

Ashlar	square-edged stonework with even faces
Bailey	defended courtyard of a castle
Ball-flower	globular ornament consisting of a three-petalled flower enclosing a small ball
Barbican	outer defence protecting a gateway
Berm	strip of ground between the base of the curtain wall and the ditch
Buttery	storeroom for wine and other beverages
Chamfer	surface created by removing a square edge obliquely
Cistern	storage tank for water
Corbel	projecting stone used to support a timber beam or joist of a roof or floor
Crucks	pair of curved timbers extending from ground to roof ridge supporting wall and roof of a building
Drystone wall	stone wall built without mortar or clay
Forebuilding	building which projects from a keep and houses the entrance staircase
Garderobe	latrine
Keep	the main tower of a castle, usually free-standing
Mortise	socket in timber into which another piece of wood or tenon is jointed
Motte	mound of earth supporting a tower and palisade
Mural tower	tower built on the line of the curtain wall
Padstone	stone on which a timber post is set
Palisade	strong timber fence, usually set on an earth rampart
Pantry	storeroom for bread and other foodstuffs
Pent roof	lean-to roof
Piscina	in a chapel, basin with a drain for washing the vessels after Mass
Plinth	projecting base of a wall
Postern	small gateway, secondary to the main entrance
Quoins	dressed stones at the corner of a building
Rendering	plastering on the outside of a wall, often lime-washed
Revetment	retaining wall of stone or timber of an earth bank or sides of a ditch
Ringwork	embanked enclosure, generally circular in plan
Romanesque	the architecture of the eleventh and twelfth centuries in Europe, sometimes called Norman in England
Sallyport	see Postern
Shell-keep	masonry wall around the perimeter of a motte, replacing a timber palisade
Shuttering	planking used, for example, to keep wet plaster in position until dry
Sillbeam	horizontal timber at the base of a building into which upright posts can be jointed

Solar	private withdrawing room, usually on an upper floor
Soleplate	horizontal timber at the base of a framed construction
Stringcourse	a projecting horizontal band of masonry running around a building
Tenon	see Mortise
Wall-walk	sentry path immediately behind the battlements of a castle or town wall
Ward	see Bailey
Wattle-and-daub	a combination of laths and clay used to infill panels in a timber-framed building

Bibliography

Abbreviations

RCAHM Royal Commission on Ancient and Historical Monuments (Scotland)

RCHM Royal Commission on Historical Monuments (England)

The standard list of abbreviated titles of periodicals given in the Council for British Archaeology's *Signposts for archaeological publication* (2nd edn 1979) has been followed in this bibliography.

Aberg, F.A. (1975), 'The excavations, 1959–1961', in C. Platt and R. Coleman-Smith, *Excavations in Medieval Southampton 1953–1969*, 1: 176–229. Leicester.

Addyman, P.V. (1965), 'Late Saxon settlements in the St. Neots area I. The Saxon settlement and Norman castle at Eaton Socon, Bedfordshire', *Proc. Cambridge Antiq. Soc.* **58**: 38–73.

Addyman, P.V. (1973), 'Excavation at Ludgershall Castle, Wiltshire, England (1964–1972)', *Château Gaillard* **6**: 7–13.

Addyman, P.V. and Priestley, J. (1977), 'Baile Hill, York: a report on the Institute's excavations', *Archaeol. J.* **134**: 115–56.

Alcock, L. (1963), *Dinas Powys: An Iron Age, Dark Age and Early Medieval Settlement in Glamorgan.* Cardiff.

Alcock, L. (1966), 'Castle Tower, Penmaen: a Norman ring-work in Glamorgan', *Antiq. J.* **46**: 178–210.

Alcock, L. (1967), 'Excavations at Degannwy Castle, Caernarvonshire, 1961–6', *Archaeol. J.* **124**: 190–201.

Alcock, L. (1987), 'Castle-studies and the archaeological sciences: some possibilities and problems', in J.R. Kenyon and R. Avent (eds), *Castles in Wales and the Marches: Essays in honour of D.J. Cathcart King*, 5–22. Cardiff.

Alcock, L., King, D.J.C., Putnam, W.G. and Spurgeon, C.J. (1967–8), 'Excavations at Castell Bryn Amlwg', *Montgomeryshire Collect.* **60**: 8–27.

Alcock, N.W. and Buckley, R.J. (1987), 'Leicester Castle: the Great Hall', *Medieval Archaeol.* **31**: 73–9.

Aldsworth, F.G. and Garnett, E.D. (1981), 'Excavations on "The Mound" at Church Norton, Selsey, in 1911 and 1965', *Sussex Archaeol. Collect.* **119**: 217–21.

Anon. (1987), 'Norman walls at Eye Castle', *Ipswich Archaeol. Trust News* **22**: 1.

Apted, M.R. (1962–3)' 'Excavation at Kildrummy Castle, Aberdeenshire, 1952–62', *Proc. Soc. Antiq. Scot.* **96**: 208–36.

Armitage, E.S. (1912), *The Early Norman Castles of the British Isles.* London.

Atkins, C. (1983), ' "The Castles", Barrow-on-Humber', *Lincolnshire Hist. Archaeol.* **18**: 91–3.

Austin, D. (1979), 'Barnard Castle, Co. Durham. First interim report: excavations in the Town Ward, 1974–6', *J. Brit. Archaeol. Ass.* **132**: 50–72.

Austin, D. (1980), 'Barnard Castle, Co. Durham. Second interim report: excavations in the Inner Ward 1976–8: the later medieval period', *J. Brit. Archaeol. Ass.* **133**: 74–96.

Austin, D. (1982), 'Barnard Castle, Co. Durham', *Château Gaillard* **9–10**: 293–300.

Avent, R. (1977), 'Laugharne Castle 1976: introduction, historical summary and excavations', *Carmarthenshire Antiq.* **13**: 17–41.

Avent, R. (1981), 'Laugharne Castle 1976–80', in R. Avent and P. Webster, *Interim reports of Excavations at Laugharne Castle, Dyfed, 1976–80 and Dryslwyn Castle, Dyfed, 1980*, 1–33. Cardiff.

Avent, R. (1983), *Cestyll Tywysogion Gwynedd/Castles of the Princes of Gwynedd*. Cardiff.

Avent, R. (1987), *Criccieth Castle*. Cardiff.

Baillie, M.G.L. (1982), *Tree-ring Dating and Archaeology*. London.

Baker, D. and Baker, E. (1979), 'The excavations: Bedford Castle', *Bedfordshire Archaeol. J.* **13**: 7–64.

Barker, P.A. (1961), 'Excavations on the town wall, Roushill, Shrewsbury', *Medieval Archaeol.* **5**: 181–210.

Barker, P.A. (1964), 'Pontesbury castle mound emergency excavations 1961 and 1964', *Trans. Shropshire Archaeol. Soc.* **57.3**: 206–23.

Barker, P.A. (1982), 'Rabies archaeologorum: a reply', *Château Gaillard* **9–10**: 220–2. (also in *Antiquity* **54** (1980): 19–20).

Barker, P.A. (1987), 'Hen Domen revisited', in J.R. Kenyon and R. Avent (eds), *Castles in Wales and the Marches: Essays in honour of D.J. Cathcart King*, 51–4. Cardiff.

Barker, P.A. and Barton, K.J. (1977), 'Excavations at Hastings Castle, 1968', *Archaeol. J.* **134**: 80–100.

Barker, P.A. and Higham, R. (1982), *Hen Domen, Montgomery: A timber castle on the English-Welsh border*, **1**. London.

Barker, P.A. and Higham, R. (1983), 'Hen Domen, Powys', *W. Midlands Archaeol.* **26**: 93–5.

Barker, P.A. and Higham, R. (1985), 'Hen Domen, Montgomery (Powys), interim report 1985', *W. Midlands Archaeol.* **28**: 18–19.

Barker, P.A. and Higham, R. (1988), *Hen Domen, Montgomery: A timber castle on the English-Welsh border. Excavations 1960–1988: a summary report*. Worcester.

Barley, M.W. (1976), 'Town defences in England and Wales after 1066', in M.W. Barley (ed.), *The Plans and Topography of Medieval Towns in England and Wales*, 57–71. London.

Barry, T.B. (1987), *The Archaeology of Medieval Ireland*. London.

Bartlett, J. (1970), 'North Walls excavation', *Kingston upon Hull Mus. Bull.* **4**: 1–23.

Barton, K.J. (1964), 'The excavation of a medieval bastion at St. Nicholas's Almhouses, King Street, Bristol', *Medieval Archaeol.* **8**: 184–212.

Barton, K.J. (1979), *Medieval Sussex Pottery*. Chichester.

Barton, K.J. (1980), 'Excavations at the Chateau des Marais (Ivy Castle), Guernsey', *Rep. Trans. Soc. Guernesiaise* **20.5**: 657–702.

Barton, K.J. and Holden, E.W. (1977), 'Excavations at Bramber Castle, Sussex, 1966–67', *Archaeol. J.* **134**: 11–79.

Bateman, J. and Redknap, M. (1986), *Coventry: Excavations on the town wall 1976–1978*. Coventry.

Bauer, T.C. (1981), 'Die houten brug van "Rozengaard" te Brunssum (L)', in T.J. Hoekstra, H.L. Janssen and I.W.L. Moerman (eds), *Liber Castellorum: 40 variaties op het thema kasteel*, 248–56. Zutphen.

Beresford, G. (1974), 'The medieval manor of Penhallam, Jacobstow, Cornwall', *Medieval Archaeol.* **18**: 90–145.

Beresford, G. (1977a), 'Excavation of a moated house at Wintringham in Huntingdonshire', *Archaeol. J.* **134**: 194–286.

Beresford, G. (1977b), 'The excavation of the deserted medieval village of Goltho, Lincolnshire', *Château Gaillard* **8**: 47–68.

Beresford, G. (1987), *Goltho: The development of an early medieval manor c. 850–1150*. London.

Besteman, J.C. (1981), 'Mottes in the Netherlands: a provisional survey and inventory', in T.J. Hoekstra, H.L. Janssen and I.W.L. Moerman (eds), *Liber Castellorum: 40 variaties op het thema kasteel*, 40–59. Zutphen.

Besteman, J.C. (1985), 'Mottes in the Netherlands', *Château Gaillard* 12: 211–24.

Biddle, M. (1964), 'The excavation of a motte and bailey castle at Therfield, Hertfordshire', *J. Brit. Archaeol. Ass.* 3rd ser. 27: 53–91.

Biddle, M. (1969), 'Excavations at Winchester 1968: seventh interim report', *Antiq. J.* 49: 295–329.

Biddle, M. (1970), 'Excavations at Winchester, 1969: eighth interim report', *Antiq. J.* 50: 277–326.

Biddle, M. (1975), 'Excavations at Winchester, 1971: tenth and final interim report: part I', *Antiq. J.* 55: 96–126.

Biddle, M. (ed.) (1976), *Winchester in the Early Middle Ages*. Oxford.

Biddle, M. and Clayre, B. (1983), *Winchester Castle and the Great Hall*. Winchester.

Blair, J. (1981), 'William fitz Ansculf and the Abinger motte', *Archaeol. J.* 138: 146–8.

Blaylock, S.R. (1985), 'Exeter Castle gatehouse', *Exeter Archaeol. 1984–5*: 18–24.

Bond, C.J. (1987), 'Anglo-Saxon and medieval defences', in J. Schofield and R. Leech (eds), *Urban Archaeology in Britain*, 92–116. London.

Boon, G.C. (1986), *Welsh Hoards 1979–1981*. Cardiff.

Border Counties Archaeological Group, (n.d.), *Oswestry Town Wall*. Oswestry.

Boüard, M. de (1973–4), 'De l'aula au donjon: les fouilles de la motte de La Chapelle à Doué-la-Fontaine (Xe–XIe siècle)', *Archéol. Médiévale* 3–4: 5–110.

Braun, H. (1935), 'Bungay Castle. Report on the excavations', *Proc. Suffolk Inst. Archaeol. Natur. Hist.* 22.2: 201–23.

Brewster, T.C.M. (1969), 'Tote Copse Castle, Aldingbourne, Sussex', *Sussex Archaeol. Collect.* 107: 141–79.

Brown, R.A. (1964), *Orford Castle, Suffolk*. London.

Brown, R.A. (1976), *English Castles* (3rd edn). London.

Brown, R.A. (1983), *Castle Rising, Norfolk* (2nd printing). London.

Brown, R.A. (1984a), *The Architecture of Castles: A visual guide*. London.

Brown, R.A. (1984b), 'Castle gates and garden gates', *Architect. Hist.* 27: 443–5.

Brown, R.A. (1985), *Castles*. Princes Risborough.

Brown, R.A. and Curnow, P.E. (1984), *Tower of London, Greater London*. London.

Brunskill, R.W. (1987), *Illustrated Handbook of Vernacular Architecture*, (3rd edn). London.

Buckley, R. and Lucas, J. (1987), *Leicester Town Defences: Excavations 1958–1974*. Leicester.

Burrow, I. (1977), 'The town defences of Exeter', *Rep. Trans. Devonshire Ass.* 109: 13–40.

Butler, L.A.S. (1974), 'Medieval finds from Castell-y-Bere, Merioneth', *Archaeol. Cambrensis* 123: 78–112.

Butler, L.A.S. (1985), 'Dolforwyn Castle, Powys, Wales: excavations 1981–4', *Château Gaillard* 12: 167–77.

Butler, L.A.S. (1986), *Dolforwyn Castle, Powys, Wales*. Leeds (duplicated typescript).

Butler, L.A.S. (1987), 'Holt Castle: John de Warenne and Chastellion', in J.R. Kenyon and R. Avent (eds), *Castles in Wales and the Marches: Essays in honour of D.J. Cathcart King*, 105–24. Cardiff.

Carter, A. (1971), 'Nottingham town wall: Park Row excavations 1968', *Trans. Thoroton Soc. Nottinghamshire* 75: 33–40.

Carver, M.O.H. (ed.) (1977–8), 'Two town houses in medieval Shrewsbury', *Trans. Shropshire Archaeol. Soc.* 61: whole issue.

Charlton, P., Roberts, J. and Vale, V. (1977), *Llantrithyd: A ringwork in South Glamorgan*. Cardiff.

Chatwin, P.B. (1955), 'Brandon Castle, Warwickshire', *Trans. Birmingham Archaeol. Soc.* **73**: 63–83.

Childe, V.G. (1938), 'Doonmore, a castle mound near Fair Head, Co. Antrim', *Ulster J. Archaeol.* 3rd ser. **1**: 122–35.

Coad, J.G. (1971), 'Recent excavations within Framlingham Castle', *Proc. Suffolk Inst. Archaeol.* **32.2**: 152–63.

Coad, J.G. (1984), *Castle Acre Castle, Norfolk.* London

Coad, J.G. and Streeten, A.D.F. (1982), 'Excavations at Castle Acre Castle, Norfolk, 1972–77: country house and castle of the Norman earls of Surrey', *Archaeol. J.* **139**: 138–301.

Coad, J.G., Streeten, A.D.F. and Warmington, R. (1987), 'Excavations at Castle Acre Castle, Norfolk, 1975–1982: the bridges, lime kilns, and eastern gatehouse', *Archaeol. J.* **144**: 256–307.

Colvin, H.M. (gen. ed.) (1963), *The History of the King's Works: 1–2. The middle ages.* London.

Colvin, H.M. (ed.) (1971), *Building Accounts of King Henry III.* Oxford.

Colvin, H.M. (gen. ed.) (1975), *The History of the King's Works: 3. 1485–1660 (part I).* London.

Colyer, C. (1975), 'Excavations at Lincoln 1970–1972: the western defences of the lower town. An interim report', *Antiq. J.* **55**: 227–66.

Cook, A.M., Maynard, D.C. and Rigold, S.E. (1969), 'Excavations at Dover Castle, principally in the inner bailey', *J. Brit. Archaeol. Ass.* 3rd ser. **32**: 54–104.

Counihan, J. (1986), 'Mrs Ella Armitage, John Horace Round, G.T.Clark and early Norman castles', in R.A. Brown (ed.), *Anglo-Norman studies VIII: Proceedings of the Battle Conference 1985*, 73–87. Woodbridge.

Cowgill, J., de Neergaard, M. and Griffiths, N. (1987), *Medieval Finds from Excavations in London: 1. Knives and scabbards.* London.

Craster, O.E. (1950–1), 'A medieval limekiln at Ogmore Castle, Glamorgan', *Archaeol. Cambrensis* **101**: 72–6.

Craster, O.E. (1967), 'Skenfrith Castle: when was it built?', *Archaeol. Cambrensis* **116**: 133–58.

Credland, A.G. (1980), 'Crossbow remains', *J. Soc. Archer-Antiq.* **23**: 12–19.

Cruden, S. (1963), *The Scottish Castle*, (rev. edn). Edinburgh.

Cunliffe, B.W. (1962), 'The Winchester city wall', *Proc. Hampshire Fld Club Archaeol. Soc.* **22.2**: 51–81.

Cunliffe, B.W. (1977), *Excavations at Portchester Castle: 3. Medieval: the outer bailey and its defences.* London.

Cunliffe, B.W. (1985), 'The structural sequence: the archaeological evidence', in B.W. Cunliffe and T. Munby, *Excavations at Portchester Castle: 4. Medieval: the inner bailey*, 5–71. London.

Cunliffe, B.W. and Munby, J. (1985), *Excavations at Portchester Castle: 4. Medieval: the inner bailey.* London.

Curnow, P.E. and Thompson, M.W. (1969), 'Excavations at Richard's Castle, Herefordshire, 1962–1964', *J. Brit. Archaeol. Ass.* 3rd ser. **32**: 105–27.

Curzon, Marquis of Kedleston (1926), *Bodiam Castle, Sussex.* London.

Daniels, R. (1986), 'The medieval defences of Hartlepool, Cleveland: the results of excavation and survey', *Durham Archaeol. J.* **2**: 63–72.

Davey, N. (1961), *A History of Building Materials.* London.

Davis, A. (1985), 'Aberystwyth Castle', *Archaeol. Wales* **25**: 35–6.

Davis, A. (1986), 'Aberystwyth Castle', *Archaeol. Wales* **26**: 51–2.

Davison, B.K. (1967), 'Three eleventh-century earthworks in England: their excavation and implications', *Château Gaillard* **2**: 39–48.

Davison, B.K. (1969), 'Aldingham', *Current Archaeol.* **2.1**: 23–4.

Davison, B.K. (1971–2), 'Castle Neroche: an abandoned Norman fortress in south Somerset', *Somerset Archaeol. Natur. Hist.* **116**: 16–58.

Davison, B.K. (1977), 'Excavations at Sulgrave, Northamptonshire, 1960–76: an interim report', *Archaeol. J.* **134**: 105–14.

Davison, B.K. (1986), *The New Observer's Book of Castles*, (2nd edn). Harmondsworth.

Drewett, P.L. (1975), 'Excavations at Hadleigh Castle, Essex, 1971–1972', *J. Brit. Archaeol. Ass.* 3rd ser. **38**: 90–154.

Drewett, P.L. (1976), 'The excavation of the Great Hall at Bolingbroke Castle, Lincolnshire, 1973', *Post-Medieval Archaeol.* **10**: 1–33.

Drewett, P.L. and Freke, D.J. (1974), 'The Great Hall at Bolingbroke Castle', *Medieval Archaeol.* **18**: 163–5.

Drury, P.J. (1982), 'Aspects of the origins and development of Colchester Castle', *Archaeol. J.* **139**: 302–419.

Dunning, G.C. (1936), 'Alstoe Mount, Burley, Rutland', *Antiq. J.* **16**: 396–411.

Durham, B., Halpin, C. and Palmer, N. (1983), 'Oxford's northern defences: archaeological studies 1971–1982', *Oxoniensia* **48**: 13–40.

Eddy, M.R. (1983), 'A Roman settlement and early medieval motte at Moot Hill, Great Driffield, North Humberside', *E. Riding Archaeol.* **7**: 40–51.

Elliott, H. and Stocker, D. (1984), *Lincoln Castle*. Lincoln.

Ellison, M., Finch, M. and Harbottle, B. (1979), 'The excavation of a 17th-century pit at the Black Gate, Newcastle-upon-Tyne, 1975', *Post-Medieval Archaeol.* **13**: 153–81.

Emery, A. (1985), 'Ralph, Lord Cromwell's manor at Wingfield (1439–*c.* 1450): its construction, design and influence', *Archaeol. J.* **142**: 276–339.

Ewart, G. (1985), *Cruggleton Castle: Report of excavations 1978–1981*. Dumfries.

Ewart, G. (1987a), 'Auldhill, Portencross', *Discovery Excav. Scot. 1987*: 48.

Ewart, G. (1987b), 'Dundonald Castle', *Discovery Excav. Scot. 1987*: 52.

Fairclough, G. (1982), 'Edlingham Castle: the military and domestic development of a Northumbrian manor. Excavations 1978–80: interim report', *Château Gaillard* **9–10**: 373–87.

Fairclough, G. (1984), 'Edlingham Castle, Northumberland: an interim account of excavations, 1978–82', *Trans. Ancient Monuments Soc.* new ser. **28**: 40–60.

Fasham, P.J. (1983), 'Excavations in Banbury, 1972: second and final report', *Oxoniensia* **48**: 71–118.

Faulkner, P.A. (1963), 'Castle planning in the fourteenth century', *Archaeol. J.* **120**: 215–35.

Flight, C. and Harrison, A.C. (1978), 'Rochester Castle, 1976', *Archaeol. Cantiana* **94**: 27–60.

Flight, C. and Harrison, A.C. (1986), 'The southern defences of medieval Rochester', *Archaeol. Cantiana* **103**: 1–26.

Ford, W.J. (1971), 'Castle Bromwich Castle', *Archaeol. J.* **128**: 214–15.

Frere, S.S., Stow, S. and Bennett, P. (1982), *Excavations on the Roman and Medieval Defences of Canterbury*. Maidstone.

Glasscock, R.E. (1975), 'Mottes in Ireland', *Château Gaillard* **7**: 95–110.

Good, G.L. and Tabraham, C.J. (1981), 'Excavations at Threave Castle, Galloway, 1974–78', *Medieval Archaeol.* **25**: 90–140.

Gooder, E., Woodfield, C. and Chaplin, R.E. (1963–4), 'The walls of Coventry', *Trans. Birmingham Archaeol. Soc.* **81**: 88–138.

Green, C. (1970), 'Excavations on the town wall, Great Yarmouth, Norfolk, 1955', *Norfolk Archaeol.* **35.1**: 109–17.

Grew, F. and de Neergaard, M. (1988), *Medieval Finds from Excavations in London: 2. Shoes and pattens*. London.

Grimes, W.G. (1968), *The Excavation of Roman and Mediaeval London*. London.

Guilbert, G.C. (1974), 'Llanstephan Castle: 1973 interim report', *Carmarthenshire Antiq.* **10**: 37–48.

Haggarty, G. and Tabraham, C. (1982), 'Excavation of a motte near Roberton, Clydesdale, 1979', *Trans. Dumfriesshire Galloway Natur. Hist. Antiq. Soc.* 3rd ser. **57**: 51–64.

Hague, D.B. and Warhurst, C. (1966), 'Excavations at Sycharth Castle, Denbighshire, 1962–63', *Archaeol. Cambrensis* **115**: 108–27.

Harbottle, B. (1967), 'An excavation at the Gunner Tower, Newcastle upon Tyne, 1964', *Archaeol. Aeliana* 4th ser. **45**: 123–37.

Harbottle, B. (1982), 'The castle of Newcastle upon Tyne: excavations 1973–1979', *Château Gaillard* **9–10**: 407–18.

Harbottle, B. and Ellison, M. (1981), 'An excavation in the castle ditch, Newcastle upon Tyne, 1974–6', *Archaeol. Aeliana* 5th ser. **9**: 75–250.

Harrison, A.C. (1972), 'Rochester east gate, 1969', *Archaeol. Cantiana* **87**: 121–57.

Harvey, A. (1911), *The Castles and Walled Towns of England*. London.

Haslam, J. (1977–8), 'The excavation of the defences of Devizes, Wilts., 1974', *Wiltshire Archaeol. Mag.* **72–3**: 59–65.

Hassall, T.G. (1976), 'Excavations at Oxford Castle, 1965–1973', *Oxoniensia* **41**: 232–308.

Hebditch, M. (1968), 'Excavations on the medieval defences, Portwall Lane, Bristol, 1965', *Trans. Bristol Gloucestershire Archaeol. Soc.* **87**: 131–43.

Heighway, C. (1983), *The East and North Gates of Gloucester and Associated Sites: Excavations 1974–81*. Bristol.

Helliwell, L. and Macleod, D.G. (1981), *Documentary Evidence and Report on Excavations 1959–61 on behalf of the Rayleigh Mount Local Committee of the National Trust*. Rayleigh.

Herrnbrodt, A. (1958), *Der Husterknupp: eine niederrheinische Burgenlage des frühen Mittelalters*. Cologne.

Hertz, J. (1982), 'Danish medieval drawbridges', *Château Gaillard* **9–10**: 419–31.

Higham, R.A. (1977), 'Excavations at Okehampton Castle, Devon. Part 1: The motte and keep', *Proc. Devon Archaeol. Soc.* **35**: 3–42.

Higham, R.A. (1982a), 'Dating in medieval archaeology: problems and possibilities', in B. Orme (ed.), *Problems and Case Studies in Archaeological Dating*, 83–107. Exeter.

Higham, R.A. (1982b), 'Early castles in Devon, 1068–1201', *Château Gaillard* **9–10**: 101–16.

Higham, R.A. (1984), *Okehampton Castle, Devon*. London.

Higham, R.A., Allan, J.P. and Blaylock, S.R. (1982), 'Excavations at Okehampton Castle, Devon. Part 2: The bailey', *Proc. Devon Archaeol. Soc.* **40**: 19–151.

Hillaby, J. (1985), 'Hereford gold: Irish, Welsh and English land. Part 2', *Trans. Woolhope Nat. Fld Club* **45.1**: 193–270.

Hodges, R. (1980), 'Excavations at Camp Green, Hathersage (1976–77) – a Norman ringwork', *Derbyshire Archaeol. J.* **100**: 25–34.

Hodgson, J. (1986), *Southampton Castle*. Southampton.

Holden, E.W. (1967), 'The excavation of a motte at Lodsbridge Mill, Lodsworth', *Sussex Archaeol. Collect.* **105**: 103–25.

Holdsworth, P. (ed.) (1987), *Excavations in the Medieval Burgh of Perth 1979–81*. Edinburgh.

Holmes, E.F. (1988), *Sewing Thimbles*. Finds Research Group 700–1700 datasheet 9.

Hope-Taylor, B. (1950), 'The excavation of a motte at Abinger in Surrey', *Archaeol. J.* **107**: 15–43.

Hope-Taylor, B. (1950–1), 'Excavations at Mote of Urr. Interim report: 1951 season', *Trans. Dumfriesshire Galloway Natur. Hist. Antiq. Soc.* 3rd ser. **29**: 167–72.

Hough, P.R. (1978), 'Excavations at Beeston Castle 1975–1977', *J. Chester Archaeol. Soc.* **61**: 1–23.

Houlder, C.H. (1957), 'Recent excavations in Old Aberystwyth', *Ceredigion* **3.2**: 114–17.

Hurst, H.R. (1984), 'The archaeology of Gloucester Castle: an introduction', *Trans. Bristol Gloucestershire Archaeol. Soc.* **102**: 73–128.

Hurst, H.R. (1986), *Gloucester, the Roman and Later Defences*. Gloucester.

Hurst, J.G. (1961), 'The kitchen area of Northolt Manor, Middlesex', *Medieval Archaeol.* **5**: 211–99.

Hurst, J.G. (1963), 'Excavations at Barn Road, Norwich, 1954–55', *Norfolk Archaeol.* **33.2**: 131–79.

Hurst, J.G. and Golson, J. (1955), 'Excavations at St. Benedict's Gates, Norwich, 1951 and 1953', *Norfolk Archaeol.* **31.1**: 1–112.

Ivens, R.J. (1983), 'Deddington Castle, Oxfordshire. A summary of excavations 1977–1979', *S. Midlands Archaeol.* **13**: 34–41.

Ivens, R.J. (1984), 'Deddington Castle, Oxfordshire, and the English honour of Odo of Bayeux', *Oxoniensia* **49**: 101–19.

Johnson, S. (1980), 'Excavations at Conisbrough Castle 1973–1977', *Yorkshire Archaeol. J.* **52**: 59–88.

Johnson, S. (1984), *Conisbrough Castle, South Yorkshire*. London.

Jones, A. (1910), *The History of Gruffydd ap Cynan*. Manchester.

Jones, P.N. and Renn, D.F. (1982), 'The military effectiveness of arrow loops: some experiments at White Castle', *Château Gaillard* **9–10**: 445–56.

Jones, T. (ed.) (1973), *Brut y Tywysogyon or Chronicle of the Princes: Red Book of Hergest*, (2nd edn). Cardiff.

Jope, E.M. (1952–3), 'Late Saxon pits under Oxford Castle mound: excavations in 1952', *Oxoniensia* **17–18**: 77–111.

Jope, E.M. and Threlfall, R.I. (1946–7), 'Recent mediaeval finds in the Oxford district. 2. Excavations at Deddington Castle, Oxon., 1947', *Oxoniensia* **11–12**: 167–8.

Jope, E.M. and Threlfall, R.I. (1959), 'The twelfth-century castle at Ascot Doilly, Oxfordshire: its history and excavation', *Antiq. J.* **39**: 219–73.

Keen, L. (1983), 'The Umfravilles, the castle and the barony of Prudhoe, Northumberland', in R.A. Brown (ed.), *Anglo-Norman Studies V: Proceedings of the Battle Conference 1982*, 165–84. Woodbridge.

Keen, L. (1987), 'Roofing tiles and bricks', in G. Beresford, *Goltho: The development of an early medieval manor c. 850–1150*, 169–71. London.

Kent, J.P.C. (1968), 'Excavations at the motte & bailey castle of South Mimms, Herts., 1960–1967', *Barnet Distr. Local Hist. Soc. Bull.* **15**: whole issue.

Kenyon, J.R. (1978), *Castles, Town Defences, and Artillery Fortifications in Britain: A bibliography 1945–74*. London.

Kenyon, J.R. (1983), *Castles, Town Defences, and Artillery Fortifications in Britain and Ireland: A bibliography* **2**. London.

Kenyon, J.R. (1988), *Raglan Castle*. Cardiff.

Kerr, M. and Kerr, N. (1983), *Anglo-Saxon Architecture*. Princes Risborough.

King, D.J.C. (1972), 'The field archaeology of mottes in England and Wales: eine kurze Ubersicht', *Château Gaillard* **5**: 101–12.

King, D.J.C. (1978), 'Pembroke Castle', *Archaeol. Cambrensis* **127**: 75–121.

King, D.J.C. (1983), *Castellarium Anglicanum: An index and bibliography of the castles in England, Wales and the islands* (2 vols). New York.

King, D.J.C. and Alcock, L. (1969), 'Ringworks of England and Wales', *Château Gaillard* **3**: 90–127.

King, D.J.C. and Cheshire, M. (1982), 'The town walls of Pembroke', *Archaeol. Cambrensis* **131**: 77–84.

King, D.J.C. and Perks, J.C. (1962), 'Carew Castle, Pembrokeshire', *Archaeol. J.* **119**: 270–307.

King, D.J.C. and Renn, D.F. (1971), 'Lidelea Castle – a suggested identification', *Antiq. J.* **51**: 301–3.

Klingelhofer, E. (1976–7), 'Barrack Street excavations, Warwick, 1972', *Trans. Birmingham Warwickshire Archaeol. Soc.* **88**: 87–104.

Knight, J.K. (1963), 'The keep of Caerleon Castle', *Monmouthshire Antiq.* **1**.3: 23–4 [*sic*: should read 71–2].

Knight, J.K. (1983), 'Montgomery: a castle of the Welsh March, 1223–1649', *Château Gaillard* **11**: 169–182.

Knight, J.K. (1987), 'The road to Harlech: aspects of some early thirteenth-century Welsh castles', in J.R. Kenyon and R. Avent (eds), *Castles in Wales and the Marches; Essays in honour of D.J. Cathcart King*, 75–88. Cardiff.

Knight, J.K. and Talbot, E.J. (1968–70), 'The excavation of a castle mound and round barrow at Tre Oda, Whitchurch', *Trans. Cardiff Natur. Soc.* **95**: 9–23.

Leach, G.B. (1960), 'Excavations at Hen Blas, Coleshill Fawr, near Flint – second report', *Flintshire Hist. Soc. Publ.* **18**: 13–60.

Leach, P. (ed.), 1984), *The archaeology of Taunton: Excavations and fieldwork to 1980.* Gloucester.

Le Maho, J. (1983), 'Genèse d'une fortification seigneuriale: les fouilles de la motte de Mirville (XIe–XIIe siècles)', *Château Gaillard* **11**: 183–91.

Le Maho, J. (1984), *La Motte Seigneuriale de Mirville (XIe–XIIe s.): Recherches historiques et archéologiques.* Rouen.

Le Maho, J. (1985), 'Note sur l'histoire d'un habitat seigneurial des XIe et XIIe siècles en Normandie: Mirville (S. Mme)', in R.A. Brown (ed.), *Anglo-Norman Studies VII: Proceedings of the Battle Conference 1984*, 214–23. Woodbridge.

Le Maho, J. (1987), 'Notre-Dame-de-Gravenchon (Seine Maritime). La Fontaine-Saint-Denis', in 'Chroniques des fouilles médiévales en France', *Archéol. Médiévale* **17**: 247–50.

Le Patourel, J. (1966), 'Knaresborough Castle', *Yorkshire Archaeol. J.* **41**.4: 591–607.

Lewis, J.H. (1984), 'Excavation at Bothwell Castle, Lanarkshire, 1981', *Glasgow Archaeol. J.* **11**: 119–28.

Lewis, J.M. (1960), *Carreg Cennen Castle, Carmarthenshire.* London.

Lewis, J.M. (1968. 'The excavation of the 'new building' at Montgomery Castle', *Archaeol. Cambrensis* **117**: 127–56.

Lewis, J.M. (1975), 'Recent excavations at Loughor Castle (south Wales)', *Château Gaillard* **7**: 147–57

Liebgott, N.-K. (1983), 'An outline of Danish castle studies', *Château Gaillard* **11**: 193–206.

Lightfoot, K.W.B. (1979), 'The medieval town defences of Swansea: the Whitewalls excavation, 1978–79', *Gower* **30**: 76–9.

Lightfoot, K.W.B. (1983), 'Cae Castell, Rumney, Cardiff: final interim report', *Glamorgan–Gwent Archaeol. Trust Annu. Rep. 1981–82:* 1–7.

Lloyd, J.D.K. and Knight, J.K. (1981), *Montgomery Castle, Powys/Castell Trefaldwyn*, (2nd edn). Cardiff.

London Museum (1967), *Medieval Catalogue*, (3rd imp). London.

Macdonald, A.D.S. and Laing, L.R. (1974–5), 'Excavations at Lochmaben Castle, Dumfriesshire', *Proc. Soc. Antiq. Scot.* **106**: 124–57.

MacGregor, A. (1975–6), 'Two antler crossbow nuts and some notes on the early development of the crossbow', *Proc. Soc. Antiq. Scot.* **107**: 317–21.

Mackenzie, W.M. (1933–4), 'Clay castle-building in Scotland', *Proc. Soc. Antiq. Scot.* **68**: 117–27.

McNeill, T.E. (1975), 'Ulster mottes: a checklist', *Ulster J. Archaeol.* 3rd ser. **38**: 49–56.

Mahany, C. (1977), 'Excavations at Stamford Castle, 1971–6', *Château Gaillard* **8**: 223–45.

Mahany, C. (1978), 'Stamford: castle and town', *S. Lincolnshire Archaeol.* **2**: whole issue.

Maloney, J. and Harding, C. (1979), 'Dukes Place and Houndsditch: the medieval defences', *London Archaeol.* **3.13**: 347–54.

Markuson, K.W. (1980), 'Excavations on the Green Lane access site, Barnstaple, 1979', *Proc. Devon Archaeol. Soc.* **38**: 67–90.

Marshall, D.N. (1983), 'Excavations at Macewen's Castle, Argyll, in 1968–69', *Glasgow Archaeol. J.* **10**: 131–42.

Martin, D. (1973), *Bodiam Castle Medieval Bridges*. Robertsbridge.

Maxwell-Irving, A.M.T. (1981), 'Cramalt Tower: historical survey and excavations 1977–9', *Proc. Soc. Antiq. Scot.* **111**: 401–29.

Mayes, P. (1967), *Sandal Castle: Excavations 1966*. Wakefield.

Mayes, P. and Butler, L. (1983), *Sandal Castle Excavations 1964–1973: A detailed archaeological report*. Wakefield.

Meeson, R.A. (1978–9), 'Tenth Tamworth excavation report, 1977: the Norman bailey defences of the castle', *Trans. S. Staffordshire Archaeol. Hist. Soc.* **20**: 15–28.

Megaw, J.V.S. (1961), 'An end-blown flute or flageolet from White Castle', *Medieval Archaeol.* **5**: 176–80.

Mercer, E. (1975), *English Vernacular Houses*. London.

Miles, H. (1971–2), 'Excavations at Rhuddlan, 1969–71: interim report', *Flintshire Hist. Soc. Publ.* **25**: 1–8.

Miles, T.J. (1986), 'The excavation of a Saxon cemetery and part of the Norman castle at North Walk, Barnstaple', *Proc. Devon Archaeol. Soc.* **44**: 59–84.

Moorhouse, S. (1971), 'Excavations at Burton-in-Lonsdale: a reconsideration', *Yorkshire Archaeol. J.* **43**: 85–98.

Morgan, W.L. (1899), 'Excavations at the Old Castle Camp, Bishopston, Gower', *Archaeol. Cambrensis* 5th ser. **16**: 249–58.

Morley, B.M. (1976), 'Hylton Castle', *Archaeol. J.* **133**: 118–34.

Morley, B.M. (1981), 'Aspects of fourteenth-century castle design', in A. Detsicas (ed.), *Collectanea Historica: Essays in memory of Stuart Rigold*, 104–13. Maidstone.

Munby, J. and Renn, D. (1985), 'Description of the castle buildings', in B.W. Cunliffe and J. Munby, *Excavations at Porchester Castle: 4. Medieval: the inner bailey*, 72–119. London.

Murray, H. and Ewart, G. (1978–80), 'Two early medieval timber buildings from Castle Hill, Peebles', *Proc. Soc. Antiq. Scot.* **110**: 519–27.

Musson, C.R. and Cain, R. (1982), 'Tomen Llansantffraid, Cwmdeuddwr, Rhayader', *Archaeol. Wales* **22**: 41.

Olsen, O. (1982), 'Rabies archaeologorum', *Château Gaillard* **9–10**: 213–19, (also in *Antiquity* **54** (1980): 15–19).

O'Neil, B.H. St J. (1944–5), 'Criccieth Castle, Caernarvonshire', *Archaeol. Cambrensis* **98**: 1–51.

Oswald, A. (1962–3), 'Excavation of a thirteenth-century wooden building at Weoley Castle, Birmingham, 1960–61: an interim report', *Medieval Archaeol.* **6–7**: 109–34.

Owles, E. (1971), 'The West Gate of Ipswich', *Proc. Suffolk Inst. Archaeol.* **32.2**: 164–7.

Oxley, J. (ed.) (1986), *Excavations at Southampton Castle*. Southampton.

Palmer, N. (1976), 'Excavations on the outer city wall of Oxford in St. Helen's Passage and Hertford College', *Oxoniensia* **41**: 148–60.

Pinder, A. and Davison, B. (1988), 'The excavation of a motte and bailey castle at Chalgrave, Bedfordshire, 1970', *Bedfordshire Archaeol.* **18**: 33–56.

Pitt-Rivers, A.H.L.F. (1883), 'Excavations at Caesar's Camp near Folkestone, conducted in June and July, 1878', *Archaeologia* **47.2**: 429–65.

Platt, C. (1978), *Medieval England: A social history and archaeology from the Conquest to A.D. 1600*. London.

Platt, C. (1982), *The Castle in Medieval England and Wales*. London.

Ponsford, M.W. (n.d), *Bristol Castle: A short summary of the recent excavations*. Bristol.

Ponsford, M.W. (1971), 'Nottingham town wall: Park Row excavations 1967', *Trans. Thoroton Soc. Nottinghamshire* 75: 5–32.

Ponsford, M.W. (1987), 'Bristol' in M. Aston and R. Iles (eds), *The Archaeology of Avon: A review from the Neolithic to the middle ages*, 144–59. Bristol.

Pounds, N.J.G. (1979), 'The Duchy Palace at Lostwithiel, Cornwall', *Archaeol. J.* 136: 203–17.

Probert, L.A. (1967), 'Deepweir Tump', *Archaeol. Wales* 7: 22.

Radford, C.A.R. (1986), *Restormel Castle*. London.

Radley, J. (1972), 'Excavations in the defences of the city of York: an early medieval stone tower and the successive earth ramparts', *Yorkshire Archaeol. J.* 44: 38–64.

Rahtz, P.A. (1960), *Pleshey Castle: First interim report*. Colchester.

Rahtz, S. and Rowley, T. (1984), *Middleton Stoney: Excavation and survey in a north Oxfordshire parish 1970–1982*. Oxford.

RCAHM (1963), *Stirlingshire: An inventory of the ancient monuments* 1. Edinburgh.

RCHM (1959), 'Wareham west walls', *Medieval Archaeol.* 3: 120–38.

RCHM (1960), 'Excavations in the west bailey at Corfe Castle', *Medieval Archaeol.* 4: 29–55.

RCHM (1972a), *An Inventory of the Historical Monuments in the County of Cambridge. 2. North-east Cambridgeshire*. London.

RCHM (1972b), *An Inventory of the Historical Monuments in the City of York. 2. The defences*. London.

Renn, D.F. (1957), 'South Mymms Castle', *Barnet Distr. Rec. Soc. Bull.* 10: whole issue.

Renn, D.F. (1960), 'The keep of Wareham Castle', *Medieval Archaeol.* 4: 56–68.

Renn, D.F. (1961), 'The round keeps of the Brecon region', *Archaeol. Cambrensis* 110: 129–43.

Renn, D.F. (1969), 'The Avranches traverse at Dover Castle', *Archaeol. Cantiana* 84: 79–92.

Renn, D.F. (1973), *Norman Castles in Britain*, (2nd edn). London.

Renn, D.F. (1987), ' "Chastel de Dynan": the first phases of Ludlow', in J.R. Kenyon and R. Avent (eds), *Castles in Wales and the Marches: Essays in honour of D.J. Cathcart King*, 55–73. Cardiff.

Renn, D.F. (1988), 'Hen Domen compared: the evidence for wooden castle buildings in Britain and Normandy', in A. Burl (ed.), *From Roman Town to Norman Castle: Papers in honour of Philip Barker*, 56–67. Birmingham.

Reynolds, N. (1975), 'Investigations in the Observatory Tower, Lincoln Castle', *Medieval Archaeol.* 19: 201–5.

Rigold, S.E. (1954), 'Totnes Castle: recent excavations by the Ancient Monuments Department, Ministry of Works', *Rep. Trans. Devonshire Ass.* 86: 228–56.

Rigold, S.E. (1967), 'Excavations at Dover Castle 1964–1966', *J. Brit. Archaeol. Ass.* 3rd ser. 30: 87–121.

Rigold, S.E. (1969), 'Recent investigations into the earliest defences of Carisbrooke Castle, Isle of Wight', *Château Gaillard* 3: 128–38.

Rigold, S.E. (1971), 'Eynsford Castle and its excavation', *Archaeol. Cantiana* 86: 109–71.

Rigold, S.E. (1973), 'Timber bridges at English castles and moated sites', *Château Gaillard* 6: 183–93.

Rigold, S.E. (1975), 'Structural aspects of medieval timber bridges', *Medieval Archaeol.* 19: 48–91.

Rigold, S.E. (1976), 'Structural aspects of medieval timber bridges: addenda', *Medieval Archaeol.* 20: 152–3.

Rigold, S.E. and Fleming, A.J. (1973), 'Eynsford Castle: the moat and bridge', *Archaeol. Cantiana* **88**: 87–116.

Rimington, F.C. and Rutter, J.G. (1967), *Ayton Castle: Its history & excavation.* Scarborough.

Rodwell, K.A. (1976), 'Excavations on the site of Banbury Castle, 1973–4', *Oxoniensia* **41**: 90–147.

Ross, C.D. (1951), 'The household accounts of Elizabeth Berkeley, Countess of Warwick, 1420–1', *Trans. Bristol Gloucestershire Archaeol. Soc.* **70**: 81–105.

Round, J.H. (1902), 'The castles of the Conquest', *Archaeologia* **58.1**: 313–40.

Rowland, T.H. (1987), *Medieval Castles, Towers, Peles and Bastles of Northumberland.* Morpeth.

Salamagne, A. (1988), 'Pour une approche typologique de l'architecture militaire: l'exemple de la famille monumentale des tours-portes de plan curviligne', *Archéol. Médiévale* **18**: 179–213.

Salzman, L.F. (1952), *Building in England down to 1540: A documentary history.* Oxford.

Sandall, K. (1986), 'Aisled halls in England and Wales', *Vernacular Architect.* **17**: 21–35.

Saunders, A.D. (1970), 'Excavations at Launceston Castle 1965–69: interim report', *Cornish Archaeol.* **9**: 83–92.

Saunders, A.D. (1977a), 'Five castle excavations: report on the Institute's research project into the origins of the castle in England: introduction', *Archaeol. J.* **134**: 1–10.

Saunders, A.D. (1977b), 'Excavations at Launceston Castle 1970–76: interim report', *Cornish Archaeol.* **16**: 129–37.

Saunders, A.D. (1978), 'A stone lamp from Launceston Castle, Cornwall', *Antiq. J.* **58**: 366–7, 385.

Saunders, A.D. (1980), 'Lydford Castle, Devon', *Medieval Archaeol.* **24**: 123–86.

Saunders, A.D. (1981), 'Launceston Castle', *Cornish Archaeol.* **20**: 220–1.

Saunders, A.D. (1982), 'Launceston Castle excavations in 1981. An interim report', *Cornish Archaeol.* **21**: 187–8.

Saunders, A.D. (1984), *Launceston Castle, Cornwall.* London.

Schofield, J. (1975–6), 'Excavations south of Edinburgh High Street, 1973–4', *Proc. Soc. Antiq. Scot.* **107**: 155–241.

Sellers, E.E. and Sellers, J.E. (1968), 'Essex: Great Easton', *Trans. Essex Archaeol. Soc.* 3rd ser. **2.2**: 159–60.

Sellers, J.E. and Sellers, E.E. (1966), 'Excavations at Great Easton: second interim report', *Trans. Essex Archaeol. Soc.* 3rd ser. **2.1**: 97.

Shoesmith, R. (1982), *Hereford City Excavations. 2. Excavations on and close to the defences.* London

Simpson, G. and Hatley, V. (1953), 'An excavation below Bishop Tunstal's Chapel, Durham Castle', *Antiq. J.* **33**: 56–64.

Simpson, G.C. and Webster, B. (1985), 'Charter evidence and the distribution of mottes in Scotland', in K.J. Stringer (ed.), *Essays on the Nobility of Medieval Scotland*, 1–24. Edinburgh.

Simpson, W.D. (1985), *Bothwell Castle*, (3rd edn), revised by D.J. Breeze and J.R. Hume. Edinburgh.

Smith, C. (1988), *The Exchequer Gate, Denbigh: A report on excavations in 1982 and 1983.* Newcastle upon Tyne.

Smith, J.T. (1965), 'The structure of the timber kitchen at Weoley Castle, Birmingham', *Medieval Archaeol.* **9**: 82–93.

Smith, P. (1988), *Houses of the Welsh Countryside: A study in historical geography*, (2nd edn). London.

Smith, T.P. (1985), 'Why did medieval towns have walls?', *Current Archaeol.* **8.12**: 376–9.

Spurgeon, C.J. (1977), 'Aberystwyth Castle and borough to 1649', in I.G. Jones (ed.), *Aberystwyth 1277–1977*, 28–45. Llandysul.

Spurgeon, C.J. (1987a), 'Mottes and castle-ringworks in Wales', in J.R. Kenyon and R. Avent (eds), *Castles in Wales and the Marches: Essays in honour of D.J. Cathcart King*, 23–49. Cardiff.

Spurgeon, C.J. (1987b), 'The castles of Glamorgan: some sites and theories of general interest', *Château Gaillard* **13**: 203–26.

Spurgeon, C.J. and Thomas, H.J. (1980), 'Cae-castell, Rhyndwyclydach', *Archaeol. Wales* **20**: 71, 73.

Stamper, P.A. (1984), 'Excavations on a mid-twelfth century siege castle at Bentley, Hampshire', *Proc. Hampshire Fld Club Archaeol. Soc.* **40**: 81–9.

Stewart, I.J. (1988), 'Note on the *tabula* set', in T. Darvill, 'Excavations on the site of the early Norman castle at Gloucester, 1983–84', *Medieval Archaeol.* **32**: 31–5.

Stewart, I.J. and Watkins, M.J. (1984), 'An 11th-century bone *tabula* set from Gloucester', *Medieval Archaeol.* **28**: 185–90.

Stewart, M.E.C. and Tabraham, C.J. (1974), 'Excavations at Barton Hill, Kinnaird, Perthshire', *Scot. Archaeol.Forum* **6**: 58–65.

Stiesdal, H. (1969), 'Late earthworks of the motte and bailey type: a summary', *Château Gaillard* **4**: 219–20.

Stocker, D. (1983), 'Lincoln Castle', *Archaeol. Lincoln 1982–1983:* 18–27.

Streeten, A.D.F. (1976), 'Excavations at Lansdowne Road, Tonbridge, 1972 and 1976', *Archaeol. Cantiana* **92**: 105–18.

Swanton, M.J. (1972), 'Castle Hill, Bakewell', *Derbyshire Archaeol. J.* **92**: 16–27.

Tabraham, C.J. (1986), *Kildrummy Castle*. Edinburgh.

Tabraham, C.J. (1987), 'Smailholm Tower: a Scottish laird's fortified residence on the English border', *Château Gaillard* **13**: 227–38.

Tabraham, C.J. and Good, G.L. (1981), 'The artillery fortification at Threave Castle, Galloway', in D.H. Caldwell (ed.), *Scottish Weapons and Fortifications 1100–1800*, 55–72. Edinburgh.

Talbot, E.J. (1966), 'Timber breastworks', in L. Alcock,'Castle Tower, Penmaen: a Norman ring-work in Glamorgan', *Antiq. J.* **46**: 207.

Talbot, E.J. (1972), 'Lorrha motte, County Tipperary', *N. Munster Antiq. J.* **15**: 8–12.

Talbot, E.J. (1974), 'Early Scottish castles of earth and timber – recent field-work and excavation', *Scot. Archaeol. Forum* **6**: 48–57.

Talbot, E.J. and Field, B.V. (1966–7), 'The excavation of Castell Madoc ringwork, Lower Chapel, Breconshire: an interim report', *Brycheiniog* **12**: 131–2.

Tatton-Brown, T. (1978), 'The Sandown Gate at Sandwich', *Archaeol. Cantiana* **94**: 151–6.

Taylor, A.J. (1969), 'Evidence for a pre-Conquest origin for the chapels in Hastings and Pevensey castles', *Château Gaillard* **3**: 144–51.

Taylor, A.J. (1986a), *Conwy Castle and Town Walls*, (rev. edn). Cardiff.

Taylor, A.J. (1986b), *The Welsh castles of Edward I*. London.

Thompson, M.W. (1957), 'Excavation of the fortified medieval hall of Hutton Colswain at Huttons Ambo, near Malton, Yorkshire', *Archaeol. J.* **114**: 69–91.

Thompson, M.W. (1960), Recent excavations in the keep of Farnham Castle, Surrey', *Medieval Archaeol.* **4**: 81–94.

Thompson, M.W. (1966), The origins of Bolingbroke Castle, Lincolnshire', *Medieval Archaeol.* **10**: 152–8.

Thompson, M.W. (1967), 'Excavations in Farnham Castle keep, Surrey, England, 1958–60', *Château Gaillard* **2**: 100–5.

Thompson, M.W. (1968), 'A single-aisled hall at Conisbrough Castle, Yorkshire', *Medieval Archaeol.* **12**: 153.

Thompson, M.W. (1969), 'Further work at Bolingbroke Castle, Lincolnshire', *Medieval Archaeol.* **13**: 216–17.

Thompson, M.W. (1974), 'Old Bolingbroke Castle', *Archaeol. J.* **131**: 314–17.

Thompson, M.W. (1987), *The Decline of the Castle*. Cambridge.

Thorburn, J. (1983), 'Aberystwyth Castle', *Archaeol. Wales* **23**: 51–2.

Todd, M. (1974), 'Excavations on the medieval defences of Newark, 1972', *Trans. Thoroton Soc. Nottinghamshire* **78**: 27–53.

Todd, M. (1977), 'Excavations on the medieval defences of Newark, 1976', *Trans. Thoroton Soc. Nottinghamshire* **81**: 41–54.

Turner, D.J. (1986), 'Bodiam, Sussex: true castle or old soldier's dream house?', in W.M. Ormrod (ed.), *England in the Fourteenth Century*, 267–77. Woodbridge.

Turner, D.J. (1987), 'Archaeology of Surrey, 1066–1540', in J. Bird and D.G. Bird (eds), *The Archaeology of Surrey to 1540*, 223–61. Guildford.

Turner, D.J. and Dunbar, J.G. (1969–70), 'Breachacha Castle, Coll: excavations and field survey, 1965–8', *Proc. Soc. Antiq. Scot.* **102**: 155–87.

Turner, H.M. (1970), *Town Defences in England and Wales: An architectural and documentary study* AD *900–1500*. London.

Wacher, J.S. (1975), 'The excavations, 1956–1958', in C. Platt and R. Coleman-Smith, *Excavations in Medieval Southampton 1953–1969*, 1, 140–74. Leicester.

Wainwright, G. (1971), 'The excavation of a fortified settlement at Walesland Rath, Pembrokeshire', *Britannia* **2**: 48–108.

Waterman, D.M. (1954), 'Excavations at Clough Castle, Co. Down', *Ulster J. Archaeol.* 3rd ser. **17**: 103–63.

Waterman, D.M. (1959), 'Excavations at Lismahon, Co. Down', *Medieval Archaeol.* **3**: 139–76.

Webster, L.E. and Cherry, J. (1973), 'Medieval Britain in 1972', *Medieval Archaeol.* **17**: 138–88.

Webster, L.E. and Cherry, J. (1975), 'Medieval Britain in 1974', *Medieval Archaeol.* **19**: 220–60.

Webster, L.E. and Cherry, J. (1976), 'Medieval Britain in 1975', *Medieval Archaeol.* **20**: 158–201.

Webster, L.E. and Cherry, J. (1978), 'Medieval Britain in 1977', *Medieval Archaeol.* **22**: 142–88.

Webster, P. (1987), 'Dryslwyn Castle', in J.R. Kenyon and R. Avent (eds), *Castles in Wales and the Marches: Essays in honour of D.J. Cathcart King*, 89–104. Cardiff.

Wedlake, W.J. (1965–6), 'The city walls of Bath ...', *Proc. Somersetshire Archaeol. Natur. Hist. Soc.* **110**: 85–107.

West, S.E. (1963), 'Excavations at Cox Lane (1958) and at the town defences, Shire Hall Yard, Ipswich (1959)', *Proc. Suffolk Inst. Archaeol.* **29.3**: 233–303.

White, R.H. (1986), *Peel Castle Excavations. Final report (1): the Half Moon Battery*. Douglas.

Wilcox, R. (1980. 'Excavations at Farleigh Hungerford Castle, 1973–76', *Somerset Archaeol. Natur. Hist.* **124**: 87–109.

Williams, B. (1987), 'Excavation of a medieval earthwork complex at Hillesley, Hawkesbury, Avon', *Trans. Bristol Gloucestershire Archaeol. Soc.* **105**: 147–63.

Williams, F. (1977), *Pleshey Castle, Essex (XII–XVI century): Excavations in the bailey, 1959–1963*. Oxford.

Williams, J.H. (1982), 'Four small excavations on Northampton's medieval defences and elsewhere', *Northamptonshire Archaeol.* **17**: 60–73.

Wilson, D.M. and Hurst, D.G. (1965), 'Medieval Britain in 1964', *Medieval Archaeol.* **9**: 170–220.

Wilson, D.M. and Hurst, D.G. (1966), 'Medieval Britain in 1965', *Medieval Archaeol.* **10**: 168–219.

Wilson, D.M. and Hurst, D.G. (1968), 'Medieval Britain in 1967', *Medieval Archaeol.* **12**: 155–211.

Wilson, D.M. and Moorhouse, S. (1971), 'Medieval Britain in 1970', *Medieval Archaeol.* **15**: 124–79.

Wilson, G.M. (1976), *Treasures of the Tower: Crossbows*. London.

Wood, M. (1965), *The English Mediaeval House*. London.

Yeoman, P.A. (1984), 'Excavations at Castlehill of Strachan, 1980–81', *Proc. Soc. Antiq. Scot.* **114**: 315–64.

Young, C.J. (1983a), 'The Lower Enclosure at Carisbrooke Castle, Isle of Wight', in B. Hartley and J. Wacher (eds), *Rome and her Northern Provinces*, 290–301. Gloucester.

Young, C.J. (1983b), 'Carisbrooke Castle to 1100', *Château Gaillard* **11**: 281–8.

Youngs, S.M. and Clark, J. (1981), 'Medieval Britain in 1980', *Medieval Archaeol.* **25**: 166–228.

Youngs, S.M., Clark, J. and Barry, T. (1985), 'Medieval Britain and Ireland in 1984', *Medieval Archaeol.* **29**: 158–230.

Youngs, S.M., Clark, J. and Barry, T. (1986), 'Medieval Britain and Ireland in 1985', *Medieval Archaeol.* **30**: 114–98.

Youngs, S.M., Clark, J. and Barry, T. (1987), 'Medieval Britain and Ireland in 1986', *Medieval Archaeol.* **31**: 110–91.

Index

227